CW00433166

Intelligent Faith

A Celebration of 150 Years of
Darwinian Evolution

First published by O Books, 2009
O Books is an imprint of John Hunt Publishing Ltd., The Bothy, Deershot Lodge, Park Lane, Ropley,
Hants, SO24 0BE, UK
office1@o-books.net
www.o-books.net

Distribution in:	South Africa
	Stephan Phillips (pty) Ltd
UK and Europe	Email: orders@stephanphillips.com
Orca Book Services	Tel: 27 21 4489839 Telefax: 27 21 4479879
orders@orcabookservices.co.uk	
Tel: 01202 665432 Fax: 01202 666219	Text copyright John MacDonald Smith
Int. code (44)	& John Quenby 2008
USA and Canada	Design: Stuart Davies
NBN	ISBN: 978 1 84694 229 7
custserv@nbnbooks.com	
Tel: 1 800 462 6420 Fax: 1 800 338 4550	All rights reserved. Except for brief quotations
	in critical articles or reviews, no part of this
Australia and New Zealand	book may be reproduced in any manner without
Brumby Books	prior written permission from the publishers.
sales@brumbybooks.com.au	
Tel: 61 3 9761 5535 Fax: 61 3 9761 7095	The rights of John MacDonald Smith & John
	Quenby as author have been asserted in
Far East (offices in Singapore, Thailand,	accordance with the Copyright, Designs and
Hong Kong, Taiwan)	Patents Act 1988.
Pansing Distribution Pte Ltd	
kemal@pansing.com	A CIP catalogue record for this book is available
Tel: 65 6319 9939 Fax: 65 6462 5761	from the British Library.

Printed by Digital Book Print

O Books operates a distinctive and ethical publishing philosophy in
all areas of its business, from its global network of authors to
production and worldwide distribution.

Intelligent Faith

A Celebration of 150 Years of
Darwinian Evolution

Editors

John MacDonald Smith

John Quenby

BOOKS

Winchester, UK
Washington, USA

CONTENTS

Contributors

Rowan Williams; Denis Alexander; R.I. Vane-Wright; Andrew Robinson and Christopher Southgate; Simon Conway Morris; R.J. Berry; Rod Davies; Ruth Page; Paul Badham; Anthony Phillips; Jonathan Clatworthy; Harriet Harris; Russell Stannard; Ian James; John Strain; Richard Harries

Acknowledgements

The editors are very grateful to the able and talented multi-disciplinary group of colleagues who have allowed us to include their contributions in the following collection.

We are grateful also for the Modern Churchpeople's Union's support for the project since its inception; and the good wishes and support of our friends and colleagues with whom we have discussed it.

Our publisher has given us a continued sense of being supported which we appreciate as we do their final production of this volume of essays.

Finally we are especially grateful to Bernadette Smith, who amidst her own studies and writing has found time to use her IT skills to put the project into a suitable shape for publication and has offered her support throughout.

Any errors are, of course, the Editors' responsibility.

The Editors

Preface

By the Archbishop of Canterbury

Sometimes the impression is given these days that there is a 'debate between science and religion' – and that it is essentially a dialogue of the deaf. It suits some people who relish oversimplification to present the situation in these terms; but in fact this is a fiction. The majority of those who hold a strong religious faith are positive about the scientific method and relaxed about evolution; and plenty of serious scientists see no conflict at all between what they do and what religious faith teaches.

It is essential to carry forward the clarifying of these matters. The belief of Christians and others in divine creation is not a theory about the mechanics of the early days of the universe. It is the conviction that all specific forms of reality depend upon the unceasing activity of God. Belief in the distinctive vocation of human beings in a complex universe is not a theory about how God intervened to insert intelligent life into a body but a conviction that human beings from the first moment they can be called human have a particular responsibility, growing towards a conscious sharing in God's contemplative joy and loving care towards all that exists, and experiencing relation with God.

These essays are a significant contribution to the clarifying task. Written by expert and imaginative thinkers in the field, they should help substantially towards exploding certain stereotypes about science and religion and enable a more sensible public discussion about the questions that both the scientist and the theologian or philosopher want to raise.

Archbishop Rowan Williams
Lambeth Palace, Michaelmas 2008

Introduction

John MacDonald Smith

If a machine is expected to be infallible, it cannot also be intelligent. There are several theorems which say almost exactly that. But these theorems say nothing about how much intelligence may be displayed if a machine makes no pretence at infallibility. *Alan Turing*

As is well known a serious and continuous attempt to undermine a developing partnership between science and theology began a century ago in America with the founding of the movement for Biblical literalism known as fundamentalism. What has been called the 'American Scenario' (Corner, 1988: 52), six day creation of a young earth, dispensationalism, the Rapture, were all part of a rather eccentric doctrinal system which should have had no reasonable expectation of lasting. Certainly its bizarre account of prehistory, with dinosaurs and children playing together did nothing to heal what John Habgood has called the 'uneasy truce' (Soundings, 1962: 23ff) between science and theology and equally did nothing for aggressively atheistic scientism except increase its annoyance.

Univocalism seemed to be the name of the game and the sophistication of an earlier age in its treatment of the Bible was forgotten. Turing was shown to be right: creationism and literalism gained increasing currency in a growing constituency partly through publicity for legal actions such as the Stokes Trial and more recently in Harrisburg in 2005. These were brought to test its legality when taught in schools as science. The pressure continues with educational conflict in Louisiana and the production of a film: *Expelled: No Intelligence Allowed* (New Scientist, 12 July, 2008) which is also anti-Darwinian.

To interpret the Bible literally as an infallible source of truth, as has recently been demonstrated by some Anglicans, leads to some very unintelligent ideas. Perhaps in a small way Intelligent Design marks a retreat from this position. But it still commits the error of identifying methodological naturalism with pointlessness, meaninglessness, and purposelessness and it thinks it corrects this by an appeal, as its often cited bacterial flagellum argument shows, to the 'it can't be done' argument. But this is the end of science.

Further, Intelligent Design is an expression of a feeling of uncertainty among some Americans which comes close to insecurity. World events, it is thought, have pushed the West into a corner where its perceived responsibilities require a supporting narrative which many people will understand as myth. The Bible is read literally: there will be Armageddon in the Holy Land; Jesus will return and so on. Hence in 2004 a survey found that 37% of Americans wanted creationism taught in schools – not just alongside evolution but in place of it.

Moral standards and community values it seems are collapsing and anything else goes; and there is a retreat from so called, 'scientific materialism'. The Center for the Renewal of Science and Culture, an important member of a network of I.D – supporting organisations funding foundations and lobby groups has this aim. In its manifesto it refers to 'The Wedge Strategy': a wedge is to be driven into the 'tree' of 'materialistic science' at its nearest point, which is Darwinian evolution. I D calls for a new, faith –based science with the worrying consequence that this leads to a dismissal of what ID theorists have called the 'chimeras of popular science': global warming, pollution and ozone depletion along with the pursuit of ruthless free-market economics. Regime change may alter this picture. We shall see.

There are consequences for education. Intelligent Design may be largely an American phenomenon, but it has made inroads into the United Kingdom. Enquiries made of the department of

Education regarding the permissibility of teaching Intelligent Design in UK schools – notably New Labour's City Academies – are met with an ambiguous response. It seems that the DOE is not clear that ID is neither science, nor theology, and it is clear that formal discussion in class would not go outside the syllabus.

This compromise with the idea that any old rubbish will do, could go far to undermine confidence in significant science, which many pupils will have only half-understood in any case. In turn, it could undermine a sense of trust that the universe is a rational, intelligible, contingent creation whose nature is understood through the patient and painstaking application of the experimental method. That would mean that the nature of God who created such a cosmos will also be misunderstood. In an age of post modernist multi-this-or-that, the idea that any madcap scheme can be invented on no grounds at all gets encouraged by somebody and so acquires currency. Intellectual standards decline and the notion of truth is eroded. The real harm done by ID is that it is an item in a market place of shoddy ideas sold off to the easily fooled at knock-down prices.

In addition there is, fundamentally important, the never-to-be forgotten figure of Charles Darwin, whose double anniversary falls this year. The ideas which he stimulated lie at the heart of our understanding of the natural world. They offer an elegant scientific account which elicits a positive response from and gives much to theology. The sixteen papers which follow have been contributed by men and women of real merit in their different fields of study and cover a very wide area. All are influenced directly or indirectly by the thought of Charles Darwin. In our understanding of the nature of God; in the way we express our faith in God; in the way we understand the Bible, and especially its account of Creation, besides the more specifically scientific ideas, these areas have been touched by Darwin. It will also be shown how through and by means of the developed understanding of scientific ideas to which Darwinism has given rise in part or in whole, there is also the possibility of illuminating the way we understand God and express our believing and trusting in God. This, we suggest, is intelligent faith.

References

Mark Corner in *Theology Against the Nuclear Horizon*, SCM, 1988, p 52

Soundings, OUP, 1962, pp 23 ff.

New Scientist, 12 July, 2008; 12 April, 2008. See also *New Scientist* for October 2005 which offers an entire section on fundamentalism of various kinds.

Evolution – Intelligent and Designed?

Denis R. Alexander

Evolution seems to have been in the news quite a bit recently, and that trend is likely to increase with the double Darwin centenary – 1809 being the year of his birth and 1859 the publication date of the *Origin of Species*. As an evolutionary biologist, it is extraordinary, I think, the extent to which evolution continues to be utilised for all kinds of ideological agendas and I suspect we will see that trend continuing during the double centenary celebrations.

Of course there is a tendency for all the Big Theories of science to be hijacked for ideological purposes of various kinds, but evolution seems to have suffered more than others. The typical process is that a big theory in science becomes highly successful, and then various interest groups move in to try and utilise the prestige of the scientific theory in support of their particular ideology. Unfortunately the end result is that in the public consciousness the actual meaning of the label given to the theory itself changes, and so 'Theory X' becomes socially transformed into 'Theory Y'.

And so in the history of evolutionary theory we see evolution being used in support of capitalism, communism, racism, fascism and many other 'isms' besides, many of them mutually exclusive – and that in itself should warn us that there is a powerful process of social transformation going on here. And I think that process helps to explain much of the recent conflict that we've been seeing in the public domain, especially in the US, between evolution and religious belief.

Some of the conflict of course comes from the recent writings of the so-called 'new atheists' as they attempt to invest evolutionary theory with an atheistic agenda, of whom Richard

Dawkins is probably the best known. I am not sure whether the new atheists fully realise the way in which they are following in this long historical tradition of investing evolution with an ideological agenda. As biologists we are left with this continual struggle to rescue Darwin from the ideologues, from the creationists on one side and from the new atheists at the other extreme, so that evolution can get on with the biological task that it's really good at – which of course is to provide the best scientific explanation we have for the origins of biological diversity.

Certainly the secular narrative is that evolutionary history is incompatible with a providentialist account of the world. According to the late paleontologist Stephen Jay Gould, we are a 'momentary cosmic accident,' albeit a 'glorious accident.' Summing up his view, Gould writes: 'Wind back the tape of life to the early days of the Burgess Shale; let it play again from an identical starting point, and the chance becomes vanishingly small that anything like human intelligence would grace the replay'.

The philosopher Daniel Dennett agrees – Dennett asks whether the complexity of biological diversity can 'really be the outcome of nothing but a cascade of algorithmic processes feeding on chance? And if so, who designed that cascade?' Dennett answers his own rhetorical question by saying: 'Nobody. It is itself the product of a blind, algorithmic process'. 'Evolution is not a process that was designed to produce us'.

So Gould, Dennett and quite a collection of other popular commentators would like to insist that a proper understanding of the evolutionary process excludes any possibility of understanding it as displaying any evidence of plan, purpose or design.

Are they right? And how does all this relate to the Intelligent Design movement which has gained a high profile in the States, and spilled over to a much smaller extent to this country? To address these questions I think we need to start by looking more carefully at this slippery little word 'design'. In fact the word is used with so many different nuances in our contemporary culture, that it's possible to have a lengthy conversation about design in biology, and all those involved have completely different ideas in their heads about what the conversation is all about.

Here is Voltaire's take on intelligent design: God's intelligent design was demonstrated 'as much in the meanest insect as in the planets... The disposition of a fly's wings or of the feelers of a snail is sufficient to confound you', wrote Voltaire as he carried on an imaginary debate with an atheist in his Dictionary of Philosophy, published in 1764. The language of design is of course very old – it goes back to the Stoic philosophers in the pre-Christian era.

And here is Darwin on a bad day at Down House nearly a century later as he studied the breeding habits of the jelly-fish: 'What a Book a Devil's Chaplain might write on the clumsy, wasteful, blundering low and horribly cruel works of nature!' wrote Darwin to the botanist Joseph Hooker on 13 July, 1856.

Two views of the biological world, one with the rose-tinted glasses on, seeing it all as evidence of god's design, and one with the dark glasses on, seeing the waste and the cruelty. A reminder that the task of natural theology has always faced profound ambiguities when tackling the question of design and purpose in biology, long before Darwin came along.

Now the term 'design' can be used with three quite distinct meanings:

Meaning A: An arrangement of form and appearance, with overtones of purpose. Bacteria seem to know what they're doing – feeding, multiplying and so forth, so we can readily say that they're biologically designed for that purpose – they evolved to feed and to multiply. But when we look at rocks, they don't seem to be doing much, so we wouldn't usually think about using the word 'designed' for rocks. So someone like Richard Dawkins can very happily agree that 'We have seen that living things are too improbable and too beautifully 'designed' to have come into existence by chance'. Dawkins is using the word 'design' here in this rather innocuous sense.

Meaning B is 'Specific detailed plan'. This is the language of the engineer or the architect. Now of course if we think of God as a kind of heavenly engineer, then we have some problems. For example, if you're an earthly engineer then you're not expected to build 100 bridges followed by a process of natural selection whereby 99 fall down, but you don't mind as long as one actually works and carries the traffic safely. Your career in engineering would not be a very long one were that to be your strategy. But of course God as a kind of heavenly engineer tinkering around with nature is certainly no part of Christian theology. Personally I'm thankful I don't worship an engineer, even a heavenly one (no disrespect intended to engineers). Neither will you find the word 'design' used in the Bible bearing anything like this particular meaning.

But there is a third and more general meaning of the term 'design' and that is 'to have intentions and purposes'. It is the language of agency and of intentionality, the language of authorship. It is what J.K.Rowling has in mind when she writes out the notes for 7 Harry Potter novels yet to be written – the details may change as she goes along, but the ending was always pretty clear from the beginning. And that kind of idea of design flags up immediately a quite different and I think much more interesting question about biology.

That brings us to a very important point, which is that there is a big difference between arguments that try and lead *from* design in biology *to* God or a Designer - the bottom-up approach of natural theology - and arguments that *start* with God and go the other way, from a prior belief in God to an appreciation of the idea of design and purpose in the created order. All scientists, as much as anybody else in an occupation or profession, encompass their knowledge within an overarching metaphysical framework.

So atheism, which I take to be a metaphysical world-view just as much as theism, for both lie beyond science, can be used to encompass biology. So the atheist will tend to interpret all biological data within the overarching matrix or world-view of atheism. Dawkins makes this point rather well: 'The universe we observe had precisely the properties we should expect if there is, at bottom, no design, no purpose, no evil and no good, nothing but blind pitiless indifference.' Not surprising - the atheist's reading of the biological text is clearly going to be one that lacks any notion of ultimate purpose, let alone a designer or God, because that is built into the starting presupposition.

Contrast that with the flow from God to design. In this case biology is being incorporated *within* a Christian theistic worldview, and so the whole biological narrative is told within that framework. The emphasis here is the kind of thing that many of us write in the Discussion sections of our scientific papers: 'the data are consistent with the model that such-and-such'. And so the Christian, who encloses the circle of biology within their theistic world-view, might want to say, 'well taken overall the biological world in general and evolutionary history in particular is *consistent with* a God who has plans and intentions for humankind'.

So we can now come to evolutionary theory and ask ourselves, well, is that the case? Biologists have long lived with the reality that their field of investigation is one of great complexity. This has led to a tradition of thinking that it's a rather messy research field, one devoid of general principles leading to firm predictions, one in which stochastic events dominate and have the final say. It is precisely such a tradition that has nurtured the anti-providentialist interpretations of the kind that Dennett, Gould and Dawkins wish to make. But the onset of genomics, the increased understanding of genes in development in the evolutionary process - so-called evo-devo - new insights into structural biology, and the ability of computing power to elucidate the emergent properties of complex biological systems, have all combined to give us a very different understanding of the evolutionary process than the one we had even a decade or so ago.

Now it is not my intention to try and present a bottom-up argument from the processes of evolution as if one could derive from these processes in themselves a providentialist understanding of the world, for the simple reason that I don't think such an inference can readily be established in this way. Instead I have a more modest goal, which is to suggest that recent biological data collected over the past decade render the claims made by writers such as Gould and Dennett less plausible. In other words my claim is that our current understanding of biological processes does not exclude a providentialist understanding of the world, and indeed for the dispassionate investigator might tip the balance of probability in a providentialist rather than a non-providentialist direction. Indeed, if we define our terms carefully, then we can indeed say that evolution has been intelligently designed for particular goals and purposes.

I will mention just 5 types of biological data that I think are relevant to this point. And the first is the rather obvious fact of the arrow of evolutionary time, an arrow associated with a striking increase in biological complexity. There is strong evidence for the existence of cells by 3.5 billion years ago and fairly good evidence for life having already started by 3.8 billion years ago. For the first 2.5 billion years of life on earth, things only rarely got bigger than 1 millimetre across, about the size of a pin-head. No birds, no flowers, no animals wandering around, no fish in the sea, but at the genetic level there was lots going on, with the generation of most of the genes that were later used to such effect to build the bigger, more interesting living things that we see all around us today. At the same time the oxygen levels in the atmosphere increased to the point at which more complex life-forms could be sustained.

It is not until the advent of multi-cellular life from around 1.2 billion years ago that living organisms start to get bigger, although even then they were generally on a scale of millimetres rather than centimetres. Only in the so-called 'Cambrian explosion' during the period 505-525 million years ago do we find sponges and algae grow up to 5-10 cm across, and the size of animals began to increase dramatically from that time onwards, until today we have creatures like ourselves with our brains with 10^{11} neurons with their 10^{14} synaptic connections, the most complex known entities in the universe.

So the evolutionary story is certainly not a smooth trajectory, but a narrative with long periods when not much new seemed to be happening, interspersed with times of high drama when creative novelty burst upon the scene.

What about the notion of progress? Now of course biologists tend to disapprove of notions of progress in their professional discourse, and no doubt for the best of reasons. But if you stand back and look at the process as a whole, then the impression of progress is inescapable. As Sean Carroll from the University of Wisconsin-Madison remarks in a recent review in Nature: 'Life's contingent history could be viewed as an argument against any direction or pattern in the course of evolution or the shape of life. But it is obvious that larger and more complex life forms have evolved from simple unicellular ancestors and that various innovations were necessary for the evolution of new means of living'. Carroll chooses his words carefully, but if pressed every biologist has to admit that multicellular organisms <u>are</u> more complex than bacteria, that mammals <u>are</u> in some sense more advanced than yeast, and that the human brain has more capacities than that of a mouse. So it is perverse to deny some form of directionality to the arrow of biological time.

A second interesting observation that relates evolutionary biology to the idea of purpose is that underlying biological complexity are networking principles that are turning out to be fewer and simpler than they might have been. Given that in every cell complex networks of interactions occur between thousands of metabolites, proteins and DNA, this is quite surprising. As Uri Alon from the Weizmann Institute comments: '...Biological networks seem to be built, to a good approximation, from only a few types of patterns called network motifs'...'The same small set of network motifs, discovered in bacteria, have been found in gene-regulation networks across diverse organisms, including plants and animals. Evolution seems to have 'rediscovered' the same motifs again and again in different systems...' [Nature 29 March 2007 p. 497].

The unity of the biosphere has also been underlined by greater understanding of how genetic information flows. The importance of horizontal gene transfer, that is the transfer of genetic information from one bacterium to another or from viruses to bacteria, has been increasingly recognised. Microbes, it is turning out, are like gene-swapping collectives, to use the evocative phrase of Carl Woese. Bacterial viruses are used as repositories of genetic information that can be used to reconstruct their genomes under some circumstances. As Carl Woese comments, 'It seems that there is a continuity of energy flux and informational transfer from the genome up through cells, community, virosphere and environment.' [Nature 25 Jan 2007, p. 369].

This has been underlined by the report from the Craig Venter Institute that came out in Science in 2007 regarding a parasitic bacteria called Wolbachia which infects a high proportion of insects as well as other invertebrates. Until recently it has been thought that only bacteria commonly swap genes between themselves, but the Science paper reports that a fruit fly called Drosophila actually contains the complete genome of Wolbachia – that is one million base pairs, the letters of the genetic alphabet – incorporated into one of its chromosomes. Many other organisms, such as bees and worms, were also found to contain Wolbachia genes, some of which are active in making RNA, which means that they might have a functional role in their host organisms. So this provides yet another way in which information can be passed on from one genome to another during the course of evolution. The process of evolution is a communal exercise, one step leading to another, with everything dependent upon everything else.

The very limited array of protein structures used by living organisms compared to the astronomically huge number of possible structures is also very striking. Proteins are made up of a specified sequence of 20 different amino-acids and a single protein may contain hundreds of amino acids, generating billions of possible sequences. Yet if you look at all the known proteins in the world, and their structural motifs, based on all the genomes that have been sequenced so far, you find that the great majority can be assigned to only 1400 protein domain 'families'. In other words, all living things are united not only by having the same genetic code, but also by possessing an elegant and highly restricted set of protein structures.

And much recent literature suggests also that proteins can only evolve along certain quite restricted pathways because of the internal constraints built into their own structures. Note what a research group from Harvard say in the Abstract of their recent paper in *Science*: 'We conclude that much protein evolution will be similarly constrained. This implies that the protein tape of life may be largely reproducible and even predictable'.

So-called fitness landscapes play an important role in evolutionary discourse. These traditionally represent topographical pictures of the adaptation of different populations to local ecological niches, but are now being applied to fitness landscapes in the context of enzyme structure and function. Again it turns out that the evolutionary pathways to arrive at a particular function of a particular enzyme are remarkably constrained. As the authors conclude in a recent paper on this topic: 'That only a few paths are favoured also implies that evolution might be more reproducible than is commonly perceived, or even be predictable.'

The fourth type of biological data that are highly relevant to the question of purpose in the evolutionary narrative relate to the phenomenon of convergence. Convergence refers to the repeated evolution in independent biological lineages of the same biochemical pathway, or organ or structure. Simon Conway Morris, Professor of Palaeobiology at Cambridge, has recently drawn attention to convergence in his fine book 'Life's Solution – Inevitable Humans in a Lonely Universe' (CUP 2003). For example, the convergence of mimicry of insects and spiders to an ant morphology has evolved at least 70 times independently. Compound and camera eyes taken together have evolved more than 20 different times during the course of evolution. If you live in a planet of light and darkness, then you need eyes – that's what you're going to get.

In a commentary on Gould's idea of contingency, that we cited earlier, Prof. Conway Morris writes that: '[I]t is now widely thought that the history of life is little more than a contingent muddle punctuated by disastrous mass extinctions that in spelling the doom of one group so open the doors of opportunity to some other mob of lucky-chancers. ...Rerun the tape of the history of life... and the end result will be an utterly different biosphere. Most notably there will be nothing remotely like a human...Yet, what we know of evolution suggests the exact reverse: convergence is ubiquitous and the constraints of life make the emergence of the various biological properties [e.g. intelligence] very probable, if not inevitable' [Life's Solution, pp 283-4].

So yes the rolling of the genetic dice is a wonderful way of generating both novelty and diversity, but at the same time it appears to be restrained by necessity to a relatively limited number of living entities. If you live in a universe with this kind of physics and chemistry, and on a planet with these particular properties, then this is what you are likely to get. If we imagine design space in the evolutionary process as a matrix of millions of little boxes, each box representing a possible genome, then the number of boxes that can be filled successfully appears to be really small. Biological diversity is definitely not a case of 'anything can happen'. Only some things can happen.

So we are living in an ordered Universe, not at all a random Universe, but an anthropically fruitful one in which there is a biological narrative culminating in us as its observers. And I have introduced 5 ways in which recent insights into the process of evolution are consistent with this plan-like character of life on this planet:

- The arrow of evolutionary time leading to increased biological complexity.
- A restrained set of networking principles appear to underlie biological complexity
- Evolution is an interconnected, communal process characterised by a high degree of information flow.
- The high level of constraint on protein evolution and structure.
- The striking phenomenon of convergence

Now we cannot really say that the biological diversity we observe is 'inevitable' – for our experience of life is based on exactly n = 1 – but remembering that the universe is likely to have a uniform biochemistry, the data so far suggest that life anywhere in the universe might look rather similar. This seems to be more consistent with a providentialist account for the overall meaning of biological diversity, including ourselves, in which God has intentions and purposes for the universe, and render less plausible the claims made by Gould, Dennett and others that evolutionary history is a totally random walk that might have ended up quite differently.

In fact it is intriguing to note that just as Christians have often utilised disastrous god-of-the-gaps type arguments, seeking to place their argument for God in the present gaps in our scientific knowledge, so is it possible that here we have an atheism-of-the-gaps type of argument in which atheists seek to support their disbelief in God based on interpretations of scientific data which appear initially plausible due to lack of knowledge about the data, but appear less believable as our understanding of the process – in this case the evolutionary process – becomes more complete.

So is the created order intelligent? Metaphorically, yes, for its very intelligibility reflects that of the mind of the Creator who has brought order and complexity out of disorder. Is it designed? In the sense of the heavenly engineer, I suggest no, not in that sense. But in the sense of a created order reflecting the purposes of God for humankind, then I would suggest certainly yes.

Now in the last part of my talk I want us to focus on a rather different use of the words 'Intelligent' and 'Design' which have been combined together to describe the Intelligent Design movement, which I'm going to call ID. ID is an anti-Darwinian movement that started in the States during the early 1990's through the writings of people like Philip Johnson, Michael Behe, Bill Dembski and others. It is quite distinct from the earlier American creationist movements, so we need to summarise its claims carefully. People have unfortunately attached the termi-nology of Intelligent Design to all kinds of ideas that are not really part of this ID movement, and I think that if we want to discuss claims made by a new movement, then the least that we can do is to try and understand the claims being made as accurately as we can.

ID suggests that there is one big arrow going from biology to design and from design to a designer, so I would want to call it a form of strong natural theology.

So now what I'd like to do is to flag up what I think are three very significant problems with the ID position:

Problem 1 is a problem from science – in reality ID has none of the characteristics that make it recognizable as a scientific theory. The purpose of scientific theories in biology is to explain the relationships between all those components of the created order which comprise living matter. And a further important criterion of biological explanations in science is that they be testable – there must be empirical evidence that can count for or against the theory, otherwise it remains vacuous. A successful theory will therefore lead to a research programme which will aim to establish its truth status.

But ID fails on both counts. First, simply saying that something is 'designed' in biology leads to no increase in our understanding of the relationships between the various material components that comprise living matter. Second, labelling a biological entity as 'designed' leads to no experimental programme that could be utilised to test the hypothesis, a fact which presumably explains the lack of scientific publications arising from ID writers.

Problem No 2 comes from the suggestion that it is possible to define certain biological entities as 'irreducibly complex' in a meaningful fashion. In reality it just isn't possible. *All* living matter is composed of thousands of components, all of which need to work together in a coordinated fashion to produce those properties that we associate with life. All the biological 'sub-systems' that maintain cell growth and division, including all biochemical pathways, are complex without exception. I could easily argue that all of them fall within the ID criteria used to identify an 'irreducibly complex' system, since in each and every case the sub-system only functions properly providing all the components are in place.

So what we have in ID is the 'fallacy of large numbers': as soon as you have a multi-component system, then the chances of it coming into being all at once as a fully functional system are remotely small, but of course no biologist thinks that's how evolution works. Evolution works incrementally.

And it's for this reason that ID proponents are very often accused, and I think rightly so, for propounding the old god-of-the-gaps arguments that we have already mentioned, except that in this case it might be more accurate to call it the designer-of-the-gaps argument. Religious believers have always been tempted by the 'argument from personal incredulity' – 'I can't imagine how <u>that</u> could have happened, so the designer must have done it' - but this is really very weak theology. And invariably what happens is that in the fullness of time the gap in scientific knowledge closes and the designer disappears - the history of science is full of such examples. The big presupposition of Christian theism completely undermines such 'god-of-the-gaps' type of arguments. In Christian Theism God is the creator and sustainer of <u>all</u> that exists, or as Augustine succinctly put the point back in the early 5th century: 'Nature is what God does'. So in this view our current scientific ignorance is irrelevant to the question of whether a creator God exists, for all our scientific descriptions are, by definition, descriptions in some sense of God's actions. Christian theism has no hidden investments in scientific ignorance.

That brings us to Problem 3, which is that ID proponents tend to use the word 'naturalism' in a manner very different from the normal understanding of that word. Go to a dictionary and you will find 'naturalism' defined in its philosophical sense as: 'view of the world that excludes the supernatural or spiritual' (Oxford Dictionary). Go to Philip Johnson and you will find comments such as the following: 'It is conceivable that God for some reason did all the creating by apparently naturalistic processes...naturalistic substitutes like the blind watchmaker mechanism are inadequate and contrary to the evidence...' And 'theistic evolution can more accurately be described as theistic naturalism'. But according to the dictionary understanding of 'naturalism', a term like 'theistic naturalism' is an oxymoron, that is, a contradiction in terms, like calling someone a 'fascist communist'. Christian theism, the kind of theism to which Johnson is referring in this passage, refers to the belief in a creator God who is the origin and sustainer of all that exists. So God cannot possibly create by 'apparently naturalistic processes' for the simple reason that if there is a God who creates, then there are no 'naturalistic processes' because naturalism is false. Unless you are really post-modern (or very confused) you can't believe in both God and naturalism simultaneously.

We find the same type of idea in Bill Dembski's book The Design Revolution: 'There has to be a reliable way to distinguish between events or objects whose emergence additionally requires the help of a designing intelligence....The whole point of the design inference is to draw such a distinction between natural and intelligent causes'. So ID proponents envisage a biological world largely explained by 'naturalistic mechanisms' and it is against this backcloth that 'designed systems' may be detected. Indeed, if there is no such backcloth, the rest of their arguments would make little sense, since if the identification of designed entities is to be possible, then clearly a non-designed 'naturalistic' backcloth is essential, otherwise the detection of the so-called designed components would be impossible.

So theologically I see ID as profoundly deficient. ID promotes the idea of a two-tier universe, part ruled by natural forces and part designed, whereas Biblical creation doctrine sees everything that exists, without exception, as being completely dependent upon the personal triune God. In this view, all that exists without exception reflects God's overall intentions and purposes for the created order.

It's interesting to note the terminology of 'Intelligent Design' already being used in this way by Christians at the time of Darwin. Here is a 19th century cleric, James McCosh, president of the College of New Jersey (later to become Princeton University) who held strongly to Darwinian natural selection, but equally strongly believed that 'the natural origin of species is not inconsistent with intelligent design in nature or with the existence of a personal Creator of the world'. Upon looking back over 20 years as president of the College of New Jersey, McCosh remarked that 'I have been defending Evolution but, in so doing, have given the proper account of it as the method of God's procedure, and find that when so understood it is in no way inconsistent with Scripture'.

I'd like to close with some words that very much reflect this view, this time the words of a very high profile contemporary evolutionary biologist, Francis Collins, who is also a Christian, and who until recently was the Director of the National Human Genome Institute in Washington. Speaking of his experience as a Christian and as a scientist heading up the most important project in contemporary biology, Collins has remarked that:

'The work of a scientist involved in this project, particularly a scientist who has the joy of also being a Christian, is a work of discovery which can also be a form of worship. As a scientist, one of the most exhilarating experiences is to learn something.... that no human has understood before. To have a chance to see the glory of creation, the intricacy of it, the beauty of it, is really an experience not to be matched. Scientists who do not have a personal faith in God also undoubtedly experience the exhilaration of discovery. But to have that joy of discovery, mixed together with the joy of worship, is truly a powerful moment for a Christian who is also a scientist'.

Dr Denis Alexander is Director of The Faraday Institute, St Edmund's College, Cambridge. This lecture was given to The Severn Forum in 2008. Dr Alexander is the author of *Creation and Evolution*, (Monarch, 2008)

Lives of Meaning: Organismal Intelligence and the Origin of Design in Nature

R.I. Vane-Wright

"Organisms can be proud to have been their own designers."
Kalevi Kull, 2000

A personal introduction

Despite a Christian upbringing, I am not a person of faith. I am an agnostic: I do not think science (or any other discipline) is capable of proving or disproving either the existence, or the non-existence of God. God, if it does exist, is ineffable, knowable only through personal conviction. I therefore disagree with fellow scientists when they suggest human logic will eventually reveal some materially-based answer to everything (e.g. Wilson, 1998). In agreement with Wendell Berry (2000), I do not believe that science can offer such assurance—which would be just another act of faith (Midgley, 1985). With Peat (2002) I am also sceptical about any certainty of science, and with Dupré (1993) even its unity.

This lack of belief in science as a potential source of ultimate, objective truth does not lead me, however, to insist on some divine or transcendental creator. Personally, I am content to be a minuscule part of the cosmos, a small nexus in the great web of life on Earth (Capra, 1996), one of the current 6.5 billion living individuals of *Homo sapiens*. For me this is enough, but others seek "the meaning of life" and a notion of salvation in something beyond. While I personally find this unnecessary, I do not object to their felt need or recourse to faith to satisfy their yearning— unless they insist that I renounce my position.

As a natural scientist, I see it as my task to contribute my mite towards describing the universe and trying to understand how it works. In doing so, I try to use no more assumptions than necessary, and depend on the minimum number of seemingly inexplicable factors—such as the various physical constants that make life on Earth possible (see discussions of the 'anthropic principle' in Carr, 2007). In strong agreement with the views of Bohm (1980: 227), I also see it is as my task to explore specific elements of the universe by abstraction from the implicate whole, and not to try to derive the whole (or subsystems) by abstraction from explicate parts. In other words, while reductionism may offer the scientist a useful tool, it does not provide a satisfactory framework for explaining complex phenomena (Mayr, 1963: 671).

I am thus happy to join the debate represented by *Intelligent Faith*, in opposition to those who believe that Darwinian evolution, without the intervention of some supernatural force or "intelligent designer", cannot bring about the adaptation seen throughout the living world between the organism and its environment. Such a belief, in my view, rests on an outmoded view of the nature of the adaptations of organisms as perfect, each "meticulously designed for its function", carried over from the days of natural theology (Brooke, 1991: 192), exacerbated by normal-science when it reductively portrays organic evolution as a process driven solely by genes—selfish or otherwise.

Whole organisms act out "a life of meaning" (Goodwin, 2007) based on a mixture of inherited and some learned understanding of their world. Organisms, each one in its own special way, are highly intelligent, not "dumb" or "stupid" as so often claimed. To me, specific organismal intelligence is the wellspring of adaptation, the source of the seeming "design" seen in all living things. Each individual organism contributes, through its own particular life of meaning, to the design of the evolutionary lineage to which it contributes—the evolving, adaptable and adapted species. Although *mediated, constrained* and ultimately *passed on* by the selection of available mutations working within established genetic mechanisms, this process is not controlled by them. As stated succinctly by Walsh (2006: 425), "one must appeal to the capacities of organisms to explain what makes adaptive evolution adaptive".

Blind chance versus intelligent design—the only alternatives?

In this short paper I presuppose that the Earth and its biota have changed over the 4.5 billion year existence of our planet. Thus I cannot appeal to those who believe that all species were created by a supernatural agency just a few thousand years ago, and are not the product of organic evolution stretching back billions of years, and that man and dinosaurs coexisted until very recently, etc. My aim is to appeal, instead, to those who are willing to contemplate that evolution might have occurred over many millions of years—but find the evident "design" of organisms, as seen in structures such as the vertebrate eye, inconceivable as being solely due to chance.

Jehovah's Witnesses have recently been asked (*Awake!*, November 2008) to contemplate the remarkable ability of Monarch butterflies to find their way, over more than 3000 km, from the Great Lakes region of southern Canada to a small area of montane forest west of Mexico City. After some interesting observations about the neurophysiology of the Monarch, readers are challenged: "What do you think? Is the complex navigational system of the monarch butterfly the product of chance? Or is it evidence of an intelligent Designer?" No answer is given, but Witnesses are expected, I feel sure, to conclude the latter. Put like this, any suggestion that the ability of the Monarch butterfly to make such a remarkable journey is simply "the product of chance" does seem absurd.

The whole *Awake* piece is very short—less than 250 words. It starts with the statement "Using a brain that is about the size of the tip of a ballpoint pen..." Is this imagery to suggest that the butterfly has limited intelligence, or is inferior to us (with our *big* brains) in some way—rather than just different? Whatever, most of the article reports on recent work on the Monarch's circadian clock, carried out in the laboratory of Steven Reppert (e.g. Reppert, 2007; Zhu, Casselman & Reppert, 2008; Zhu *et al.*, 2008), and its key role in the Monarch's navigation. It then turns to speculation about how understanding this mechanism "could lead to new therapies for [human] neurological afflictions" (a utilitarian justification for the research, or even the existence of the Monarch itself?)—before leading finally, one sentence later, to the ID question quoted above.

The implication is that the Monarch finds its way from the Great Lakes to the Transverse Neovolcanic Belt (Brower, 1995: 340) of Central Mexico due to its possession of some remarkable brain circuitry which, because it could not have evolved by chance, must have been designed by an external agency ("an intelligent Designer") explicitly for the purpose. To me this is the equivalent of saying that, if I possess a satellite navigation system (which I did not and could not design myself) "tuned" to direct me from Canterbury to Doncaster, this explains why I make regular 400 km trips to that town. In the past I relied on printed maps. If I had to reach that part of England before there were even roads, like the Monarch, I would probably have used the sun and some form of circadian clock. How on a particular day I get from East Kent to South Yorkshire, or how a Monarch spends several weeks to get from Ontario to Central Mexico, in both cases with a high probability of success, is technically very interesting—but it tells us nothing about *why* I or the butterfly make our respective journeys. Why am I *minded* to go to Doncaster several times a year? Why is a Canadian Monarch *minded* to go to Mexico in autumn? Why is a Costa Rican Monarch *not minded* to do either, ever?

To criticise the necessarily short piece of journalism in *Awake* for what it leaves out may seem unfair. However, it is the case that this article poses a fundamental question about our understanding of nature without informing or reminding the reader of any of the relevant natural history. Moreover, that it raises this question by recourse to Cartesian mind/body dualism, even to the extent of seizing on a clock metaphor, is disturbing. As Midgley (2007: 6) points out, according to such views, "animals are really only simple, unconscious automata." Have satellite navigation, I will travel to Doncaster? Have circadian clock, the Monarch will travel to Mexico?

Why I travel to Doncaster several times a year is explicable by my (recent) family history. When I married in 1987, I gained a new family—in particular, my wife's parents. Her mother is still alive today, and we drive to Doncaster to see her when we can, as time in our busy lives permits. After a few short days we return to Canterbury, to carry on with our daily preoccupations—our local network of friends, other family members, and many commitments. Our travel, although mediated by amazing technology, is not to be understood in terms of mechanism. Had we lived out such a life 500 years ago, we would have travelled north on horseback along various Roman roads. My wife and I make these journeys because of our history, and our felt need to make a life of mutual meaning and significance by nurturing family ties.

Although Monarch butterflies surely do not have the self-awareness characteristic of the human species, their lives too can only be understood in context. To discuss "design" by reference to mechanism without ecological and historical context, as in the *Awake* article, presents a travesty of our understanding of biological systems (Capra, 1996; Goodwin, 2007).

The Monarch (*Danaus plexippus*) is a member of a distinctive and largely tropical group of over 150 species, the so-called milkweed butterflies (tribe Danaini, family Nymphalidae). Their common name comes from the specialised feeding habits of their larvae, which will only eat a narrow range of plants that mostly have white, sticky sap—most notably the so-called milkweeds themselves (family Asclepiadaceae) and various relatives. Most Danaini only occur in the Indo-Australian region, with relatively small numbers of mostly very different species in Africa, and another small set of separate species in the Americas. The Monarch belongs to a very distinctive group of three species native to South and Central America and the Caribbean. The Monarch itself is divisible into half a dozen subspecies occupying different parts of northern South America, Central America and the Caribbean. Only one of these subspecies (*Danaus plexippus plexippus*) extends into North America (it has also spread throughout the Pacific, and to various Atlantic islands, over the last 170 years), and only one (huge) sub-population of this subspecies is involved in the spectacular long-range migration that is the subject of the *Awake* article. This sub-population, and a smaller sub-population that occurs west of the Rockies, where it makes similar but less spectacular and shorter-range migrations to the California coast, has been the subject of intensive research for over 100 years. In contrast, relatively little is known about the more southerly, non-migratory populations of *D. plexippus plexippus*, or any of the Monarch's other subspecies or close relatives.

The great southerly migration to Mexico affects the eastern USA and southern Canada population once a year, starting in the Fall, with literally many millions of Monarchs arriving in the Transverse Neovolcanic Belt around 1–2 November (All Souls' and All Saints' Days). Over the following week or so the butterflies locate certain favoured spots in the mountain forests, all at about 10,000 ft altitude, where they cluster on the Oyamel fir trees so densely that sometimes their weight is sufficient to break small branches. The locations they choose offer an excellent compromise between being too hot (and therefore burning up all their fat reserves before spring) or too cold (and freezing to death). Even so, during the winter many of the butterflies die due to various causes, sometimes in huge numbers (Brower *et al.*,

2004). The following March the survivors become very active, and fly north to the southern states of the USA, where they reproduce and then die. Their sons and daughters fly further north, some as far as the Great Lakes and even beyond, where they produce a third and even fourth generation of butterflies. It is these grandchildren that undertake the remarkable Fall migration, all the way back to the same small mountain massif in Central Mexico where their grandparents overwintered, where they have never been before nor will ever return. Those that survive the coming winter, like their forebears, will fly to the southern states, mate, lay eggs and die, thus repeating the annual cycle year on year.

No other butterflies in North America do this—although quite a number do make more limited and less coordinated southerly movements in the Fall, to escape the extremely deep frosts experienced in northern USA and Canada. Instead, most North American butterfly species (as in Europe) have winter survival strategies and the physiology to endure the harsh winters *in situ*.

Not so the Monarch—frosts, and even temperatures just above zero, are fatal to this insect (Brower, 1995). So far as we know, this is true for all milkweed butterflies, which appear to be frost-intolerant in all their life stages. Why, then, do Monarchs fly north in North America into areas that are potentially fatal to them and their offspring? Is it because they have the navigational equipment to take them south again, before it is too late? Are they mere automata, slaves to their Intelligent Designer neuro-physiology—or perhaps, alternatively, the potentially selfish genes responsible for this navigational mechanism (Zhu *et al.*, 2008)? Here history and ecology must come together as *context*, if we are to make *biological* (not just mechanical) sense of this phenomenon.

Migration of the Monarch butterfly in ecological and biological context

Until the closing of the Darien Gap about 3 million years ago, South America was an island continent, rather like Australia today. About 100 million years ago, being far apart, the fauna and flora of North America and South America were very different, but when the two continents got closer, perhaps 30 million years ago, occasional faunal interchange became possible through dispersal across the slowly narrowing sea gap. On final approach, and closure of the Isthmus of Panama at Darién, a major exchange of plants and animals took place in both directions—the so-called Great American Interchange (Marshall, 1988).

As already noted, milkweed butterflies are fundamentally tropical, frost-intolerant insects. Given that all four species of Danaini found in the USA are also widespread in Central and South America (Ackery & Vane-Wright, 1984: table 29), where they form part of a significantly larger milkweed butterfly fauna, the presence of the genus *Danaus* in North America is almost certainly to be explained as part of the great Interchange. North America has a very rich milkweed flora (e.g. Woodson, 1954), with the Monarch able to exploit more than 20 different species (Scott, 1986: 230). Notably, the Monarch is the only one of the four danaines found in North America that breeds around the Great Lakes or even further north (Scott, 1986).

The available information supports the idea that *Danaus plexippus* reached what is now Central America at some time during the last 3 million years, and since then the species has extended its breeding range northwards, right up to the Great Lakes and even beyond, to take advantage of the rich milkweed flora. "However, because of their tropical origins [frost intolerance], the butterflies would have had to retreat southwards each fall to avoid freezing" (Brower, 1995: 356). An important complication is that, as the summer advances, the milkweeds that grow in the southern USA senesce, and cease to be suitable food. By mid-summer, there are no Monarchs breeding in the USA below about 33°N (with the possible exception of a permanent colony in southern Florida). In this context it is also important to note that, in Mexico, there is also a widely dispersed population of *Danaus plexippus plexippus* that does not migrate to the Great Lakes. So far as known, there is no or very limited interbreeding between the USA/Canada population that overwinters at high altitude from November–March each year, and the local population—which breeds continuously throughout the year at lower elevations.

Why don't the Monarchs from USA and Canada just mingle with the resident Mexican Monarchs, take advantage of the local opportunities to breed, and then fly northwards again in the Spring? We can perhaps imagine that when Monarchs first reached the area that is now Arizona and Texas, assuming some degree of summer senescence of milkweed plants already occurred, that by mid-summer they needed to emigrate—either south, back to Mexico, or, perhaps more easily, further north, tracking the still-suitable milkweed flora. If they did this, however, getting ever further from the south, they or their offspring would be faced with lethal frosts, and die out. Indeed, this appears to happen to many temperate butterflies that occasionally build up very large populations in the southern parts of their ranges during summer. Many individuals fly north and some are able to find suitable plants on which to breed, even into the autumn. Generally, however, these species do not have mass or well-coordinated return migrations, and the vast bulk of them die without contributing to future generations—unless they are also more or less frost-tolerant species—in which case a proportion will survive from time to time and, in favourable years, produce a local spring brood.

If, perhaps cued by rapidly shortening day-length, some individual Great Lakes area Monarchs were to fly south, rather than go still further north, or west into the Rockies, or east into the Atlantic, then they would have some chance of breeding — their Darwinian fitness would be positive, not zero. If there was a genetic component to flying south in the northern autumn then, coupled with an existing tendency to fly north at other times of the year, we can begin to imagine how the migratory phenomenon could have built up. If a way could be found that combined exploitation of the rich milkweed flora of North America during spring and summer, coupled with a reliable ability to fly south in autumn, then compared with other Monarchs in the region, any that did this would have very high relative fitness.

Once started, any change in heritable behaviour that improved this emergent migration behaviour would be favoured by natural selection. The crucial point here is simply that this would only come about as a result of the behaviour of the organism. Over time, heritable variations in individual behaviour have allowed the Monarch to internalise (assimilate) knowledge of the relevant ecology of North America. At a minimum, for a female Monarch this means mating and finding milkweed plants suitable for her larvae, in such a way that her children and grand-children will have a good chance of being able to repeat this process reliably. Thus for a Monarch in Texas in summer, this means flying north to lay eggs, so long as she is "wired", or at least her children and their children are wired to fly south in autumn. Not flying south at the appropriate time is fatal. It will be fascinating to discover if the clock-based navigational system now explored in detail by Reppert's group will be set to different "goals" in different Monarch populations and subspecies.

This has been a long discursion about the Monarch, to establish two related points: that context (historical and ecological) is fundamental to understanding critical "why" questions about evolution, and that the capacity of individual organisms, *as mediated by their behaviour*, is fundamental to setting the evolutionary trajectory of the species to which they belong. Evolution is *driven* by the behaviour (in the broadest sense of the word) of organisms, as intelligent subsystems of the great web of life, not by random mutations. The great majority of mutations will either be eliminated as deleterious or, even if potentially advantageous in some context, they will not be selected unless the organism is already operating appropriately in that context. In the process of making evolutionary change, organisms internalise (mainly as instinct) new knowledge about their environment—and this in turn means that their inherent capacity is also subject to change, opening yet further possibilities for adaptive novelty.

Objections

The account proposed above, concerning the evolution of migration in the eastern North American population of the Monarch butterfly as driven by its behaviour, is immediately open to two major objections. First, it can be interpreted as teleological—does it seek to explain the phenomenon by its purpose rather than its cause? If so, it could be rejected as an empty, circular argument. Secondly, is the proposal Lamarckian? Does it rest on the basis that the mere act of flying south at the right time of year is not only necessary but also sufficient for the behaviour to be inherited? If so, the proposal is deeply flawed as "It would require a theory of inheritance completely at variance with that receiving experimental support today" (Thain & Hickman, 1994: 352). Early 20th century accounts for the supposed inheritance of acquired characters now read like science fantasy (e.g. Rignano, 1911).

Teleology versus Teleonomy

Following the rise of Darwinism, but still operating in an essentially Cartesian mind/body dualistic framework, biologists became increasingly uncomfortable with vitalism in any form, including teleology. A good example is given by the initial and by some continuing rejection of the *Gaia* hypothesis. Critics insist that it is teleological—that it implies that homeostatic properties of the biosphere are driven by some mystical "purpose"—even though its authors, James Lovelock and Lynn Margulis, have never said that (Capra, 1996: 106–07). This unwillingness to embrace any suggestion of teleology has led, according to Walsh (2006), to a position where the notion that the "capacity" of organisms can shape their own developmental or evolutionary trajectory has been rejected, for fear of being seen non-objective, or to exhibit non-population thinking (see also Winsor, 2006). Walsh proposes that we need to re-embrace the idea that the natures of organisms do play an explanatory role in biology: "Organismal natures—the goal-directed capacities of organisms to develop and maintain viability, given the material resources at their disposal—play an ineliminable role in the explanation of adaptive evolution" (Walsh, 2006: 444–45).

Walsh is not alone in this conviction. A possible turning point came with the introduction of the term "teleonomy" by the chronobiologist Colin Pittendrigh (1958), who felt a need to acknowledge the quality of apparent purposefulness seen in living organisms that relates to their evolutionary history and adaptations bestowing Darwinian fitness, without ascribing, as in teleology, any notion of conscious purpose, intention or foresight. Following this lead, some famous evolutionary biologists have embraced his term—and the spirit of the distinction intended—to affirm that the natures and capacities of whole organisms are of fundamental importance in organic evolution.

One of the first was Ernst Mayr, writing in 1965. I quote here, however, from Mayr (1963: 604–05), concerning his ideas on the role of behaviour in evolution: "A shift into a new niche or adaptive zone is, almost without exception, initiated by a change in behavior. The other adaptations to the new niche, particularly the structural ones, are acquired secondarily . . . This is not the place to discuss how the behavior changes themselves originate . . . The point that is important for us is that new habits and behavior always start in a concrete local population. If the new behavior adds to fitness, it will be favored by selection and so will all the genes that contribute to its efficiency." So Mayr saw the evolutionary sequence as: new challenge > new behaviour > natural selection improving behavioural effectiveness > further adaptations to new niche, notably structural ones.

Nobel prize-winner Jacques Monod (1972: 20) wrote: ". . . one of the fundamental characteristics common to all living beings without exception [is] that of being *objects endowed with a purpose or project*, which at the same time they show in their structure and execute through their performances [behaviour] . . . Rather than reject this idea (as certain biologists have tried to do) it must be recognised as essential to the very definition of living beings. We shall maintain that the latter are distinct from all other structures or systems present in the universe by this characteristic property, which we shall call *teleonomy*. Most strikingly, Monod (1972: 30–31) continues: "The cornerstone of the scientific method is the postulate that nature is objective. In other words, the *systematic* denial that 'true' knowledge can be reached by interpreting phenomena in terms of final causes—that is to say, of 'purpose'... Objectivity nevertheless obliges us to recognize the teleonomic character of living organisms, to admit that in their structure and performance they decide on and pursue a purpose. Here therefore, at least in appearance, lies a profound epistemological contradiction. In fact the central problem of biology lies with this very contradiction, which, if it is only apparent, must be resolved, or else proved to be radically insoluble, if that should turn out indeed to be the case." [All emphases original.]

Systems scientist Peter A. Corning has written extensively and very richly about the evolution of organic and social complexity, with special reference to the role and importance of synergism, and pitting his vision against conventional neo-Darwinism that focuses on "the reductionist, mechanistic, gene-centered approach to evolution epitomized by the selfish gene metaphor" (Corning, 2005: 1). He writes: "... it may be appropriate to deploy the notion of *teleonomic selection* (or neo-Lamarckian selection) to characterise the proximate "mechanism" of value-driven, self-controlled behavioural changes. As the evolved products of evolution have gained greater power to exercise teleonomic control over their relationships to the environment (and to each other), natural selection has become a dog that is increasingly wagged by its tail. Teleonomic selection has become an important instigator of evolutionary change and complexification." (Corning, 2005: 118.)

In an earlier work Corning stated: "... the mechanisms that determine the relationship between an organism and its environment, are neither random nor the result of phylogenetic inertia and ecologoical pressures... Instead, they involve *teleonomic selection*, a modernized, cybernetic version of Organic Selection [see below]... if the cybernetic model is accepted as an accurate representation of the essential nature of animal behaviour, this implies a much more complex and active role for the [whole] organism as an agency of evolutionary change. In the cybernetic model, internal goals orient the actions and reactions of an animal; learning and innovation are highly directed processes in which goals... will tend to focus behavioural changes on the solution of preexisting adaptational problems... with the process (and outcomes) having a teleonomic, goal-orientated (and frequently "creative") aspect. Thus *teleonomic selection* denotes a purposive internal selective process, the second order effects of which may be evolutionary changes via natural selection." (Corning, 1983: 48).

Thus Ernst Mayr, and to an even greater extent Jacques Monod and Peter Corning, are in agreement that what can be called progressive evolution (roughly equivalent to directional selection, as opposed to stabilising selection) is frequently, if not exclusively, led by changes in purposive behaviour. Subsequently, the effectiveness and heritability of such changes can be improved by natural selection operating on genetic mutations and recombinations.

Does the Pittendrigh-Mayr-Monod-Corning endorsement of the central role of teleonomic selection in the evolution of adaptation mean that this formulation of the evolutionary process escapes the fatal accusation of circularity—of saying, in effect, that Monarchs migrate to Mexico because that is their purpose? Personally, I am satisfied that Monarchs in eastern USA and Canada migrate to Mexico annually because it is part of a novel adaptation to take advantage of the rich milkweed flora of North America which, given that they remain frost intolerant, requires "the butterflies... to retreat southwards each fall to avoid freezing" (Brower, 1995: 356). I am not satisfied with the idea that the Monarchs fly to Mexico each fall because they have a mechanism that allows them to do so. For me the neurological clockwork is surely something that has been acquired (or tuned) secondarily (cf. Mayr, as quoted above), but is now critical for the efficient and reliable functioning of this remarkable adaptation that is only manifest in every third or fourth generation—and may also play a triggering role in the process.

Not all biologists or philosophers accept the distinction between teleology and teleonomy. Hull (1982), for example, has been particularly dismissive of this as no more than a change in terminology, a sleight-of-hand to reintroduce final causes and essentialism back into biology where population thinking had supposedly triumphed. While many may still be inclined to agree with Hull, his thinking on essentialism has recently been challenged by Winsor (e.g. 2006) and Walsh (2006), as already indicated above. If we accept as a working hypothesis that teleonomic selection does not depend on circular reasoning, and is therefore a valid candidate for the creation of new purposive behaviours and structures that appear to be "designed" for particular ends, then we need next to look at the accusation of Lamarckism. Can teleonomic selection operate without invoking the inheritance of acquired characters?

Lamarckism, natural selection, organic selection and genetic assimilation

The classic example of speculative Lamarckism is the idea that giraffes evolved long necks and forelegs because of competition for food. Needing to stretch up to reach ever-higher leaves on forage trees, any consequent increase in the length of their necks and forelimbs would appear in their offspring, which would thus have a selective advantage over those whose parents had stretched up less, or not at all. The process repeated over generations supposedly led to the form of the giraffe seen today (Rignano, 1911: 198).

The discoveries of Gregor Mendel and August Weismann paved the way for our current understanding of genetics. Although the idea that Lamarckism could act together with natural selection persisted among some mainstream evolutionary biologists into the 1930s (Rensch, 1983), and even though there is now some evidence of somatic inheritance (e.g. Richards, 2006), the sort of process described above for evolution of the giraffe exists only in the realms of fantasy. However, there remains the problem of a link between plastic changes in individual behaviour, as discussed above, and the incorporation of genetic changes capable of evoking and enhancing such behaviour in descendants.

The organic selection movement at the end of the 19th century, embracing in particular the ideas of James Mark Baldwin, Conway Lloyd Morgan and Henry Fairfield Osborn, represents a radically different attempt to consider how this could come about (Baldwin, 1902). The proposal was that individual learning could guide the evolutionary process. Learnt abilities that positively effect fitness would be replaced in subsequent generations by inherited mechanisms that save the cost of learning—thus behaviours initially acquired by learning could later become instinctive. This was not conceived as happening by a direct, Lamarckian mechanism, but by an indirect "screening" effect, such that individuals that more readily exhibited the behaviour, or performed the behaviour more effectively, would be favoured by selection (Corning, 1983: 38).

This two-step process, involving a sequential dynamic between the benefit of learning and its cost, can be repeated again and again, so that the growing instinctive knowledge (or intelligence) that the organism has about managing effective interactions and relationships within normal and (within limits) abnormal environments, can be the basis for progressive, adaptive evolution. Such evolution would not be random—even though, as we now envisage, it would be dependent for its rate of attainment of heritable change on genetic recombination and chance mutation.

Despite Baldwin's (1902) extensive synthesis, and his enthusiastic support from the formidable Darwinian Edward Bagnall Poulton, the interesting ideas of organic selection were swept aside by the rapid emergence of Mendelian genetics at the very beginning of the 20th century (Waddington, 1957: 165). According to the Mendelians, mutation and structural change were primary (Corning, 1983: 39)—and this view still prevails widely today: hence the erroneous idea that evolution by natural selection is all a matter of chance—because it is thought of as *driven* by random mutation, rather than *constrained* by it (in terms of rate of progress etc.). Thus even behavioural change is seen as the *result* of evolutionary novelty, not as one of its most potent *causes*, as Baldwin and his contemporaries imagined.

However, not all was lost. Simpson (1953) reignited interest in organic selection when he dubbed it the "Baldwin effect"—

although insisting, at the same time, that the mechanism did not really differ from conventional natural selection. During the same period, Waddington (e.g. 1953) began to explore organic selection within the emergent framework of cybernetics and systems theory. Quoting also Huxley (1942: 304), Waddington (1957: 154) pointed out that, unless a non-Lamarckian link could be demonstrated between the plastic emergence of the novelty (e.g. new behaviour), and the subsequent emergence of genetic factors in the population that produce the same or similar pheno-typic trait, then organic selection is trivial. It depends either on Lamarckism and is therefore wrong, or on normal selection and is therefore redundant.

Waddington was interested in the possibility mutation might not always be random, and could in some way be potentiated by feedback from an environmental stimulus. He pursued this through his ideas on developmental "canalisation" and potential remodelling the "epigenetic landscape" (Waddington, 1957: fig. 30). These notions gave rise to what Waddington termed "genetic assimilation"—a process related to but more sophisticated than organic selection with respect to how the initially acquired trait would become genetically fixed. "The older discussions of the Larmarckian problem of 'the inheritance of acquired characters' usually missed the point that all characters of all organisms are to some extent acquired, in that the environment has played some part—possibly only permissive, but often also to some extent directive—in their formation, and that equally all characters are to some extent inherited, since an organism cannot form any structure for which it does not have the hereditary potentialities. The question we should ask is... whether... the ability to acquire the character differs hereditarily in different individuals in a population, and if so what will be the effect of natural selection on the potentialities of later generations... Whenever a population has been tested for the ability of its members to acquire characters during their lifetime under the influence of abnormal environments, it is found that different individuals differ in their hereditary potentialities in this respect." (Waddington, 1961: 91.)

Waddington carried out a variety of experiments on the development of *Drosophila* under various forms of environmental stress, and was able to interpret some of his results in terms of his theory of genetic assimilation. He concluded at one point: ". . . only certain [some] of the results of evolution... make us feel that more than pure chance must have been at work, and it is in connection with these phenomena that we can see ways in which such cybernetic processes as genetic assimilation and the guidance of the effects of mutations might be of importance. Organismic thinking has some contributions to make to evolutionary theory, as a complement to the atomistic outlook, whether that is put in terms of simple causation or of random chance." (Waddington, 1961: 98.)

Current status of organic selection and genetic assimilation

What is the current status of the Baldwin effect and genetic assimilation? Interest remains very active (e.g. Wcislo, 1989; Turney, Whitley & Anderson, 1996; Eshel & Matessi, 1998; Weber & Depew, 2003; Grether, 2005; Crispo, 2008) but, to some extent, controversial (e.g. de Jong, 2005). Pigliucci, Murren & Schlichting (2006: 2366) suggest that resistance may be due to a misconception that these ideas constitute "a threat to the Modern Synthesis", whereas they are instead "a welcome expansion of its current horizon". Even so, the notion that these ideas are potentially "subversive" should be countenanced—insofar as they may reflect a shift from modernism (e.g. orthodox Darwinism) to post-modernism, as implied in a recent account of the evolutionary views of Jakob von Uexküll (Kull, 2004).

Crispo (2007) notes that the Baldwin effect and genetic assimilation are now frequently confounded in the literature. She helpfully clarifies that the selective regimes—orthoplasy in the

Baldwin effect (term introduced by Baldwin, 1902: 142), genetic assimilation in Waddington's scheme—are not only different, but both also involve the wider concept of *genetic accommodation*: heritable changes that occur in response to novel inductions.

Regardless of whether some special mechanism (e.g. genetic assimilation) is necessary, or if 'conventional' natural selection is all that is required (as Huxley, Simpson and Mayr all claimed), a considerable weight of opinion now favours the idea that behaviour plays a key role in the evolution of populations and species (e.g. West-Eberhard, 2003; Bateson, 2004, 2005; Corning, 2005). Thus, although mutation may be random, the direction of evolution is not, as it is often shaped by the emergence of novel plastic behaviour, notably when faced with new environmental challenges, within the framework of an organism's inherited behavioural/phenotypic repertoire. "Adaptive evolution is a two-step process: first the generation of variation by development, then the screening of that variation by selection." (West-Eberhard, 2003: 139.) "The decision-making and adaptability of the organism is recognized as an important driver of evolution and is increasingly seen as an alternative to the gene-focused views." (Bateson, 2005: 31.) There has been "A flood of publications on the role of behavior, social learning, and cultural transmission as pacemakers of evolutionary change" (Corning, 2005: 1.)

Thus a butterfly can switch to a novel host plant without genetic change—both in theory (Mameli, 2004) and in reality (Singer & Thomas, 1996)—and by some process of genetic accommodation, this shift may later become fixed in the population (also both in theory and practice—see the same references). Or a butterfly can first learn to go and then instinctively fly in a new direction at a critical time of year—as appears to have been the case with the Monarch. With time, it can do this better and better, in the case of the North American populations of *Danaus plexippus plexippus*, evolving neurological structures and systems that can fly it all the way to Mexico with an astonishing degree of success.

Conclusion

Perhaps the greatest interest in these systems lies in the relationship between individual learning and racial instinct, and its impact on evolution, including human evolution (Weber & Depew, 2003; Corning, 2005). This was recognised very early by the organic selectionists: "We reach a point of view which gives to organic evolution a sort of intelligent direction after all; for of all the variations tending in the direction of an instinct, but inadequate to its complete performance, only those will be supplemented and kept alive which the intelligence ratifies and uses for the animal's individual accommodations. The principle of selection applies strictly to the others or to some of them. So natural selection eliminates the others; and the future development of instinct must at each stage of a species evolution be in the directions thus ratified by intelligence." (Baldwin, 1902: 69.)

We can thus see organismal intelligence as the sum total of what each organism has learned and committed to "racial memory" about how to deal with its own environment (*umwelt*, or self-centred world), and successive changes in that environment. To me, this specific animal, plant, fungal, even "protistal" intelligence is the foundation on which organic (natural) selection can act, *and is thereby augmented*. This *is* the creative force of evolution, and why, as Kalevi Kull (2000) has so nicely expressed it, "organisms can be proud to have been their own designers". Once life has begun, there need be no *telos*, final cause or external designer—just the inexorable internal workings of intelligent, self-organizing, autonomous yet coherent populations of organisms as they live, develop, reproduce and die in their ever-changing world. Through acting according to their own (evolving) intelligence, organisms seek lives of meaning within their umwelt. In this context, we ought also to consider why so many humans underestimate, fail to appreciate, or even deny the enormous intelligence that is possessed by other organisms—but that is a different story, another essay.

Acknowledgements

I would like to acknowledge my gratitude to NESTA (National Endowment for Science, Technology and the Arts) for support during 2005–2008. I also thank Neil Spurway, and the editors, for the opportunity to contribute to this volume.

References

Ackery, Phillip R. & Vane-Wright, Richard I. 1984. *Milkweed butterflies: their cladistics and biology*. Ithaca: Cornell University Press.

Awake. 2008. Was it designed? The navigational system of the butterfly. *Awake!*, November 2008: 10.

Baldwin, James Mark. 1902. *Development and Evolution. Including psychophysical evolution, evolution by orthoplasy, and the theory of genetic modes*. New York: Macmillan.

Bateson, Patrick. 2004. The active role of behaviour in evolution. *Biology and Philosophy* 19(2): 283–298.

Bateson, Patrick. 2005. The return of the whole organism. *Journal of Biosciences* 30: 31–39.

Berry, Wendell. 2000. *Life is a Miracle. An essay against modern superstition*. Washington, DC: Counterpoint.

Bohm, David. 1980 (2002 edition). *Wholeness and the Implicate Order*. Abingdon, UK: Routledge.

Brooke, John Hedley. 1991. *Science and Religion. Some historical perspectives*. Cambridge, UK: CUP.

Brower, Lincoln P. 1995. Understanding and misunderstanding the migration of the Monarch butterfly (Nymphalidae) in North America: 1857–1995. *Journal of the Lepidopterists' Society* 49(4): 304–385.

Brower, L.P., Kust, D.R., Rendón Salinas, E., García-Serrano, E.,

Kust, K.R., Miller, J., Fernandez del Rey, C. & Pape, K. 2004. Catastrophic winter storm mortality of Monarch butterflies in Mexico during January 2002. *In* Oberhauser, K. & Solensky, M.J. (eds), *The Monarch Butterfly: biology and conservation*, pp. 151–166. Ithaca: Cornell University Press.

Capra, Fritjof. 1996 (1997 edition). *The Web of Life. A new synthesis of mind and matter.* Flamingo (HarperCollins).

Carr, Bernard (ed.) 2007. *Universe or Multiverse?* Cambridge: CUP.

Corning, Peter A. 1983. *The Synergism Hypothesis. A theory of progressive evolution.* New York: McGraw-Hill.

Corning, Peter A. 2005. *Holistic Darwinism. Synergism, cybernetics, and the bioeconomics of evolution.* Chicago: University of Chicago Press.

Crispo, Erika. 2007. The Baldwin effect and genetic assimilation: revisiting two mechanisms of evolutionary change mediated by phenotypic plasticity. *Evolution* 61(11): 2469–2479.

Crispo, Erika. 2008. Modifying effects of phenotypic plasticity on interactions among natural selection, adaptation and gene flow. *Journal of Evolutionary Biology* 21: 1460–1469.

de Jong, Gerdien. 2005. Evolution of phenotypic plasticity: patterns of plasticity and the emergence of ecotypes. *New Phytologist* 166: 101–118.

Dupré, John. 1993 (1995 paperback edition). *The Disorder of Things. Metaphysical foundations of the disunity of science.* Cambridge, Mass: Harvard University Press.

Eshel, Ilan & Matessi, Carlo. 1998. Canalization, genetic assimilation and preadaptation: a quantitative genetic model. *Genetics* 149: 2119–2133.

Goodwin, Brian. 2007. *Nature's Due. Healing our fragmented culture.* Edinburgh: Floris.

Grether, Gregory F. 2005. Environmental change, phenotypic plasticity, and genetic compensation. *The American Naturalist* 166(4): E115–E123.

Hull, David L. 1982. Philosophy and biology. *In* Fløistad, G. (ed.), *Contemporary Philosophy, A New Survey* 2: *Philosophy of Science*, pp. 280–316. The Hague: Nijhoff.

Huxley, Julian. 1942. *Evolution. The modern synthesis*. London: Allen & Unwin.

Kull, Kalevi. 2000. Organisms can be proud to have been their own designers. *Cybernetics and Human Knowing* 7(1): 45–55.

Kull, Kalevi. 2004. Uexküll and the post-modern evolutionism. *Sign Systems Studies* 32(1/2): 99–114.

Mameli, Matteo. 2004. Nongenetic selection and nongenetic inheritance. *British Journal for the Philosophy of Science* 55, 35–71.

Marshall, Larry G. 1988. Land mammals and the Great American Interchange. *American Scientist* 76: 380–388.

Mayr, Ernst. 1963. *Animal Species and Evolution*. Cambridge, Mass: Harvard University Press.

Midgley, Mary. 1985 (2006 edition). *Evolution as a Religion. Strange hopes and stranger fears*. Abingdon, UK: Routledge.

Midgley, Mary (ed.). 2007. *Earthy Realism. The meaning of Gaia*. Exeter, UK: Imprint Academic.

Monod, Jacques. 1972. *Chance and Necessity. An essay on the natural philosophy of modern biology* (English edition, translated by Austryn Wainhouse). London: Collins.

Peat, F. David. 2002. *From Certainty to Uncertainty. The story of science and ideas in the Twentieth Century*. Washington, D.C: Joseph Henry Press.

Pigliucci, Massimo, Murren, Courtney J. & Schlichting, Carl D. 2006. Phenotypic plasticity and evolution by genetic assimilation. *Journal of Experimental Biology* 209: 2362–2367.

Pittendrigh, Colin S. 1958. Adaptation, natural selection, and behavior. *In* Roe, A. & Simpson, G.G. (eds), *Behavior and Evolution*, pp. 390–416. New Haven: Yale University Press.

Rensch, Bernhard. 1983. The abandonment of Lamarckian explanations: the case of climatic parallelism of animal characteristics. *In* Grene, M. (ed.), *Dimensions of Darwinism*, pp. 31–42. Cambridge: Cambridge University Press.

Reppert, Steven M. 2007. The ancestral circadian clock of monarch butterflies: Role in time-compensated sun compass orientation. *Cold Spring Harbor Symposia on Quantitative Biology* **72**: 113–118.

Richards, Eric J. 2006. Inherited epigenetic variation—revisiting soft inheritance. *Nature Reviews Genetics* 7: 395–401.

Rignano, Eugenio. 1911. *Upon the Inheritance of Acquired Characters* (English edition, translated by Basil C.H. Harvey). Chicago: Open Court.

Scott, James A. 1986. *The Butterflies of North America*. Stanford, Ca: Stanford University Press.

Simpson, George Gaylord. 1953. The Baldwin effect. *Evolution* 7: 110–117.

Singer, Michael C. & Thomas, Christopher D. 1996. Evolutionary responses of a butterfly metapopulation to human and climate-caused environmental variation. *American Naturalist* 148: S9–S39.

Thain, Michael & Hickman, Michael. 1994. *The Penguin Dictionary of Biology* (9th edn). London: Penguin Books.

Turney, Peter, Whitley, Darrell & Anderson, Russell W. 1996. Evolution, learning, and instinct: 100 years of the Baldwin effect [editorial]. *Evolutionary Computation* 4(3): iv-viii.

Waddington, Conrad H. 1953. Genetic assimilation of an acquired character. *Evolution* 7: 118–126.

Waddington, Conrad H. 1957. *The Strategy of the Genes*. London: Allen & Unwin.

Waddington, Conrad H. 1961. *The Nature of Life*. London: Allen & Unwin.

Walsh, Denis. 2006. Evolutionary essentialism. *British Journal for the Philosophy of Science*, 57: 425–448.

Wcislo, William T. 1989. Behavioral environments and evolutionary change. *Annual Review of Ecology and Systematics* 20:

137–169.

Weber, Bruce & Depew, David (eds) 2003. *Evolution and Learning: the Baldwin Effect reconsidered.* Cambridge, Mass: MIT Press.

West-Eberhard, Mary Jane. 2003. *Developmental Plasticity and Evolution.* Oxford: Oxford University Press.

Wilson, Edward O. 1998 (1999 edition). *Consilience. The unity of knowledge.* New York: Vintage (Random House).

Winsor, Mary P. 2006. The creation of the essentialism story: an exercise in metahistory. *History and Philosophy of the Life Sciences* 28: 149–174.

Woodson, Robert E. Jnr. 1954. The North American species of *Asclepias* L. *Annals of the Missouri Botanical Garden* 41: 1–211.

Zhu, Haisun, Casselman, Amy & Reppert, Steven M. 2008. Chasing migration genes: A brain expressed sequence tag resource for summer and migratory monarch butterflies (*Danaus plexippus*). PLoS ONE 3(1): e1345 doi:10.1371/journal.pone.0001345.

Zhu, H., Sauman, I., Yuan, Q., Casselman, A., Emery-Le, M., Emery, P. & Reppert, S.M. 2008. Cryptochromes define a novel circadian clock mechanism in monarch butterflies that may underlie sun compass navigation. *PLoS Biology* 6(1): e4doi:10.1371/journal.pbio.0060004.

Dick Vane-Wright, entomologist, and a Zoology graduate from University College London, spent his professional life at the Natural History Museum, London. In 2003 he received the degree of Doctor of Science, *honoris causa*, from the University of Copenhagen. Currently Honorary Professor of Taxonomy at DICE, University of Kent, he continues to work on a wide variety of projects related to entomology, biodiversity and conservation.

Intelligent Design and the Origin of Life

Andrew Robinson and Christopher Southgate

Introduction: The ultimate chicken-and-egg conundrum

At first sight the origin of life presents the ultimate 'chicken-and-egg' conundrum. Organisms – at least the ones we know of on earth – share in common with one another a complex system including DNA (deoxyribonucleic acid), RNA (ribonucleic acid) and proteins. The DNA of living things consists of long chains composed of four nucleotides (designated by A, T, C, and G) arranged like a sequence of letters. The sequence of nucleotides acts like a code, containing the 'information' required to make a protein. Proteins consist of sequences of amino acids. The shape of each protein is determined largely by the order in which the amino acids are arranged, and the functional properties of the protein depend on its shape. Each of the twenty amino acids that occur in proteins is 'coded' for by a triplet of nucleotides. For example, GGC codes for the amino acid glycine. The expression of a DNA sequence into an amino acid sequence depends on the function of certain specialised proteins acting as enzymes (an enzyme is a protein that speeds up the rate of a particular chemical reaction by acting as a catalyst) It takes place in two steps: 'transcription' into messenger RNA (mRNA) and 'translation' of mRNA into protein. A protein called RNA polymerase is needed to transcribe the DNA sequence into a messenger (mRNA) sequence. The translation of the mRNA sequence into an amino acid sequence requires another kind of RNA molecule, called transfer RNA (tRNA). Each tRNA molecule acts as an 'adaptor'. At one end of the molecule is a triplet nucleotide sequence which 'recognises' the corresponding triplet on the mRNA molecule. At the other end of the tRNA molecule is a binding site to which the required amino acid has already been attached. That attachment of the correct amino acid to the particular kind of tRNA molecule depends on another set of proteins, called amino-acyl tRNA synthetases. To add to the complexity, the process by which the tRNA molecules become temporarily attached to the mRNA molecule, so that the amino acids joined to the tRNA molecules are connected up into a chain to form the required protein, depends on another complex structure called a ribosome. Ribosomes are themselves made up out of subunits of another kind of RNA molecule together with other specialised proteins.

It will be clear from this brief (and simplified!) description of the transcription and translation mechanisms that the manufacture of a protein from the corresponding DNA sequence is a complex process. The reason that it poses a chicken-and-egg kind of problem can be put quite simply: DNA is needed in order to make proteins because the DNA sequence stores the 'information' needed to put together the correct amino acid sequence to make any particular protein. But specialised proteins are needed to transcribe the DNA sequence into an RNA sequence, and other specialised proteins are needed to translate the RNA sequence into a protein. So which came first – the proteins that are needed to transcribe and translate the DNA, or the DNA that is needed to specify the order of amino acids necessary to make these proteins? At first sight the problem seems to be a perfect example of two concepts central to intelligent design (ID) theory: 'irreducible complexity' (Behe 2006) and 'complex specified information' (Dembski 2001). In this chapter we will consider each of these concepts in the light of the problem of the origin of life. In the case of irreducible complexity we will offer some responses to ID theory that are broadly equivalent to the responses that can be offered in relation to other examples of biological complexity. In the case of complex specified information we shall suggest that, in addition, ID theory (and, for that matter, much current scientific thought in biology) is confused about what it means by 'information'.

Irreducible complexity and the emergence of life

According to Intelligent Design theorist Michael Behe, 'irreducible complexity' presents an insurmountable challenge to Darwinism:

> By 'irreducibly complex' I mean a single system composed of several well matched, interacting parts that contribute to the basic function, wherein the removal of any one of the parts causes the system to effectively cease functioning. An irreducibly complex system cannot be produced directly (that is, by continuously improving the initial function, which continues to work by the same mechanism) by slight successive modifications of the precursor system, because any precursor to an irreducibly complex system that is missing a part is by definition nonfunctional. (Behe 2006, 39)

Behe's everyday illustration of his concept of irreducible complexity is a household mousetrap (Behe 2001, 93). The mousetrap consists of several components – platform, spring, holding bar, catch, hammer – all of which are necessary to the effective working of the trap. If any of the components were removed then mice would never be caught. We may safely admit that the same is true of the mechanism of protein synthesis outlined above. If any of the major parts of the mechanism were removed then proteins would not get made. The question for origin of life research, then, is whether Behe is correct that such an 'irreducibly complex' system could not, even in principle, be produced by slight successive modifications of a precursor system.

One of the most promising ways around this apparent problem is the possibility that before proteins and DNA came onto the scene there was a pre-biotic system of replicating molecules consisting only of RNA – the 'RNA world' hypothesis. This hypothesis was first proposed in the 1960s and gained experimental support when it was shown in the 1980s that RNA molecules can themselves act as catalysts in a manner similar to the function that in most biological reactions are performed by protein enzymes (see Orgel 2002, 142). An RNA molecule that can act as a catalyst is called a ribozyme (just as a protein that can act as a catalyst is called an enzyme). As explained above, genetic 'information' is normally stored as a DNA sequence, and the transcription and translation of this sequence normally requires protein catalysts. However, it is possible to imagine RNA performing both the functions that in present-day organisms are performed by DNA (as an 'informational' molecule) and proteins (as enzymes). According to the RNA-world hypothesis the catalytic functions of ribozymes would subsequently have been taken over by proteins (which are catalytically more versatile than RNA) and the genetic, 'informational', function of the RNA sequence would have been taken over by DNA (which is chemically more stable than RNA and is therefore a better 'information storage' medium). At the moment we cannot be sure that life emerged through an RNA-world scenario, though the centrality of RNA to some very fundamental biological processes such as the function of ribosomes (see above) provides some circumstantial evidence. The important point is that the RNA-world hypothesis is an example of one way in which an 'irreducibly complex' system could in principle arise from simpler precursors. Furthermore, the hypothesis is the subject of active and ongoing scientific research (for example, see De Lucrezia, Anella, and Chiarabelli 2007). It is also possible that an RNA world developed in tandem with other forms of proto-biology, such as primitive systems of lipid vesicles (see details of Szostak's work at http://genetics.mgh.harvard.edu/szostakweb/index.html) and / or the self-organising properties of some autocatalytic chemical systems (Kauffman 2007). Until recently these different scenarios

(RNA world, vesicle systems, self-organisation) have tended to be considered as competing alternative hypotheses; the fact that origin of life research is reaching the point at which these concepts and experimental systems can be experimentally combined is evidence of the fruitfulness of current lines of enquiry.

It is important to acknowledge that the concept of an RNA world would not, on its own, answer all the problems of the origin of life. One problem is that nucleotides themselves (the building blocks of RNA) are complicated molecules; it may be difficult (though not impossible) for them to arise directly in pre-biotic conditions (i.e. from chemical processes not themselves dependent on life). We need not conclude, however, that an RNA world could not have had a natural origin. One possibility is that the first 'genetic' system did not involve RNA, but some other chain of chemical building blocks that were more likely to arise on the early earth and / or were more easily replicated in the absence of protein enzymes. One candidate that has been considered is PNAs (peptide nucleic acids), in which the sugar-phosphate backbone of RNA or DNA is replaced by a simpler kind of chemical bond (Orgel 2002, 152). Experiments have shown that PNA molecules (and other analogues of nucleic acids) can interact with RNA in a way that might allow a transition from a pre-RNA world to an RNA world. An implication of the possibility of one or more pre-RNA worlds is that the first steps towards the origin of life may have left little or no trace in the biochemistry of current living organisms (Orgel 2002, 151). This serves to underline the difficulties that origin of life research faces. We are dealing with events that took place nearly 4 billion years ago in terrestrial conditions that are very different from those with which we are familiar (Schopf 2002). In addition, we are not simply looking for the origin of a familiar kind of system, such as a fully functioning complex single-celled organism. Rather, we are asking what kinds of system might plausibly have arisen in the pre-biotic conditions of the early earth *and* have had the potential for subsequent evolution into more familiar life-forms. This is an immensely difficult scientific task, but the difficulty of the challenge does not justify an *a priori* assumption that irreducible complexity (to use Behe's term) could not have arisen by natural processes.

Before moving on to consider the concept of 'complex specified information', let us briefly note three other misconceptions, alongside the premature attribution of 'irreducible complexity', that seem to keep recurring in ID arguments relating to the origin of life:

ID theorists sometimes point out that Darwin and his contemporaries had no idea of the internal complexity of biological cells. For example, the German biologist Ernst Haeckel (1834-1919) once described cells as 'homogenous globules of plasm' (Meyer 2001, 103; see also Dembski and Ruse 2007, 16). Darwin therefore had no reason to question how such a complex structure as a biological cell first appeared – his theory assumed the initial existence of 'one or a few simple forms'. If Darwin did not know about the biochemical and structural complexity of the cell then, so the ID argument goes, Darwinism does not deal with the origin of this complexity, but only with the evolution of life *after* living cells had come into being (Meyer 2001, 103). The fallacy of this argument is that the fact that Darwin had no way of knowing the full complexity of cells does not imply that Darwinian theory (the concept of evolution by natural selection) will be unable to explain such complexity.

The claim is sometimes made that Darwinian evolution cannot explain the origin of life because natural selection cannot occur until there is a replicating system, and organisms do not reproduce unless they already have the full protein-RNA-DNA system outlined above. ID theorists like to quote the great Ukrainian evolutionary biologist Theodosius Dobzhanksy (1900-1975), who remarked that 'pre-biological evolution is a contradiction in terms' (Lennox 2007, 187). The problem with this argument is that natural selection does not require that the reproducing organisms (or proto-biotic entities) must replicate using the same biochemical machinery as today. Rather, the logical requirements for evolution by natural selection are very general: all that is necessary is that the organism / entity is capable of replication with variation, and that some of that variation is heritable (i.e., has a tendency to be passed from one generation to the next). These very general requirements could be met by systems other than the DNA-based replication system with which we are familiar – for example, they could be met by an RNA molecule capable of catalysing its own replication (see above).

ID theorists like to point out that experiments on the origin of life are conducted by an experimenter who designs the conditions under which the experiment will be carried out. For example, in 1953 Stanley Miller published the results of some now famous experiments in which he passed electrical sparks through a gas mixture to simulate the effect of lightening occurring within the atmosphere of the early earth. He left the apparatus running for a week, after which he was able to show that the reaction products included amino-acids, the building blocks of proteins. Since then a large amount of scientific work has been done on the pre-biotic synthesis of organic molecules, and we also know that such molecules are produced naturally elsewhere in the universe, because they are present in significant amounts in meteorites (Miller and Lazcano 2002). ID theorists argue that the fact that origin of life experiments such as those of Miller have to be carefully designed in order to produce useful results is evidence that life requires design (Meyer 2001, 106). The fallacy in this argument is that it misconstrues such experiments as direct attempts to reconstruct the exact events that led to the emergence of life. Experiments of this kind are much better thought of as like the many small pieces of detective work that collectively may solve a crime. Miller was asking a specific question (can organic molecules be produced by non-biological processes in certain conditions that may mimic the early earth?) and carefully designed an experiment to test his hypothesis. That the experimental set-up required a designer does not justify an inference that the actual processes that led to the emergence of life required anything equivalent to a purposeful experimenter in the background.

Information and the origin of life

We turn now to another concept from ID theory, that of 'complex specified information'. William Dembski argues that the key criterion for recognising the hand of design is 'specified complexity', which he defines by the presence in a system of three features: contingency, complexity, and specification (Dembski 2001, 178). These three features can be illustrated with an example that he draws from the film *Contact,* based on a Carl Sagan novel in which researchers in SETI (the Search for Extraterrestrial Intelligence) detect a radio signal consisting of a sequence of 1126 beats and pauses. When the series of beats and pauses are expressed as a sequence of 1s and 0s it is found to correspond to a representation of the prime numbers from 2 to 101 (Dembski 2001, 176-177). The sequence is *contingent* in that it seems unlikely to have been produced by necessity from any natural process. It is *complex* in that it is not so simple that it could reasonably be explained by chance (as a sequence corresponding to, say, only the first three prime numbers might be). And it is *specified* in that it is a pattern that it is reasonable to suppose had been chosen before the event of its transmission. To illustrate the specificity criterion with another example, winning the lottery is highly improbable because the sequence of numbers on your own lottery ticket is specified in advance of the draw. Your sequence is one of several million that might come up and is individually improbable; that *someone* will win the lottery is probable, because one of the millions of (individually improbable) sequences *is* likely to occur. (Note that our lottery example would not meet Dembski's second criterion, that of complexity, because the number on the ticket, though specified before the draw, could have been generated, say, by a random number generator.)

ID theorists have argued that nucleotide sequences in the DNA of living organisms exhibit specified complexity of the kind defined by Dembski and that such sequences therefore constitute strong evidence of design. For example, Stephen Meyer argues that the probability of DNA randomly assembling into a sequence corresponding to the amino acid sequence of a functioning protein is vanishingly small (Meyer 2001, 110). The Darwinist will of course point out that evolution by natural selection offers a way in which such sequences could evolve by the random occurrence of small changes, with changes that confer a small selective advantage in terms of survival and repro-duction being preserved. Meyer rejects this Darwinian view on the grounds that natural selection requires replication, and repli-cation requires functioning proteins and nucleic acids – an argument that we criticised in the previous section. He goes on to consider, and reject, the possibility that DNA might self-assemble into functional sequences by a spontaneous *self-organ-ising* process (Meyer 2001, 111-114). Again, we can certainly agree with Meyer that this scenario is implausible, but this is not a role that origin of life researchers would consider for self-organising processes. Self-organising processes may well have a role in producing or stabilising some of the order in the pre-biotic systems form which life emerged (Kauffman 1995; Depew and Weber 1998; Kauffman 2000; Kauffman and Clayton 2006; Kauffman 2007), but it would not be expected to account in any simple way for the specificity of functional amino acid and nucleotide sequences. Having rejected chance, natural selection, and self-organisation as the sources of the specified complexity of functional DNA, Meyer concludes – by analogy with the specified complexity of a sentence in English or of the lines of code in a computer software programme – that design by an intelligent agent must be invoked (Meyer 2001, 115). In keeping with Dembski's definition of complex specified information, Meyer puts this argument in 'informational' terms. According to Meyer, systems that have both specificity and complexity have 'information content' (Meyer 2001, 114). The problem of the origin of life, Meyer argues, is the problem of the origin of biological information (Meyer 2001, 108), a statement with which some origin of life researchers would agree (Küppers 1990). Meyer goes on to argue that, 'our experience with information-intensive systems (especially codes and languages) indicates that such systems always come from an intelligent source', and hence we must infer 'the past action of an intelligent cause' (Meyer 2001, 115).

Meyer's argument against a natural origin of biological 'information' of the sort found in the 'specified complexity' of functional DNA sequences is vulnerable to the same kinds of criticism as we have already made of the application of the concept of 'irreducible complexity' to origin of life questions (see above). We wish to focus here on the way in which both ID theorists *and* many origin of life researchers appear to be confused about the concept of 'information'. The nature of the confusion is illustrated by Meyer's use of the same term, information, to refer both to the sequence of 1126 ones and zeros corresponding to the prime numbers between 2 and 101 and to a meaningful sentence in English. We agree with Meyers that both of these exhibit specified complexity according to Dembski's definition. We also agree that there *is* an information concept in terms of which both can be analysed, namely, Claude Shannon's mathematical theory of information (Shannon and Weaver 1949). However, the mathematical theory of communication is concerned with something much narrower than the everyday use of the word 'information'. Whilst the mathematical theory is very powerful in appropriate contexts it is liable to lead us to dead ends (scientific and theological) if too much is expected of it. This is such an important point that it is worth considering briefly what Shannon's concept is intended to measure. Briefly, the mathematical theory of information provides a way of measuring the amount by which our 'uncertainty' is decreased if we receive a 'signal' consisting of a sequence of 'symbols'. The reduction in uncertainty refers to the comparison of the signal 'received' with the number of possible signals that could have been be 'sent'. For example, if a device can produce 2 possible symbols (0 or 1), each of which is equally likely, we do not start with a very high degree of uncertainty: we already know that the signal will be either a 1 or a 0. When the device produces a symbol (say, a 1), our uncertainty is reduced, but not from a very high level. (If there is noise in the system then our reduction of uncertainty will not be to zero because even if we receive a 1 we cannot be sure that a 1 was sent: the mathematical theory of information can also deal mathematically with this problem of noise). If the device can produce any one of 4 symbols (e.g., ACTG – the 'letters' of the DNA 'code'), and again supposing that each is equally likely, then when we know which symbol actually occurs at any particular site then the quantitative reduction in our uncertainty will be greater than if only two symbols had been possible at that site. The units of the measure of information provided by the mathematical theory of infor-mation are 'bits'. A single 'letter' in the two-symbol example (0s and 1s) carries 1 bit of information (reduces our uncertainty by 2 bits per symbol); a single letter in the 4-letter DNA alphabet carries 2 bits of information.

The technological ramifications of the discovery of a quanti-tative measure of information lie at the heart of the revolution in information and communication technology that has occurred in the last generation or so. But, crucially, *the mathematical theory of information has nothing to do with meaning*. Meyers is perfectly correct to say that a sentence in English, a string of 'code' in binary form in a computer programme, or a sequence of 1s and 0s received from space, share with one another a property that we may call 'information', provided that what he means is that they can all be analysed using the mathematical theory of information. But such an analysis can tell us nothing about what such 'messages' *mean* – nothing, in other words, about the process of *interpretation*.

What, it may be asked, has interpretation got to do with the origin of life? Isn't interpretation a capacity limited to humans and perhaps a few 'higher' animals? At this point the reader must be warned that the ideas we are going to present are not (yet) part of the mainstream of thinking about the origin of life. But we introduce these ideas here (a) because, negatively, they highlight the limitations of the information concept that ID theory – and much scientific origin of life work – has tended to focus on, and (b) more positively, they are the starting point for the more constructive theological approach that we shall mention at the end of this chapter.

Consider, then, a bacterium swimming up a glucose gradient. The bacterium is *interpreting* the presence of glucose molecules as a sign of 'dinner over there' (cf. Kauffman 2000, 111). And the action of swimming in that direction may prove to be a misinterpretation: perhaps there will not prove to be enough glucose over there to make the swim worthwhile, or perhaps the molecule responded to was not glucose after all. We have been exploring the hypothesis that by focusing on what amounts to the mathematical concept of information applied to 'informational' macromolecules such as RNA and DNA, origin of life research has – to use what is perhaps an unlikely expression in this context – been missing the elephant in the room. The elephant is interpretation. The question is, can interpretation be defined in a sufficiently robust and general way that it can be applied not only to the level of bacteria but also to very simple proto-biotic entities?

(Robinson 2007; Southgate and Robinson 2008). Another way of putting this is to say that we already know that the last universal common ancestor (LUCA) of all the major branches of the evolutionary tree must have been a complex bacterium-like organism. All living organisms, we contend, are capable of interpreting their environments in a primitive way. We may therefore infer that the LUCA was able to make interpretations. It is important to understand, however, that LUCA was not the point at which life originated. Between the lifeless earth of about 4 billion years ago, when there were no interpreting entities, and the time when LUCA lived, the capacity for interpretation emerged. How and why, then, did that capacity emerge?

To answer that question we must try to get a clearer idea of what it is to make an interpretation or – to put it a little more precisely – to interpret a sign. The field of biosemiotics attempts to apply semiotic theory to biological systems, drawing particularly on C. S. Peirce's triadic concept of the sign (e.g., Hoffmeyer 1996). According to Peirce, interpretation involves a triadic relation between a sign, the object represented by the sign, and an 'interpretant', where the interpretant is a purposeful response to the sign, not necessarily made consciously. Biosemiotics has generally struggled to show that the putatively triadic sign-processes it identifies are not, in fact, reducible to purely mechanical events. However, a recent scholarly reconsideration and reconstruction of Peirce's semiotics (Short 2007) offers a very promising way of giving an account of interpretation that is fully naturalistic (i.e., it does not involve any mysterious or supernatural causes) and yet irreducible to mere sequences of mechanical events (in other words, mechanistic explanations cannot provide a full explanation of the processes in question). Interestingly in the context of this discussion of ID, the key to this naturalistic but non-reductive account of interpretation would be the re-introduction of a concept of purpose – of final causation – into respectable scientific discourse. (The bacterium's movement up a glucose gradient only counts as an interpretation because it is done for a *purpose*, namely, getting a 'meal', and because it may fail to achieve its purpose if it has made a misinterpretation.) The hypothesis that Southgate and I have been exploring is that interpretation may have been an important, currently overlooked, factor in the emergence of life. A simple autocatalytic system capable of replication (recall that replication does not imply RNA or DNA), or perhaps even a single molecule, would gain a selective advantage if it were able to interpret its environment, for example by changing from a stable unreactive configuration to a less stable, but reactive configuration in the presence of the substrate molecules needed for replication. The entity could interpret its environment by responding (changing from 'unreactive' to 'reactive' configuration) in the presence of a sign (the presence of one or a few relevant substrate molecules, or of something usually associated with the presence of substrate). This interpretation would result in fulfilment of the entity's 'purpose' (ultimately that of reproduction) if the sign indeed turns out to be associated with the presence of the object that it is taken to represent (e.g., presence of enough substrate molecules to allow growth or replication).

If, as I have suggested above, the relevance of interpretation to the origin of life turns out to be distinct from the question of how 'informational' macromolecules such as RNA and DNA arose, should we conclude that the 'information' in such molecules has nothing to do with semantics and meaning? And if that is the case, is the general enthusiasm for nucleic acids as the apparent key to life misplaced? Biologists appear to be divided on this question. At one extreme, Richard Dawkins has no hesitation about referring to DNA as a code containing the instructions for making the organism (Dawkins 1976, 22-23). Ironically, in this respect ID theorists share some of the assumptions about the informational content of DNA that are favoured by ultra-reductionist biologists like Dawkins. At the other extreme, some

Developmental Systems Theorists deny that there is anything particularly special about the biological function of DNA, which should be understood as merely one 'developmental resource' among many (Oyama 1985; Griffiths and Gray 1994; Oyama, Griffiths, and Gray 2001). This view is often accompanied by a high degree of scepticism about the usefulness of the term 'information' in biology, which, it is argued, is at best metaphorical and at worst positively misleading. Our own view is that in this respect Developmental Systems Theory (DST) is in danger of throwing the baby out with the bathwater. DST has provided an important and compelling criticism of the idea that DNA somehow contains 'instructions' or a 'programme' for making the organism as a whole. But in a more limited sense it may still be legitimate to regard nucleotide triplets as standing for (representing) the corresponding amino acids (Godfrey-Smith 2000). The important, if perhaps controversial, point that we wish to make is that the informational function (in the semantic rather than mathematical sense) of DNA is probably better thought of as a good trick that life has discovered, rather than the key to life itself. If we ever discover life on other planets we may or may not find that DNA and / or RNA are involved; it would certainly be interesting to know. I expect, however, that if the entities in question cannot be shown to be interpreting their environments then we will hesitate to call them living.

The metaphysics of meaning

Debates about Intelligent Design tend to be conducted in negative terms: ID theorists do not think that science can deliver all that it promises by way of natural explanations; scientists (and probably most theologians) do not think that ID is science. We would like to finish on a more constructive note. William Dembski, one of founders of the ID movement, offers the following reflections on the ultimate metaphysical (as opposed to scientific) significance of ID theory:

The primary challenge, once the broader implications of design for science have been worked out, is therefore to develop a relational ontology in which the problem of being resolves thus: to be is to be in communion, and to be in communion is to transmit and receive information. Such an ontology will not only safeguard science and leave adequate breathing space for design, but will also make sense of the world as sacrament. The world is a mirror representing the divine life. The mechanical philosophy was ever blind to this fact. Intelligent design, on the other hand, readily embraces the sacramental nature of physical reality. Indeed, intelligent design is just the *Logos* theology of John's Gospel restated in the idiom of information theory. (Dembski 2001, 191-192)

Many Christian theologians would find themselves in sympathy with what Dembski claims is his broader aim, that of developing a relational ontology with which to ground the claim that being is communion (cf. Zizioulas 1985). But does communion really consist of the transmitting and receiving of information? Not, we suggest, if information is conceived in terms of Shannon's mathematical theory of communication or Dembski's own 'complex specified information'. But perhaps communion *does* consist of the seeking, finding, and making of *meaning*. And the interesting metaphysical question then is not 'where does information come from?', but rather, 'what does the world have to be like in order that meaning can emerge from matter?'.Elsewhere one of us has drawn attention to the parallels between C. S. Peirce's semiotics and the Christian doctrine of the Trinity (Robinson 2004). Where Dembski says that the world is a 'mirror' reflecting the divine life, we would like to propose that meaning and interpretation are *vestiges of the Trinity in creation*, and that creaturely life is grounded by, and participates in, the communion of meaning-making that constitutes the divine life. According to this model, for example, the Holy Spirit, the mediator between the Father (source of all being) and Son (Word / Logos), is the ground of all interpretation and meaning in the created order. Recall, for example, the role of the Spirit at Pentecost (Acts 2) in making apparently unintelligible languages intelligible. And if, as we have suggested above, interpretation proves to be a necessary property for the emergence of life, a property without which we would not be prepared to acknowledge an entity as living, then we would have a biological and philosophical correlate of the affirmation in the Niceno-Constantinopolitan creed that the Spirit is 'the Lord, the giver of life'.

Interestingly, if this perspective gives rise to any kind of argument for the existence of God then it would be a cosmological argument rather than a design argument. Design arguments claim to recognise design in the world and infer from that the existence of a designer. (ID theorists often describe their approach as an inference *to* design, but the implied existence of a designer is never far away). The standard cosmological argument, on the other hand, follows from the question 'why is there something rather than nothing?'. A form of cosmological argument relating to interpretation might start with the question, 'why is it that anything makes sense or has meaning; why is the world intelligible?'. Design arguments, but not cosmological arguments, are always in danger of reducing God to a god-of-the-gaps and of reducing the status of the world to that of a manufactured artefact. Dembski refers to ID theory as embracing 'the sacramental nature of physical reality', but in everyday experience designed objects perform instrumental functions. The things we love purely for themselves are not designed; one's children are precious in a way that one's computer is not. If God loves us creatures it is, we hope, because we are God's children, not because we are God's artefacts. The best way of affirming the 'sacramental' nature of physical reality, and of life in particular, is not by looking for evidence of design, but by asking whether it is coherent to understand the created order as so constituted as to be oriented towards participation in the divine life. We suggest that the most appropriate contemporary idiom for restating the Logos theology of John's Gospel is not, as Dembski suggests, information theory (in either the mathematical or ID sense) but semiotic theory, the theory of signs and meanings.

References

Behe, Michael. 2001. Darwin's Breakdown: Irreducible Complexity and Design at the Foundation of Life. In *Signs of Intelligence: Understanding Intelligent Design*, edited by W. A. Dembski and J. M. Kushiner. Grand Rapids, MI: Brazos Press.

———. 2006. *Darwin's Black Box: The Biochemical Challenge to Evolution (10th Anniversary Edition)*. New York: Free Press.

Dawkins, Richard. 1976. *The Selfish Gene*. Oxford: Oxford University Press.

De Lucrezia, Davide, Fabrizio Anella, and Cristano Chiarabelli. 2007. On the Chemical Reality of the RNA World. *Origins of Life and Evolution of Biospheres* 37 (4-5):379-385.

Dembski, William A. 2001. Signs of Intelligence: A Primer on the Discernment of Intelligent Design. In *Signs of Intelligence: Understanding Intelligent Design*, edited by W. A. Dembski and J. M. Kushiner. Berkeley: University of California Press.

Dembski, William A, and Michael Ruse. 2007. Intelligent Design: A Dialogue. In *Intelligent Design: William A Dembski and Michael Ruse in Dialogue*, edited by R. B. Stewart. Minneapolis, MN: Fortress Press.

Depew, David J., and Bruce H. Weber. 1998. What Does Natural Selection Have to Be Like In Order to Work with Self-Organisation? *Cybernetics and Human Knowing* 5 (No. 1):18-31.

Godfrey-Smith, Peter. 2000. On the Theoretical Role of "Genetic Coding". *Philosophy of Science* 67:26-44.

Griffiths, P. E., and R. D. Gray. 1994. Developmental Systems and Evolutionary Explanation. *The Journal of Philosophy* XCI (No.

6):277-304.

Hoffmeyer, Jesper. 1996. *Signs of Meaning in the Universe*. Bloomington: Indiana University Press.

Kauffman, Stuart. 2007. Origin of Life and the Living State. *Origins of Life and Evolution of Biospheres* 37 (4-5):315-322.

Kauffman, Stuart A. 1995. *At Home in the Universe: The Search for the Laws of Self-Organization and Complexity*. Harmondsworth: Penguin.

———. 2000. *Investigations*. Oxford: Oxford University Press.

Kauffman, Stuart, and Philip Clayton. 2006. On emergence, agency, and organization. *Biology and Philosophy* 21 (4):500-520.

Küppers, Bernd-Olaf. 1990. *Information and the Origin of Life*. Cambridge, Massachusetts: MIT Press.

Lennox, John C. 2007. Intelligent Design: Some Critical Reflections on the Current Debate. In *Intelligent Design: William A Dembski and Michael Ruse in Dialogue*, edited by R. B. Stewart. Minneapolis: Fortress Press.

Meyer, Stephen C. 2001. Word Games: DNA, Design, and Intelligence. In *Signs of Intelligence: Understanding Intelligent Design*, edited by W. A. Dembski and J. M. Kushiner. Grand Rapids, MI: Brazos Press.

Miller, Stanley L, and Antonio Lazcano. 2002. Formation of the Building Blocks of Life. In *Life's Origin: The Beginnings of Biological Evolution*, edited by W. J. Schopf. Berkeley: University of California Press.

Orgel, Leslie E. 2002. The Origin of Biological Information. In *Life's Origin: The Beginnings of Biological Information*, edited by J. W. Schopf. Berkeley: University of California Press.

Oyama, Susan. 1985. *The Ontogeny of Information: Developmental Systems and Evolution*. Cambridge: Cambridge University Press.

Oyama, Susan, Paul E. Griffiths, and Russell D. Gray, eds. 2001. *Cycles of Contingency: Developmental Systems and Evolution*.

Cambridge, MA: MIT Press.

Robinson, Andrew. 2007. Emergence and the origin of life. *Reviews in Science and Religion* 49 (May):29-37.

Robinson, Andrew J. 2004. Continuity, Naturalism and Contingency: A Theology of Evolution Drawing on the Semiotics of C.S. Peirce and Trinitarian Thought. *Zygon: Journal of Religion and Science* 39 (1):111-136.

Schopf, William J. 2002. When Did Life Begin? In *Life's Origin: The Beginnings of Biological Evolution*, edited by W. J. Schopf. Berkeley: University of California Press.

Shanks, Niall. 2004. *God, The Devil, and Darwin: A Critique of Intelligent Design Theory*. Oxford: Oxford University Press.

Shannon, C. E., and W. Weaver. 1949. *The Mathematical Theory of Communication*. Urbana: University of Illinois Press.

Short, T. L. 2007. *Peirce's Theory of Signs*. Cambridge: Cambridge University Press.

Southgate, Christopher, and Andrew Robinson. 2008. Interpretation and the Emergence of Life. *Poster presented at the International Society for the Study of the Origin of Life, XVth Conference, 24-29 August, Florence, Italy.*

Zizioulas, John D. 1985. *Being and Communion: Studies in Personhood and the Church*. Crestwood, NY: St Vladimir's Seminary Press.

Andrew Robinson is an Honorary University Fellow in Theology at the University of Exeter. He trained in Physiology and Medicine and holds a PhD in Theology.

Christopher Southgate is a Research Fellow in Theology at the University of Exeter. He has published widely on the science-and-religion debate and was the co-ordinating editor of *God, Humanity and the Cosmos* (T&T Clark, 1999, 2005). He has recently published *The Groaning of Creation; God, Evolution and the Problem of Evil* (Westminster John Knox Press, 2008). The authors' current work on Information and the Origin of Life has been funded by the Science and Transcendence Advanced Research Series (CTNS, Berkeley, Calif).

Darwin's Compass: How Evolution Discovers the Song of Creation

Simon Conway Morris

It was G.K. Chesterton (1913) who trenchantly reminded us that, if one was going to preach, then it was more sensible to expend one's energies on addressing the converted rather than the unconverted. It was the former, after all, that were – and even more so are – in constant danger of missing the point and sliding away from the Faith into some vague sort of syncretistic, gnostic, gobbledegook. Chesterton, as ever, was right and should you think this is just another of his tiresome paradoxes may I urge you to re-read him: his prescience concerning our present situation and, worse, where we are heading is astounding. Yet, it might seem a little odd in a lecture devoted to the ancient and ongoing debate between science and religion to invoke at its onset the name of Chesterton. Well, no, I don't think so. First, as Stanley Jaki (1986) has reminded us, it is over-simplistic to regard Chesterton as anti-science. What Chesterton regarded with the deepest alarm was not science, but its mis-use. Indeed long before the time of Chesterton, others already saw the dangers of unprincipled meddling where hubris and ignorance marched hand-in-hand. Robert Boyle was one such.

Indeed, from the time of Boyle we should ask how far we have come. So far as the science-religion debate is concerned the linearity of history looks curiously circular. What exactly has changed? In Boyle's time we see science, albeit in nascent form, already beginning to grasp limitless possibilities in knowledge while at the same time the drumbeat of Hobbesian materialism is clearly heard. As Reijer Hooykaas (1987) has remarked the reductionists were abroad, and amongst the atomists there were leanings towards naturalism, if not atheism. Somewhat mysteriously the barriers between science and religion, if not already in place, certainly were in the process of construction. And today? Who hasn't met the scientist who boomingly – and they always boom – declares that those who believe in the Deity are unavoidably crazy, "cracked" as my dear father would have said, although I should add that I have every reason to believe he was – and now hope is – on the side of the angels. Conversely, the religious reaction was, and remains, to shy away from the implications of science. Better to doubt evolution, the age of the Earth, even the world itself, than imperil one's soul. The devout Boyle remained confident that this divide was false and pernicious. Yet even in his time Boyle's vigorous faith and orthodoxy, rather than simple observance of the customary pieties, was perhaps more unusual than we realize. Of Boyle himself it was written that he is "said to be a learned and witty man of science *in spite* of his religious convictions" (Hooykaas, 1987: 59). If that raised eyebrows in the time of Charles II, today the same sentiments are likely to provoke mute astonishment.

It is surely telling that the apparent disagreements between science and religion are so often treated with a bluntness and unsubtlety that in any normal discourse would be dismissed as juvenile. Hear the sounds of debate? Then sure enough within minutes we will be reminded of Galileo before the Inquisition or Bishop Wilberforce being mangled by T.H. Huxley. So often the terms of reference are condescending and dismissive, with the supposedly losing side being equated with flat-earthers. If at all possible the additional sins against political correctness are also heaped against the doors of religious discourse. This is bad enough, but the discussion is usually based on a chronic chrono-logical snobbery that supposes individuals dead for many years, if not centuries, were singularly unfortunate not to have lived in our times among people who not only know but are *right*. It would also be a mistake to overlook the fact that the undoubted continued hostility between science and religion in no small part is exacerbated by the sleight-of-hand whereby a materialist philosophy is illicitly imported to bolster a particular world-view of science. It remains an astonishing piece of window-dressing: meaning is smuggled into a world which by definition lacks meaning. Boyle himself knew the enemy. He was more than prepared, in the words of Hooykaas, (1987: 58) to be the one who "unmasks their pride ..... exposes their narrow mindedness [and] .... shows up their arrogance".

So how are we to be true heirs of Robert Boyle, legitimate scientists but inspired by faith, willing not only to conduct the debate, but win it? The present-day auguries are hardly auspicious. Too often our arguments, our world-picture, even our data, are cringingly presented, in a combination of nervousness and accommodation. Do I really have to remind you of our opponents' visceral aversion to religious thought and practice? To be labelled as the credulous believers in fairy tales, bottomless receptacles for wish-fulfilment, blind to the undoubted evils of the world, are common enough jibes. So too is our opponents' almost limitless degree of patronizing. Think of Daniel Dennett's parody of religious thought in the form of his "Skyhooks" (Dennett, 1995). Is he so naïve as to imagine the orthogonal intersection with our world of other realities is akin to some sort of elevator or a London Underground escalator? Nor should we forget that the attitude of our opponents is not one of benign disdain, but a deep-seated animus. Nor are they reluctant to pronounce on matters, such as reproductive technology or genetically modified food, with a conviction and assurance which in other contexts they would despise as symptomatic as the worst of dogmatic interference by the Pope or similar. These things matter, and as Peter Kreeft reminds us they not only matter, they matter absolutely.

Polemic and rhetoric have their places, but we are here not only to honour Boyle, but to re-examine how science and religion not only must co-exist – and I hope nobody here has fallen for

Stephen Jay Gould's (2001) reckless canard of science and religion defining independent magisteria of influence (and by way of further parenthesis should they toy with this superficially appealing idea be warned they face logical incoherence) – but far more importantly how science reveals unexpected depths to Creation while religion informs us what on earth (literally) we are going to do about it. From this perspective the impoverished world picture which the western world has been busy painting with a meager palette of predominantly browns and greys on a scruffy piece of hardboard (rescued from the attic) might not only be re-illuminated, but in this new blaze of light the wonder might become deeper – and the risks clearer.

I think it almost goes without saying that of all the areas of science concerned with this dialogue that of organic evolution is the most sensitive, in some ways the most vulnerable. This is hardly surprising; the stakes are the highest because where we humans came from, who we are, and what we represent must be questions of central importance. In other areas of science, on the other hand, the temperature of engagement is lower, and even in quiet corners scenes of cordiality may be witnessed. Such is most obvious in terms of the astounding developments in physics. Not only with the evidence for an instantiation of Creation - the Big Bang, if you prefer - but even more powerfully the now famous evidence for cosmological fine-tuning and the implication this has for an Anthropic Universe (Rees, 1999). So peculiar and so finely balanced do the key physical constants appear to be that it is hardly surprising that many physicists have embraced the concept of not just one universe but a gadzillion of them tucked away behind black holes or hidden in other dimensions, ever present but ever invisible. And out of that gadzillion, well we are the lucky ones where everything turned out to be just, precisely right.

Theologians are suspicious, and so they should be. Alternative universes, for ever invisible? This sounds like an area for debate by such as Albertus Magnus, Thomas Aquinas and perhaps especially William of Ockham. More topically, is this concept of multiverses so very far removed in our society from the inalienable belief in our society of unlimited "choice"?, a matter not only for the deathly pursuit of consumerism, but more worryingly expressed in the enthusiasm for making religion out of a patchwork of beliefs. Yet to return to the cosmic dimension, even if we accept the possibility of multiverses, George Ellis has reminded us that the concept is highly protean. One possibility is that if indeed there are multiple universes, then they are all the *same*.

Should we choose to be parochial, and stick to just one, fourteen billion year old, universe with its physical constants just so to ensure habitality then we are not necessarily clear of the woods. Neil Manson (2000: 163-176) has emphasized that if we can accept fine-tuning we still have no notion of why the numbers are what they are, nor how they could all be systematically different yet still be combined to provide a habitable universe. Yet we must also acknowledge Howard van Till's (2000: 188-194) point that it is the interdependence of each value as much as the fine tuning of any one that is so remarkable. All this smacks of design: physicists are rightly wary and the invisible host of multiverses is ever-popular.

Somewhere, and even more mysteriously somehow, out of physics and chemistry life emerged. By natural processes surely, but by routes and in an environment of which we have no secure knowledge. Despite its physical substrate the processes of evolution, and indeed their bewildering complexity of products, seem to find no echo in any anthropic principle, no sense of particular rules analogous to the gravitational constant or nuclear strong force. The paradox of this view is that it is nevertheless just these evolutionary processes that have led - in the view of some inexorably - to a species that strangely can find meaning in such physical concepts. Some find it distinctly strange that just one species has stumbled on facts that not only inform us about the cosmos but in a deep fashion define its comprehensibility. From an evolutionary point of view, paradox or irony notwithstanding, this view in turn verges on the incomprehensible. This is because if there is a consensus amongst neo-Darwinists it is that evolution is an open-ended and indeterminate process. It cannot be over-emphasized how pervasive is this view. Organisms must be fit for purpose, but "purpose" in only a relative sense. A widely agreed corollary is just as humans are an evolutionary accident, as interesting in their own way as a duck-billed platypus or for that matter water-cress, so too is human intelligence. More than one investigator has pointed out that if indeed this is true then the SETI project, that is the Search for Extraterrestrial Intelligence, is at best quixotic and more likely based on a massive delusion. A profound irony: the one species capable of understanding the Anthropic Principle can only share his discovery with – a gerbil.

Intelligent design?

Yet even if we were to espouse this view of evolution as being utterly indeterminate, everything a fluke of history and circumstance, the organisms themselves never cease to amaze us, be it a bacterium living in the boiling water of a volcanic pool, an albatross circumnavigating the Southern Ocean, or a spider spinning its web of silk. As is repeatedly pointed out to talk about the organism as designed may indeed be a metaphor, but the integration of function, their unbelievable complexity not least at the level of biochemistry, their emergent sophistications be they in terms of navigation, exquisite sensory perception or intelligence, indeed their sheer poise, should leave us stunned. Organisms *are* astonishing, and it is our common failing that this is too often lost sight of in the attempt to depict biology as a subject only to be conducted in an atmosphere of steely rationalism. The latter is no doubt the necessary procedure for investigation so long as it is never forgotten that the things we study are *alive*. In unguarded moments some biologists will gladly admit that the way an organism is put together is remarkable. It is not the point that we understand that biochemical cycle, this enzyme, or a particular hormone, it is the way systems interact and have a dynamic interdependence that is – unless one has lost all sense of wonder – quite awe-inspiring.

Nor should we dismiss this as an unworthy emotion. From this perspective it is easy to appreciate the intellectual attraction of the quasi-scientific/quasi-theological movement known as Intelligent Design (ID). Consternation! "Order! Order!!" Gavels pounding, the Chairman with flushed face and hectic expression, swooning in the aisles with others hurriedly stepping over the recumbent and senseless bodies as they stumble to the doors, fresh air (well, of a sort), and the reassuring thunder of a busy London street. "Get me out of here! Intelligent Design? What, another recruit?" "Please revive yourselves, please return to your seats". Not a bit of it. In my opinion, Intelligent Design is a false and misleading attraction. Tonight there would be little point in reiterating the many objections raised against Intelligent Design, especially those made by the scientific colleagues, but opponents, of Michael Behe and Bill Dembski, perhaps the two principal proponents of Intelligent Design. Rather it seems to me that Intelligent Design has a more interesting failing, a theological failing. Consider a possible analogy, that of Gnosticism. Where did this claptrap come from? Who knows, but could it be an attempt to reconcile orphic and mithraic mysteries with a new, and to many in the Ancient World, a very dangerous Christianity? So too in our culture, those given over to being worshippers of the machine and the computer model, those admirers of organized efficiency, such would not expect the Creator – that is the one identified as the engineer of the bacterial flagellar motor or whatever your favourite case-study of ID might be – to be encumbered with a customary cliché of bearing a large white beard, but to be the very model of scientific efficiency and so don a very large white coat. ID is surely the deist's option, and one that turns its back not only on the richness and beauty of creation, but as importantly its limitless possibilities. It is a theology for control freaks.

To question Intelligent Design might generate a ripple of applause from any neo-Darwinians present, until they recall that this is a Boyle Lecture and theology is not a fad, a pastime for eccentrics, but in fact central to our enterprise. And now I want to persuade you that just such an approach may not only be consistent with evolution, but can also resonate with orthodox Christian theology – the Fall, the Incarnation and the End Times. Surely not; well let us see.

What is life?

My enthusiasm for life surely needs no reiteration. Let us also recall, however, how little of it we really understand. It is pretty clear that organisms are not blobs of malleable protoplasm buffeted by environmental circumstance. First, there is some intriguing evidence that at least in some circumstances organisms are predisposed – I won't use the word designed – to evolve. That is somewhat less surprising when we consider such evolvability in the context of the complexity of the developmental systems. Amongst the many oddities of life is that fact that first there is no detailed instruction manual – and in this context we can effectively ignore the genetic code – but these systems, if prodded or disrupted, are remarkably adept at self-repair. Not foolproof, of course, otherwise we would never catch a cold or, for that matter, die. Yet remarkable nonetheless. So too however neglected it may be because of its sheer familiarity, too easily we forget the remarkable homeostasis of living organisms, that is their internal balance and capacity for adjustment whatever the external environment. In any computer room along with the banks of hard disks, screens and printers there will be the steady hum of air conditioning, extracting the excess heat. Noisy and inefficient; now compare it with the temperature regulation of your brain. Not only is the integrity and integration of living systems quite astonishing, but attempts to employ machine-like analogies soon run into difficulties (Barham, 2004: 210-226) .To be sure we refer to motors, switches, transport mechanisms, fluid flow, pumps and electricity, but the reality is that organisms have a subtlety and efficiency far beyond any machine we can build. Again and again we discover that even in apparently straightforward functions there is an exactness to purpose which is eerily precise. The fact remains we have no idea of what it is about life that although obviously made of atoms no different then you find in a stone combines to form such a dynamic entity, culminating in the entirely surprising ability to become conscious. But consider even the cell. Here jostling together are innumerable chemical compounds involved in extra-ordinary biochemical cycles, including reactions that may be accelerated a billion times by protein catalysts – the enzymes – and all depending not only on carefully transmitted instructions – again depending on a truly baroque arrangement – but instructions that can be appropriately modified long after transcription from the original genetic code.

We are left in the rather extraordinary position of describing things which at one level we hardly understand. This alone should not make us confident that our attempts to mimic the products of evolution will be in any way straightforward. Notwithstanding the fact that biological systems are being used increasingly to instruct us, notably in the application of robotics, the manifest failures in the experiments on the origin or life and attempts to re-embed intelligence in an artificial context suggest a failure to grasp what it is that defines life. This is surely sobering, and whilst it is emphatically not my intention to restore vitalism, it remains the case as James Barham (2004) has rightly stressed that the sum of the parts that defines life will continue to elude us if we insist on constructing definitions that look no further than a physico-chemical basis. Of course, given the remarkable advances in our understanding of biochemistry, molecular biology and evolution as a whole it is all the more strange we have failed to develop concepts, ideas, even a language that could capture this dance of life. Or is it so surprising? We forget at our peril that language presupposes deep assumptions about the way the world is. If we decide it is arid, machine-like and meaningless then it will be all the less odd that its richness will slip through our nets.

That satisfactory definitions of life elude us may be one hint that when materialists step forward and declare with a brisk slap of the hands that this is *it*, we should be deeply skeptical. Whether the "it" be that of Richard Dawkins' reductionist gene-centred world-picture, the "universal acid" of Daniel Dennett's meaningless Darwinism, or David Sloan Wilson's faith in group selection (not least to explain the role of human religions), we certainly need to acknowledge each provides insights but as total explanations of what we see around us they are, to put it politely, somewhat incomplete.

World pictures

Yet, even if levels and mechanisms of evolution are hotly disputed – what make ye of genes, or group selection? – the fact remains that just as the sky is blue, evolution is true. So what is the problem? A rhetorical question, of course, because none of us needs to be reminded that it is the Darwinian world-picture that provides the metaphor of humans being just one tiny twig on the great tree of life – a tree which also, please note, is almost completely dead. Not only are we built of the dust of dead stars, but now we learn that we stand on a charnel house. To argue from this well-rehearsed perspective that nevertheless we are in some bizarre way also built in God's image would seem to be frankly preposterous. I will suggest that such a reading, effectively built on the assumption that size and position in themselves are important, is woefully simplistic. But there is much more at stake than simple disagreement as to whether or not one species, on one planet, in one solar system and in one galaxy of all the billions, is somehow relevant.

A world-picture that encompasses science but also the deep wisdom of theology may help us to explain how it is we can think, how we discover the extraordinary, but so too it may warn us of present dangers and future catastrophes. Not only that, but it can instruct us as to what may be the limits of desirable knowledge and risks of unbridled curiosity (Rendell & Whitehead, 2001: 309-373). This world picture could also show that far from being a series of mindless accidents history has directions and conceivably end-points. And the other world-picture; one based not just on science but wedded to a scientistic programme? Well, you know it as well as I do. Here all is ultimately meaningless. The metaphorical sparrow in the storm may still enter the warm and well-lit mead-hall, but its return to the violent night outside erases all memories and obligations. Those individuals who espouse this world-picture may, for all I know, be better and more charitable people than the theists. I wouldn't be at all surprised; the latter don't have too good a reputation for tolerance but the relative moral merits of any of us are in the final analysis only relevant to exponents of the theistic world picture; to those of scientistic inclination they might be socially useful but in the grand order of things can have no meaning in a soulless world. To repeat Peter Kreef's remark: in the end these are matters whose final resolution is beyond discussion. If correct they matter absolutely, both for us as individuals and for the sort of world we want to inhabit.

So could the study of evolution actually lead us to a far less bleak view than such secular hierophants as Dawkins repeatedly claim? It is, of course, no new suggestion that evolution may be the way God has chosen to arrange matters, and this view in its turn has been resoundingly attacked. What of the sheer waste – all those trilobites, and the pain and evil exposed generation by generation – all those ichneumon flies? Both points have been addressed elsewhere, by others more cogent in argument and skilled in debate. Concerning the latter simply recall that as evil has no reality in a meaningless world we may rightly deplore it because we too have a nervous system, but our pain and that of ichneumon fly's victims has no permanent significance that might one day be redressed. Why all the fuss? And who, of all people, are we to complain of waste? Our profligacy might also perhaps provide a point of reference when Creation is summed up.

Such views presuppose a world-picture very alien to many scientists and philosophers today. Theirs is ultimately a council of despair; one species, on one tiny planet, in a vast and ancient universe? There are several responses to this view. First, who are we to decide what is or is not appropriate? What metric do we use? One can observe that at least in terms of size, perhaps oddly, we are just in the centre, the mid-point between the unimaginably small and the cosmically vast (Trimble). Next, what if we stand on an immensity of time? Leaving aside what time is, would it make any practical difference if the beginning was a million years ago, as against the believed value of 13 billion, let alone even 100 billion years? Did the innumerable brachiopods (or whatever is your favourite fossil organism) drum their metaphorical fingers and glance at their watches, wishing the Palaeozoic would slip by just a bit more quickly? Maybe the 13 billion years is the time we need, for carbon to form, for life not only to evolve but to find itself in a neck of galactic woods which is stable enough not to frighten the horses with rogue black holes, gamma ray bursts and titanic supernovae.

Suppose this approach has some merit. Metric-sized animals that are the end-result of many billions of years of prior stellar and biological evolution may be the only way to allow at least one species to begin its encounter with God. But you may well riposte: let us reconsider organic evolution. Isn't it an open-ended process, to be sure showing an inherent evolvability, but to evolve to what? To be able to function, to reproduce, of course, but to produce in the fullness of time a very strange species, capable to great good but also terrible evil, sensitive to hidden dimensions but also credulous, able to measure the span of the universe but also allow the Flat Earth Society? As has already been made clear, the viewpoint within orthodox Darwinism is agreed and uncontroversial: humans are an accident of evolution, because *everything* produced by evolution is strictly incidental to the process. Accordingly humans are as fortuitous as a tapeworm, and by implication ultimately no more – or less – interesting. I have already suggested that if we are hardly able to define life, this alone should give us pause for thought.

I would further argue that the study of evolution itself already hints that to reduce all to the accidental and incidental may turn out to be a serious misreading of the evidence. In terms of evolution the clear evidence for organismal simplification, not to mention the repeated move to parasitism, does not negate the realities of evolutionary progress and the emergence of irreversibly complex states. More particularly the view that evolution is open-ended, without predictabilities and indeter-minate in terms of outcomes is negated by the ubiquity of evolu-tionary convergence (Conway Morris, 2003). The central point is that because organisms arrive repeatedly at the same biological solution, the camera-eyes of vertebrates and cephalopods perhaps being the most famous example, this provides not only a degree of predictability but more intriguingly points to a deeper structure to life, a metaphorical landscape across which evolution must necessarily navigate.

Converging on convergence
Concerning evolutionary convergence I could give you

innumerable examples, but the central aim of this lecture is to show the evidence now strongly suggests humans to be an evolutionary inevitability. On this basis some time-honoured theological questions may be re-addressed. What is it then concerning evolutionary convergence that can inform us about both the definition and emergence of humanness? This is a large and complex area, and in passing I will only note is that there are a number of key features such as complex vocalizations, tool-making and cultural transmission, which are both vital to the general argument and are patently evolutionarily convergent. Not only have they evolved independently a number of times, but as importantly this indicates that these features are real biological properties, defined entities which are necessary prerequisites for the evolution of humans. For reasons of time and also relative importance it is pardonable, I trust, if I choose to focus on the emergence of complex intelligence and mentality. Briefly, it is now clear that an intelligence equivalent to the primates has evolved independently at least twice, that is in the dolphins and corvids (Clayton & Emery, 2004: 1903-1907. In fact the figure is probably substantially higher (amongst other examples of intelligence that probably have evolved independently are killer whales, sperm whales, New World monkeys, parrots, and very likely octopus) but any estimate depends on questions of phylogenetic relationships (Marino, 2004: 1247-1255) and continuing debates about levels of intelligence, for example amongst the cetaceans (Rendell & Whitehead, 2001: 309-373). Even so, within at least the dolphins (Marino, 1996: 81-85) and crows (Clayton & Emery, 2004: 1903-1907) the similarities are indeed very striking. And there is good reason for such surprise. First, this primate-like intelligence has emerged in strikingly different contexts. Sitting in trees and laying eggs is one thing, living in an ocean is another, and both contrast with the evolution of the apes in jungle and savannah. Second, and even more importantly, even though dolphins are also mammals, their brain structure of the dolphins differs markedly from that of the apes, whilst that of the crows is even more distinct. Thus from radically different neural substrates the same type of mind emerges. This is surely startling, for at least two reasons. First, it reinforces our view that mind is not some sort of epiphenomenon, a simple by-product of chemistry and electrical activity in a squishy organ that happens to be located in the skull. If it was, why should it be so similar? Second, as Ed Oakes has pointed out to me if wings (also convergent) need air to fly, perhaps brains require an equivalent "mental atmosphere" to operate.

These extraordinary, and in large part only recently appreciated, similarities in mental architectures beg other profound questions. If so similar, what is it then that really defines human uniqueness? In part language of course, but even here the gap is probably narrower than we think. Consider the semantic and syntactical abilities of such animals as the dolphins, not to mention the evidence for animal vocalizations both being acquired in the same manner as human speech (including a phase of infant babbling) but having also an inherent structure in terms of the frequency distribution of different "words" (Zipf's law).

Recall also that so far as the hominid fossil record can be relied upon concerning such intangibles as awareness, language and empathy, let alone an almost universal religious instinct, the transition to full humanness was evidently a gradual process (and remember a process that is still arguably incomplete). This in turn has two very interesting implications. First, if consciousness was hovering in the wings of the theatre of evolution with its fully fledged emergence only a matter of time, then why us as against some other species still grunting in the undergrowth? Simply an accident of circumstance, being first on the block? Possibly so, but we should remember that belief in a personal God implies choice, both on our part and more importantly His. Is the history of the Jewish nation a sort of analogy?

Chosen, prodded by their true prophets, and despite diversions and disasters leading the rest of us by a route nobody expected to the Incarnation? Tricky, and possibly a dangerous argument, because of course the story doesn't stop there. Either way, the plea of "why us?" takes on new and different dimensions, but ones to which our materialist colleagues will, I fear, be blissfully oblivious.

Second, and I very much fear treading on even more problematic – but in fact related – ground, suppose that there were other species on this planet even closer in sentience to humans than either dolphins or crows? How should we treat them? Larder, zoo, nature reserve, or an invitation to tea? I suspect strongly that would be our dilemma if, for whatever reason, the Neanderthals had not disappeared. A similar question is asked by the American writer, Harry Turtledove (1988) in one of his stimulating science fiction novels based on a counter-factual world. In his book *A different flesh* we are asked to imagine a North America which is the abode of australopithecines but otherwise uninhabited by hominids, that is until the arrival of the Europeans. His story stretches over several centuries, but a central theme is how we should treat our very near cousins, creatures he calls the "sims". That question stretches from initial contacts to finally medical trials involving the deliberate infection of sims with HIV. Hypothetically with the sims and probably actually with the Neanderthals, these represent species that are so close to us that any Socratic dialogue would beg agonizing questions of moral decision. In either case humanness is in the last stages of emergence, a consciousness that is already grasping realities beyond immediate vision. We might be grateful that such a dilemma cannot arise with either the Neanderthals or the sims, until we recall that just such an emergence of mind almost certainly occurs within a few weeks of conception in the human foetus (Vining, 2004: 145).

Far from being a series of curious accidents the study of evolution poses some deep and awkward questions. I suggest, moreover, that it may illuminate in other ways who we are and our place in the world. I have already mentioned that evolutionary convergence hints at a prior "landscape" which predetermines, albeit in an extraordinarily rich way, the outcomes of the process, not least human intelligence and by implication the inevitability of contact with a different sort of Mind, an encounter with God. I want to argue that this is more than a powerful metaphor, and in doing so I now move to the heart of this Boyle Lecture. Consider music.

A universal music?

In a fascinating essay Patricia Gray (2002) and colleagues remark on the many similarities between our music and that of animals. That gap between them and humans is obvious enough, no bird in a tree astonishes us with Tallis' Forty-part motet, *Spem in alium*, but the basics of harmonics, melody, invention, inversion duetting and even riff sessions are all shared. Like consciousness, the symphony orchestra is also waiting in the wings of the theatre of evolution. Music is, therefore, a splendid example of convergence. As such one can certainly propose scientific explanations, both in terms of the physics of sound and the biology of function such as sexual matters or territoriality. The plausibility of such assumptions, not least in the famous songs of the male humpback whales, let alone their dubious extrapolation to the realms of evolutionary psychology in humans, need not detain us. This is because Gray *et al.* go on to make a much more interesting argument. Suppose, they suggest, there is a Universal Music, and the reason why all earthly song is so similar is because all are gaining access to an Ideal, a reality both "out there" but also intimately close, in a "dimension" discovered by evolution, familiar but also one that defies simple categorization. Such a view has equal applicability to intelligence, mentality and discovery of the other "invisibles" that together define our continuing search for Truth.

There is, moreover, an intriguing analogy to the discovery of music that has even more interesting theological implications. I alluded above to the mysterious origins of language. We can, of course, take a biological stance. In the context, say, of predator warnings or the demands of reproduction the howls, screeches, chattering and whistles may well make good functional sense so that our continuing research will be rewarded with fruitful insights. As with music, however, there are other approaches, other dimensions that touch wider and more remote shores. Here I have in mind J.R.R. Tolkien's fascination with words and the origins of language. His creation, or more strictly sub-creation, of Elvish might owe much to his interests in Welsh and Finnish, but it is also clear that his immense creativity and the invocation of the beautiful, mysterious and almost painfully real Middle Earth, was founded on a deep appreciation and love for languages. In some strange way the articulation of Elvish and the other languages of Middle Earth were the catalysis for the rest of his mythos. It is also evident that Tolkien, already a master philologist, was fundamentally influenced by another of the Inklings, Owen Barfield and especially his book *Poetic Diction* In essence, and as compellingly explored by Vernon Flieger (2002) Barfield and thereby Tolkien believed that from its source language had become fragmented: Flieger's metaphor is "splintered light". Originally certain words, in "primitive" times, carried an immensity of meanings that importantly touched on the unseen, if not the sacred. With the elapse of time these meanings subdivided, to be sure, precision (of a sort) was gained, but also much was lost. Paradoxically reality was blurred and disenchantment spread.

The implications of this are not difficult to grasp, but they seem to me to be extraordinarily fruitful. The sense that there are other realities, orthogonal to everyday experience, is certainly familiar: who has not entered zones of timelessness, had prescient dreams, compelling hunches or odd synchronicities? It is not my assumption that these realities are either exclusive or incompatible. In fact, there is every reason to think that individually but obliquely they collectively touch on much deeper matters, but in our present state they can be deeply disconcerting. Potentially, however, they open portals to new perspectives and possibilities. Who is not familiar with the metaphor of hearing the harmony of spheres or imagining that somehow we might engage in speech with animals? Literally these are either fanciful or folk tales, but if the New Testament tells us anything, it is that, as Tolkien finally persuaded C.S. Lewis in their celebrated night-time walk in Magdalen College, the point of Christianity and the Incarnation is that this is when myth became true and real. As I will explain at the end of this lecture in the final analysis how we got here hardly matters, but at this juncture all I need to stress is the process by which we, and evidently other sentient species, had at least the possibility of understanding a wider reality, a bed-rock of existence, was by the agency of evolution. By this process, life has ramified into a richness and complexity. We are embedded in a true Creation. Unsuspected it turns out that Darwin not only equipped us with a mechanism but also a compass whereby sentience would necessarily emerge so that ultimately the Song of Creation would also be heard. Are science and theology really so far apart?

Evolution beyond the horizon

My work on evolutionary convergence, with its claims that the roads of evolution are constrained, that not all is possible (in fact the reverse is the case: nearly all is impossible), and that the outcomes of evolution are thereby effectively inevitable, frequently provokes the question along the lines of "Fine, so what's next?" A fair question, and one which not only generates interesting responses but again touches directly on theological issues. Some predictions are pessimistic and well-rehearsed. We simply destroy ourselves, be it by global warming, viral pandemic, bio-terrorism, nuclear warfare: exit is inevitable, whether by a bang or more probably by a whimper. Other prognostications I find even more chilling. Maybe we are too clever for our own good, but not clever enough to realize that serving as a hand-maiden to machine-intelligence we are sealing our fate and embarking on the construction of a terrible world, joyless and cripplingly uninteresting, arid in all but computation. To many, and as with so much else we see around us, there is in this gloomy view a grinding sense of inevitability. In our heart of hearts it is not what we want, "but then you can't stop progress, can you? Shame really. N'other cup of tea?"

Perhaps, however, what is construed as "progress" is better viewed as the wrong road that if not swiftly abandoned will lead to a destination that we understand but one over which one day we have no control. Such thinking, of choices, decisions and acknowledgement of fault (repentance, if you prefer) is of course very germane to theological thinking. Indeed, theology may end up making some absolute and very surprising claims. Let us reconsider the rhetorical question, "Fine, so what's next?" In contrast to the musings of science the view of orthodox Christianity is, I think, fairly straightforward, even if its implications are not. If Adam is metaphorically the first man, then Jesus as Christ is the last. In one sense there is no more future. Evolution did have an end-point, it was us, and now with the Incarnation it is time to move on. To the non-theist this perspective will no doubt seem not warped, but simply mad. Robert Boyle emphatically would not have been so minded, and it is now time to see not so much whether science and religion have any relation but rather to suggest that they are intimately linked in a way that actually promises great goodness but from our present stance seems to be much more problematic.

A Faustian compact?

It would be otiose to suppose that science, along with medicine and technology, has not delivered extraordinary benefits and gifts. Nor is it disputed that there are side-effects and unforeseen consequences that can undo at least some of the good done. As a group scientists, even under existing pressures, generally maintain a high degree of integrity and are genuinely interested in what is true as against what is popular or expedient. Yet the darker side is never very far away. Discoveries and inventions, even those apparently innocuous, in the wrong hands may lead either to distortion of societies or ways of delivering death yet more widely and efficiently. So too the dangers of monopoly power and the manipulation of the market place may benefit the few and impoverish the many. The risks are most obvious in biotechnology, but in fact no area of science is free of risk. To many the benefits of science appear to be gained at the increasing expense of a Faustian compact.

Theologians have not been silent on these issues, but I suspect that we are not going to make much headway when the aim of today's culture is blatantly scientistic and deeply manipulative. Here the ultimate aim is of controlling the world in a way ostensibly for the best but in fact wedded to a naturalistic programme, that is to see no arbiter outside human agency, or worse whim. To such ears talk of the Fall, the realities of radical evil, even the danger of damnation will seem quaint, risible and medieval; nothing that is to do with the real world. Robert Boyle, in his time, was not so sure. He was deeply concerned that some areas, notably of magic and astrology, might lead into very dangerous territory where malevolence would be made manifest. The point is not whether magic and astrology are in any sense true, but to act as if they might. So too today we are unwilling to concede either the possibility of what Roger Shattuck (1997) calls "Forbidden Knowledge" or that we might be assisted by those intelligences who do not have our long-term interests at heart.

Christian theology offers insights that at the moment are deeply unfashionable, not least as to what we ought to do when we choose to eat at the tree of knowledge. It is not necessarily a viewpoint that is in any way comforting, but neither are we meant to despair. Creation, so far as we know, is infinite in its richness and promise, and while there are many avenues to discover this truth, there is no reason to think that science is not one of them and in certain situations is actually the only inkling we will have. Indeed science reminds us that Creation is far more wonderful, far more extraordinary, far more diverse, far richer than we could have ever anticipated. Nor is there any sense that we are anywhere close to a complete explanation of all we see. Rather, each discovery yields new and unexpected insights. What is also obvious is that at least materially this knowledge can be extraordinarily powerful. How we choose to use what we learn remains our central dilemma. If we ignore the theological dimension then we are heading for deep trouble. As long as we view the world as an accidental happenstance, to be treated as a utilitarian object, we not only lose sight of Creation, but also ourselves and our place in it. Well, that is a debate that is still with us, and was as familiar to Robert Boyle.

An evolutionary eschatology?

So is this the end of the matter? There is one final aspect of Creation which in my view we would do very well not to overlook. Science certainly informs us about the integrity and complexity of the world around us, and thereby are we the better equipped to appreciate its beauty. Yet whatever else it might be, just as with our lives, so the visible world and so far as we can ascertain the entire Universe cannot be permanent, at least in any recognizable form. The standard view is that given the expansion of the universe, and the new evidence that on a cosmic scale this process is accelerating, in the long term our future is not too bright. Fairly early on the Earth itself will become uninhabitable as the Sun enters old age and swells up. Present estimates indicate that within a billion years the oceans will have boiled away, and if those estimates are wrong the death of our planet would not be much postponed beyond that. Other local excitement will be the projected collision between our galaxy and the nearby Andromeda galaxy. Again it is in the distant future, but in the cosmic scale of things may get a few lines on page 176594972187 of the *Universal Herald*. After all there is nothing too unusual with this given examples of colliding galaxies are known. But as I said these are all views from the parish pump. This is because as expansion of the universe continues galaxy after galaxy will slip away over the horizon of visibility. Whereas today billions of galaxies are visible, in the distant future all will be receding from us so fast, so far away, that none of their light will ever reach us. Beyond our galaxy there will be nothing to see. So too the stars will dim, and later still even the stars will cease to exist. After that, who knows, but the laws of physics suggest an eternity of a near-emptiness populated by solitary particles that slowly decay to even more elementary particles. There is speculation as to whether some sort of intelligence would – somehow – garner enough energy to survive in this diffuse, cold, near-vacuum. The point is that even if we, in some distant future, were able to spread to other worlds, conceivably other galaxies, we would merely win an extension of existence, a postponement of the inevitable.

There is, however, another view. It will not, I warn you, be popular. Yet consider; let us assume the universe is genuinely *ex nihilo*, made out of nothing by the good grace of God. That is certainly part of the Christian orthodoxy, and so far as I can see neither the size nor the age of the Universe makes any difference to this assumption. It also appears to be consistent with the evidence from the Big Bang. We should, however, be wary about such concordism, this apparently happy marriage between cosmology and revealed religion. Not that concordance is out of the question, far from it. One should just be wary because scientific evidence is always provisional. Apparently irrefutable data or hypotheses have a curious habit of turning out to be gloriously, wonderfully wrong. From our present stance it is difficult to see what data could more satisfactorily explain many cosmological observations than the Big Bang, but we should be cautious of two things. First, to assume that the Big Bang is the same as God's Creation, and second to fool ourselves that Creation *ex nihilo* is actually in any useful way open to comprehension. What surely matters, however, is that what can be brought out of nothing might be either returned to nothing or otherwise utterly transformed.

This too, I think, accords with Orthodoxy. The world around is very real, a point again G.K. Chesterton felt so strongly that at times thinking of an alternative literally promised madness. Now, no doubt to our scientistic colleagues all this *will* seem madness. "What? The world not defined by its flaming ramparts, but consumed by them? Dear me, not only medieval, but in decidedly poor taste." Well, like death itself if one side is correct we will at least know, even if what we are greeted with is "not only medieval, but in decidedly poor taste." Well, I don't see any likely response in the mind-set of the moderns; almost any sort of eschatology will seem to be risible. Christian orthodoxy certainly suggests otherwise, and in this context, it is particularly difficult to remind ourselves how totally unlikely the Incarnation appeared, first to the Jews and very soon the ancient world. Yet, it has an inexorable logic, and so I believe does an eschatology. My hunch is that it too will be quite unlike what we expect. Nor do I think the looming disasters, notably global warming, are the actual avenue. Global warming does, however, provide a very useful mind-set of attitudes. "Well, maybe it will happen, one day, but not in my lifetime ....." But the writing is on the wall, and in the sky and within the oceans. Could the same be true of End Times?

Let me, however, conclude with one small observation. I have, uncertainly and with little skill, tried to show that Robert Boyle's concerns and beliefs remain as valid and pertinent today as they did in his time. A common complaint against such people as Boyle, or indeed any of our antecedents, is that they simply knew less, so no wonder they were the more credulous. This, however, is to fall simply into the scientistic trap, and neglects the likelihood that if some areas of worthwhile human endeavour have flourished, others have unnecessarily withered, to our common detriment. Moreover, this view turns its back on eternal verities that were as true in Boyle's, or Pontius Pilate's, times as they are in ours. That such verities are presently widely dismissed as social constructs, power games, or whatever will simply erode the good and impoverish the many but at least allow the intellectuals to dream the more easily in their many beds. Nor am I sure, despite the best efforts of such people as C.S. Lewis, Peter Kreeft and many other brilliant apologists, how these ventures would be successfully recaptured. Science when it treats creation as a true Creation, and thereby faces up to its responsibilities, may well be important. I expect Boyle would have agreed. It seems ultimately, however, that it is the knowledge and experience of the Incarnation, the wisdom and warnings given by Jesus in the Gospels, and not least the Resurrection that in the final analysis are all that matters. Again I expect Robert Boyle would have agreed.

Acknowledgements

I am most grateful to the organizers of the Boyle Lecture 2005, notably Michael Byrne and the Rector of St Mary-le-Bow, the Reverend George Bush, for their original invitation to deliver this lecture, as well as their continuing encouragement and support. I am also most grateful to Sandra Last for much technical assistance, including typing drafts of the paper under considerable pressure. Finally, I wish to acknowledge numerous friends with whom I have discussed some of the issues, as well as the University of Cambridge, and especially my Department, for support over many years as my interests have continued to evolve. I dedicate this essay to the memory of my father.

References

Barfield, O. 1952. *Poetic diction: a study in meaning*. London: Faber & Faber.

Barham, J. 2004. The emergence of biological value, in *Debating design: From Darwin to DNA* (eds W.A. Demski & M. Ruse), pp. 210-226. Cambridge University Press.

Clayton, N. & Emery, N. 2004. *Science* 306, pp. 1903-1907.

Conway Morris, S. 2003. *Life's Solution: Inevitable humans in a lonely universe*. Cambridge University Press.

Chesterton, G.K. 1913. An accident, in *Tremendous Trifles*. London: Methuen.

Dennett, D.C. 1995. *Darwin's dangerous idea: Evolution and the Meanings of Life*. London: Allen Lane, Penguin Press.

Flieger, V. 2002. *Splintered Light: Logos and Language in Tolkien's World*. Kent State University Press.

Gould, S.J. 2001. *Rock of Ages: Science and Religion in the Fullness of Life*. London: Cape.

Gray, P.M. *et al.* 2002. *Science* 291, pp. 52-54.

Hooykaas, R. 1987. *Robert Boyle: A Study in Science and Christian Belief*. University Press of America.

Jaki, S.L. 1986. *Chesterton, a seer of science*. University of Illinois Press.

Manson, N.A. 2000. *Religious Studies* 36, pp. 163-176.

Marino, L. 1996. *Evolutionary Anthropology* 5, pp. 81-85.

Marino, L. *et al.* 2004. *Anatomical Record* 281A, pp. 1247-1255.

Rendell, L. & Whitehead, H. 2001. *Behavioral and Brain Sciences* 24, pp. 309-373.

Rees, M. 1999. *Just six numbers: The Deep Forces that Shape the Universe*. London: Weidenfeld and Nicholson.

Shattuck, R. 1997. *Forbidden Knowledge: From Prometheus to Pornography*. London: Harcourt, Brace.

Trimble, V. Personal communication.

Turtledove, H. 1988. *A different flesh*. New York: Baen

van Till, H. 2000. Partnership: Science and Christian theology as partners in theorizing, in *Science and Christianity: Four Views* (ed. R.F. Carlson), pp. 188-194. Intervarsity Press.

Vining, J. 2004. *The Song Sparrow and the Child: Claims of Science and Humanity*. University of Notre Dame Press

Simon Conway Morris holds an *Ad Hominem* Chair in Evolutionary Palaeobiology, at the University of Cambridge. He is a Fellow of St John's College, and also of the Royal Society. His *Life's Solution: Inevitable Humans in a Lonely Universe* (Cambridge University Press) addressed the importance of evolutionary convergence. His interests extend to the science/religion debate and the public understanding of science, the latter including television appearances in the *1996 Royal Institution Christmas Lectures*.

Darwin's Legacy: A Regularly Misunderstood and Misinterpreted Triumph

R.J. Berry

Eight years after the *Origin of Species* appeared, Matthew Arnold, mourning the seemingly inexorable advance of science and industry, wrote a lament to the ebbing tide of faith:

The Sea of Faith
Was once, too, at the full, and round earth's shore
Lay like the folds of a bright girdle furled.
But now I only hear
Its melancholy, long, withdrawing roar.

Commentators tie Arnold's pessimism to the ferment stirred by Darwin's ideas. In fact his un-ease has much deeper roots; Darwin, Darwinism and evolution were merely a step – albeit a significant one – in our understanding of our surroundings and how we relate to it. Surveying perceptions since the end of mediaeval times, Keith Thomas (1983: 242) judged that "at the start of the early modern period, man's ascendancy over the natural world was the unquestioned object of human endeavour. By 1800 it was still the aim of most people.... but by this time the objective was no longer unquestioned". Knowledge of the world was increasing at an ever accelerating pace. At least in Europe, belief in witchcraft and evil spirits had receded; faith was becoming milder and cooler.

At the same time, geologists were massively extending the history of the Earth beyond the six thousand or so years implied by the biblical genealogies of creation (Lewis & Knell, 2001). In 1788 James Hutton, the 'father of modern geology' declared in his *Theory of the Earth* that the world was almost infinitely old. This was not speculation, but an inference from observations of the real world. It was not intended as a challenge to the scriptures, but it forced bible expositors to look again at their interpretation of Genesis. Notwithstanding the idea that the earth had a long history proved the Achilles heel of traditional natural theology. A creator could presumably design an organism perfectly adapted to a particular environment, but such perfection would disappear if the environment was not constant. Adjusting to changes in climate, to the physical structure of the Earth's surface, or to predators and competitors is possible only if organisms can adapt. All this produced considerable theological turmoil. This is not relevant here (Gillispie, 1951; Moore, 1986); suffice it to say that by 1859, the great majority of bible expositors accepted a non-literal interpretation of the early chapters of Genesis (Roberts, 1997).

In a book *The Sea of Faith* which took its title from Arnold's poem, Don Cupitt (1984: 59) described the atmosphere at the end of the eighteenth century: "Mechanistic science was allowed to explain the structure and workings of physical nature without restriction. But who designed this beautiful world-machine and set it going in the first place? Only Scripture could answer that question. So science dealt with the everyday tick-tock of the cosmic framework and religion dealt with the ultimates: first beginnings and last ends, God and the soul... It was a happy compromise while it lasted. Science promoted the cause of religion by showing the beautiful workmanship of the world... But there was a fatal flaw in the synthesis. Religious ideas were being used to plug the gaps in scientific theory. Science could not yet explain how animals and plants had originated and had become so wonderfully adapted to their environment – so that was handed over to religion. People still made a sharp soul-body distinction and the soul fell beyond the scope of science – so everything to do with human inwardness and personal and social behaviour remained the province of the preacher and moralist".

And then came Darwin, providing an easily understood way of how the world could come into being without supernatural agency. He was well aware that his ideas could be seen to be 'bestializing' human nature. Two years before the *Origin*, he wrote (22 December 1957) to Alfred Russel Wallace about his planned book on 'transmutation', "You ask whether I shall discuss 'man'. I think I shall avoid the whole subject, as so surrounded with prejudices; though I fully admit it is the highest and most interesting problem for the naturalist". In the *Origin*, he referred to human evolution only once: "I see open fields for far more important researches... Much light will be thrown on the origin of man and his history problem". Richard Dawkins (1986: 6) put it, "although atheism might have been tenable before Darwin, Darwin made it possible to be an intellectually fulfilled atheist".

Is Charles Darwin the anti-Christ? Or did Oxford theologian Aubrey Moore (1889: 99) get it right when he wrote a generation after the *Origin of Species*, that Darwin did the work of a friend under the guise of a foe by making it impossible to accept the Enlightenment assumption of an occasionally interfering absentee landlord (Porter, 2000). For Moore, Darwinism "is infinitely more Christian than the theory of 'special creation' for it implies the immanence of God in nature, and the omnipresence of His creative power... Deism, even when it struggled to be orthodox, constantly spoke of God as we might speak of an absentee landlord, who cares nothing for his property so long as he gets his rent. Yet nothing more opposed to the language of the Bible and the Fathers can hardly be imagined... For Christians the *facts of nature* are *the acts of God*. Religion relates these facts to God as their Author, science relates them to one another as integral parts of a visible order. Religion does not tell us of their interrelations, science cannot speak of their relation to God. Yet the religious view of the world is infinitely deepened and enriched when we not only recognize it as the work of God but are able to trace the relation of part to part" (Moore, 1892: 184-5).

Evolution

Charles Darwin was born in Shrewsbury on 12 February 1809. He followed his father and elder brother to Medical School in Edinburgh (1825-27), but found himself too squeamish for a medical career. He transferred to Cambridge and read for a general degree (1828-31), following this by five much more exciting years (1832-36) as a 'gentleman naturalist' on *HMS Beagle*, commissioned under the command of Robert Fitzroy to survey the southern coasts of South America. The *Beagle* went on to circumnavigate the globe, most famously spending three weeks (16 September to 20 October 1835) in the equatorial Galapagos Archipelago, 1000 km west of the South American mainland.

Darwin's assumption had been that he would seek ordination after his Cambridge degree. He wrote home at an early stage of the *Beagle*'s voyage, "Although I like this knocking about, I find I steadily have a distant prospect of a very quiet parsonage & I can see it even through a grove of Palms". After leaving Edinburgh, he had read with approval the evangelical Bishop of Chester's *Evidences of Christianity* (Sumner was later Archbishop of Canterbury 1848-62). At Cambridge, he was required to study William Paley's *Evidences of Christianity*. He found Paley's logic 'irresistible'. In his *Autobiography* he notes "The logic of this book and I may add of his *Natural Theology* gave me as much delight as did Euclid. The careful study of these works.... was the only part of the Academic Course which, as I then felt and still believe, was of the least use to me in the education of my mind" (Barlow, 1958: 59).

But during his time on the *Beagle*, he began to drift away from the idea of career as a clergyman. He did not become an atheist. In his *Autobiography*, he insisted that he continued to believe in some form of God after his return. Notwithstanding, as Janet Browne (1995: 325) comments, "It is clear that his kind of belief, though orthodox, was a very loose, English-style orthodoxy in which it was far less trouble to believe than it was to disbelieve… For Darwin, as for countless others, belonging to the Church of England was as much a statement of social position and attitude than it was a profession of any particular doctrine… No sane man could believe in miracles, he decided… Yet he went to church regularly throughout the voyage, attending the shipboard ceremonies conducted by Fitzroy and services on shore whenever possible". Years later he wrote to his friend, the botanist Joseph Hooker (12 July 1870), "My theology is a simple muddle. I cannot look at the universe as a result of blind chance, yet I can see no evidence of beneficent design, or indeed a design of any kind in the details".

A major stumbling-block for Darwin was animal suffering. He wrote (22 May 1860) to Asa Gray, Professor of Botany at Harvard who was a Christian,, "I own that I cannot see, as plainly as others do & as I shd wish to do, evidence of design & beneficence on all sides of us. There seems to me too much misery in the world. I cannot persuade myself that a beneficent & omnipotent God would have designedly created the Ichneumonidæ with the express intention of their feeding within the living bodies of caterpillars, or that a cat should play with mice. Not believing this, I see no necessity in the belief that the eye was expressly designed. On the other hand I cannot anyhow be contented to view this wonderful universe & especially the nature of man, & to conclude that everything is the result of brute force[1]. I am inclined to look at everything as resulting from designed laws, with the details, whether good or bad, left to the working out of what we may call chance. Not that this notion *at all* satisfies me. I feel most deeply that the whole subject is too profound for the human intellect... I can see no reason, why a man, or other animal, may not have been aboriginally produced by other laws; & that all these laws may have been expressly designed by an omniscient Creator, who foresaw every future event & consequence. But the more I think the more bewildered I become".

Darwin's view of the natural world altered during his time on the *Beagle* as he saw how animal species replaced one other along the length of South America and how fossils often resembled – but differed in details from – similar living forms. Notwithstanding he still retained a 'traditional' belief in a world more or less as it was at its creation. The trigger that changed his views about this seems to have been a conversation in March 1837 with John Gould, the ornithologist at the London Zoo, to whom Darwin had entrusted the bird specimens he had collected whilst on the *Beagle*. Gould's finding that the finches on the Galapagos were an entirely new group wholly confined to those islands, forced Darwin to re-think his earlier assumption of a static world (Sulloway, 1982). He made a note for himself, "the Zoology of Archipelagoes will be well worth examining, for such facts would undermine the stability of species".

By 1842, Darwin was sufficiently sure of himself to write a brief 35 page 'sketch' setting out his new understanding of evolutionary change; he expanded this into a 200 page 'Essay' in 1844. The latter formed the basis of the *Origin of Species*, published in 1859. Its starting point was a Paleyian belief that the creator used laws in his creating work (Ospovat, 1979). Darwin invoked a very simple mechanism, based on three facts and two deductions. He began with the observation that virtually all species have a large potential for increase in number (think of the number of acorns produced by an oak tree or the masses of frog spawn laid by every female frog), but (second observation) numbers remain roughly constant. The inference from this is that there must be a *struggle for existence*, with only a small proportion of young surviving. The existence of such a struggle is essentially an ecological deduction and one well understood in Darwin's time. It forced itself on Darwin's awareness when in 1838 he read 'for amusement', Thomas Malthus's *Essay on the Principles of Population*, which set out the spectre of the human population outstripping its food supply, leading to the weak and improvident succumbing in a struggle for resources. Darwin's genius was in linking to this ever-prevalent struggle for existence a third fact - heritable variation. If only a small proportion of a population survive the struggle, the likelihood is that it will include a high proportion of those with any trait which gives them some sort of advantage in their survival. Over the generations, those carrying the trait will increase at the expense of those lacking it. There would be a genetic change in the population, amounting to *natural selection* for the trait in question.

Darwin began drafting what he called his 'Big Book' on evolution in 1856, but his plans were thrown awry when in June 1858 he received a letter from Alfred Russel Wallace – written whilst recovering from fever on the Indonesian island of Ternate in the Moluccas (or Malukus) – asking him to comment on a manuscript setting out a possible mechanism for evolutionary change. Wallace's proposals were almost identical with Darwin's. Darwin felt he was morally obliged to pass on Wallace's paper for publication, but he was persuaded by his friends Charles Lyell (the leading geologist of the time) and Joseph Hooker (soon to follow his father as Director of the Royal Botanic Gardens at Kew) to allow parts of his 1844 'Essay' to be read at a meeting of the Linnean Society at the same time as Wallace's communication. Hooker recalled the Linnean Society meeting in a letter to Francis Darwin after his (Charles's) death: "I was present with Lyell at the meeting [Darwin did not attend]. We both I think said something [about] impressing the necessity of profound attention (on the part of Naturalists) to the papers and their bearing on the future of Nat. Hist. etc., etc., etc., but there was no semblance of discussion. The interest excited was intense, but the subject was too novel and too ominous for the old School to enter the lists before armouring".

Wallace's paper spurred Darwin to publish his ideas more definitively. He wrote hard through the autumn and winter of 1858-9, and by May 1859 had a manuscript to send to the publisher, John Murray. *On the Origin of Species* appeared on 24 November 1859, and sold out immediately. Adam Sedgwick, Professor of Geology at Cambridge castigated it as "a dish of rank materialism cleverly cooked and served up". Charles Kingsley, at the time Rector of Eversley in Hampshire but soon to become Regius Professor of Modern History at Cambridge, reacted entirely differently. He wrote to Darwin: "'Let God be true and every man a liar'. I find it just as noble a conception of Deity to believe that He created primal forms capable of self development... as to believe that He required a fresh act of intervention to supply the *lacunas* which He himself had made".

The fact of evolutionary change was rapidly accepted (Moore, 1979). It made sense of so many data – of comparative anatomy and physiology, of classification, of geographical distribution, of fossil relationships. The Origin received an effective imprimatur when Frederick Temple (soon to become Archbishop of Canterbury) echoed Kingsley, writing in his Bampton Lectures, "[God] did not make the things, we may say no: but He made make themselves" (Temple, 1885: 115). Ironically in the light of future history, Darwin's ideas were assimilated more readily by conservative theologians than by liberals, apparently because of the stronger doctrine of providence of the former (Livingstone, 1987). Many of the authors of the 'Fundamentals', a series of booklets produced between 1910 and 1915 to expound the 'fundamental beliefs' of Protestant theology as defined by the General Assembly of the American Presbyterian Church and which have led to the word 'fundamentalism' entering the language, were sympathetic to evolution. Princeton theologian

B.B. Warfield, a passionate advocate of the inerrancy of the Bible, argued that evolution could provide a tenable "theory of the method of divine providence in the creation of mankind".

But Darwin's 'big idea' of natural selection was less successful; it did not fit easily with conventional notions of progress or improvement, and philosophers and theologians developed alternative proposals – more metaphysical than scientific (Provine, 1971; Ruse, 1996; Bowler, 2007). Even worse, the rediscovery of Mendel's results in 1900 and the subsequent explosion of the science of genetics seemed to show that the physical basis of heredity could not be the basis of the variation expected by Darwinism. Mutations studied in the laboratory tended to have a large effect, to be deleterious, and to be inherited as recessive traits. The Darwinian expectation was that evolution progressed through small steps produced by favourable variants. In a book surveying the state of evolutionary biology published in 1907 for the Jubilee of the *Origin*, Vernon Kellogg began by describing "the death-bed of Darwinism". It was only through the work of R.A. Fisher, J.B.S. Haldane and Sewall Wright in the 1920s that genetics, palaeontology and comparative studies came together in a 'neo-Darwinian synthesis' (Huxley, 1942); this rehabilitated Darwin's original thesis and has proved resilient in the face of further discoveries – notably the challenges produced by the 'molecular revolution' of the 1960s and 70s (Mayr & Provine, 1980; Berry, 1982).

Misconceptions

Darwin was well aware of some of the implications of his ideas and knew they would be controversial. He was alarmed by the explosion in 1844 provoked by the publication of the *Vestiges of the Natural History of Creation* by Robert Chambers. Chambers wrote that when there is a choice between special creation and the operation of general laws instituted by the creator, "I would say that the latter is generally preferable as it implies a far grander view of the divine power than the other". Since there was nothing in the inorganic world "which may not be accounted for by the agency of the ordinary forces of nature", why not consider "the possibility of plants and animals having likewise been produced in a natural way".

The *Vestiges* was effectively a tract against the deism of William Paley's version of natural theology (Secord, 2000). It was an immediate best-seller. In the ten years following its publication, it sold more copies than did the *Origin* fifteen years later. But it was full of errors. For Darwin, "the writing and arrangement are certainly admirable, but the geology strikes me as bad & his zoology far worse". Others roundly condemned the book. Adam Sedgwick, Professor of Geology in Cambridge and an early mentor of Darwin lambasted it in an 85 page diatribe in the *Edinburgh Review*; he called it "A foul book [in which] gross credulity and rank infidelity join in unlawful marriage". He wrote to his fellow geologist Charles Lyell, "If the book be true, the labours of sober induction are in vain; religion is a lie; human law is a mass of folly and a base injustice; morality is moonshine; our labours for the black people of Africa were works of madmen; and man and woman are only better beasts". Nevertheless, the *Vestiges* was important because of the debate it stirred. Despite his misgivings, Darwin welcomed it on the grounds that "it has done excellent service in calling in this country attention to the subject and in removing prejudices".

The author of the *Vestiges* was widely attacked as a wild speculator, not to be taken seriously, but the criticism worried Darwin. His knowledge of the natural world was extensive, but it was not deep. He began a study of the barnacles he had collected on the *Beagle* cruise. This extended into a detailed investigation of barnacles worldwide and occupied him from 1846 to 1854 (Stott, 2003). It became much more than a self-justifying exercise: it opened Darwin's eyes to variation within species and the apparent relationships of different families. When he returned to his 'transformism' he was much more aware of biological complications in the real world than previously (Bellon, 2006).

Darwin in the *Origin* anticipated specific criticisms of his ideas. In Chapters 6 and 7 he dealt with 'difficulties' and 'miscellaneous objections' to his theory. His main points concerned the nature of species and questions about the efficacy of selection. In a later chapter, he discussed the imperfections of the fossil record. These questions are still raised by critics of evolution, but Darwin well knew that the mechanism of how variation was maintained was the key weakness of his theory. The causes of variation are repeatedly referred to in the *Origin*, and in later editions he tended to accept that some Lamarckian explanation might be necessary (that is, that the heredity of an individual might be affected by an environmental modification of its body [phenotype]).

The recognition of the physical basis of variation by the 'Mendelians' at the beginning of the twentieth century was the basis of their disagreement with the Darwinians. It led to a rift which persisted and widened for several decades. There were no real doubts that large scale evolution had occurred, but it did not seem to have been driven by natural selection. Into this apparent void, an extravagance of other evolutionary theories poured: Berg's *Nomogenesis*, Willis's *Age and Area*, Smut's *Holism*, Driesch's entelechy, Osborn's aristogenesis and orthogenesis. Invention was rife. Their common feature was some form of inner progressionist urge or *élan vital*. Unfortunately three standard and still-read histories of biology (by Nordenskiöld, Rádl and Singer) were written during this time, perpetuating the idea that evolutionary theory is an illogical mess and that Darwinism is completely eclipsed.

The scientific confusion spread into theology. The idea that evolution was driven by some sort of purpose was influentially espoused by some distinguished scientists - the zoologist Ray

Lankester and the physiologist J.S Haldane, the psychologists Lloyd Morgan, William McDougall and E.S. Russell, physicists like Oliver Lodge, and the cosmologists A.S. Eddington and James Jeans; as well as by popularisers like Arthur Thomson and politicians such as Arthur Balfour. Not surprisingly with such apparently informed authorities, these ideas were seized upon by churchmen, prominent among them being Charles Gore, and somewhat later by W.R.Inge, Hensley Henson, Charles Raven and E.W. Barnes. This cross-over of evolutionary idealism from science to theology has been elegantly chronicled by Peter Bowler (2001). It eventually died through its perceived ineffectiveness rather than conscious rejection ("The Modernists saw themselves marginalized not by the new science, of which many remained unaware, but by changing values within the churches, which brought back a sense of human sinfulness and alienation from God incompatible with the idea of progress" Bowler, *op. cit.* p. 417). One can have some sympathy with the theologians. It took the scientists a long time to reach an evolutionary synthesis, but this does not excuse uncritical use of inadequate science (Nitecki, 1988).

The scientific questions discussed by Darwin himself and the problems raised in the early 1900s together with later debates about 'adaptationism' and 'neutralism' which arose in the 1970s following the discovery of the role of DNA are often repeated by non-scientists but more tendentiously by 'special creationists'[2]. Ian Plimer, an Australian Professor of Geology has written a book *Telling Lies for God*, detailing the repeated factual falsehoods of 'creationists' even after their errors were pointed out (Plimer, 1994). In a Presidential Address to the American Association of Physical Anthropologists, Bill Pollitzer tells of his views being meretriciously misrepresented in a publication of the Creation Research Institute "circulated to millions" (Pollitzer, 1980).

Deliberate misrepresentations undoubtedly cloud the proper understanding of evolution, but they also encourage misconceptions. These began early. The debate at the British Association for the Advancement of Science Meeting in Oxford in 1860 is regularly resurrected in the media as a clash between religion represented by the Bishop of Oxford and science championed by Thomas Henry Huxley, with science triumphant, vanquishing superstition and false authority. In fact it was nothing of the kind. On the Bishop's side it was about the danger of legitimising change in an age when he believed it was having dangerous social and theological effects, while Huxley's aim was the secularisation of society - to establish the legitimacy of science against what he regarded as the improper influence of church leaders. It was reported that Wilberforce went away happy that he had given Huxley a bloody nose, while Hooker (who spoke after Huxley) told Darwin that Huxley had been largely inaudible, but that he (Hooker) "smashed Sam [Samuel Wilberforce, the Bishop] amid rounds of applause". Allegedly, most of the audience scored the occasion as an entertaining draw (Brooke, 2001). The next day, Frederick Temple preached the University sermon. He granted scientists all the laws they could discover in the universe and promised "the finger of God" in them'; the bible did not demand "confirmation of minute details" but recognition of "tone, character and spirit between the Book of God and the Book of Nature".

But the Oxford debate has continued to cast a malign shadow, giving a legacy of inevitable conflict between science and faith. This was encouraged by Huxley himself, fuelled by two much-read manifestos by the virulently anti-Roman Catholic, John William Draper (*History of the Conflict between Religion and Science*, 1875) and the ardent secularist, Andrew Dickson White, keen to promote the newly founded Cornell University where he was the first president (*A History of the Warfare of Science with Theology in Christendom*, 1886), and energetically stoked by so-called neo-atheists – Richard Dawkins, Christopher Hitchens, Daniel Dennett. Moore (1979: 99) judged that the nineteenth century did not produce "a polarisation of 'science' and 'religion' as the idea of opposed armies implies, but a large number of learned men, some scientists, some theologians, some indistinguishable, and almost all of them very religious, who experienced various differences among themselves... We conclude that the military metaphor has taken a dreadful toll in historical interpretation".

But worse came in a surge of literalism ineluctably leading to 'creationism'. It was a movement which had only very tenuous links with the earlier debates which led to the historical acceptance of Darwinism. The main begetter of this new wave was the Adventist Ellen White and her followers, notably George McCready Price whose cry was "No Adam, no Fall; no Fall, no Atonement; no Atonement, no Savior" (Numbers, 1992). At the same time, Presbyterian Albert Johnson claimed that evolution led to "sensuality, carnality, Bolshevism and the Red Flag". By the end of the 1920s, three American states (Tennessee, Mississippi and Arkansas) had passed laws banning the teaching of evolution in government-funded schools. In Dayton, Tennessee, John Scopes was tried and convicted in 1925 in the notorious "Monkey Trial" (Larson, 1997). He was fined $100, although the sentence was later overturned on a technicality, because the judge had set the fine, rather than the jury as the law required.

After this, organized 'creationism' in the US lapsed into relative quiescence. The American Scientific Affiliation, founded in 1941 by evangelical scientists concerned about the quality of Christian witness on science and religion, devoted more energy to appraising than opposing evolution. A widely read and influential book by Bernard Ramm of Baylor University in Texas sought to reconcile science and scripture on the basis of a venerable theory that there was a large time gap between the creation of the universe described in the first verse of Genesis and the events subsequently described. This 'gap theory' was espoused by the influential Scottish divine, Thomas Chalmers

(1780-1847) and popularized by the dispensationalist commentator Cyril Schofield in the Schofield Reference Bible (Ramm, 1955). The calm was shattered in 1961 when the *Genesis Flood* appeared, a book written by John Whitcomb, a bible teacher, and Henry Morris, a hydraulic engineer (Whitcomb & Morris, 1961). This rapidly became a cornerstone for 'young earth creationism'. The authors rejected the established findings of geology, palaeontology and archaeology because they believed that the world had been so ravaged by a worldwide flood; consequently (they claimed) orthodox stratigraphy cannot be applied. They argued that Genesis tells of a canopy of water which once surrounded the earth and provided the waters for Noah's flood; this protected the surface of the early earth from cosmic rays, accounting for the long lives of the patriarchs. In early editions they made much of the 'Paluxy footprints' in Texas where giant human footprints were found alongside those of dinosaurs. However, the human tracks were later shown to be a mixture of poorly formed dinosaur tracks and artefacts produced by locals to attract tourists. This 'evidence' was later omitted from 'creationist' writings, but it illustrates the sort of data used to challenge accepted scientific understandings. An attempt by the 'creationist' lobby to legitimise its beliefs as scientific and thus requiring 'equal time' in science teaching to orthodox evolutionary science (claimed as 'only a theory') was firmly rebuffed in the Arkansas courts.

Despite its incredibility, 'young earth creationism' still attracts a large number of adherents. Bibles are still produced with the date '4004 BC' heading the references at the beginning of Genesis, and a book *In Six days. Why 50 Scientists Choose to Believe in Creation* was published as recently as 1999 (Ashton, 1999). A more nuanced variant of 'creationism' is "Intelligent Design" (ID), in effect a revival of the classical argument of God as Designer. ID first came to general awareness in a book *Darwin on Trial*, written by a Californian lawyer, Philip Johnson (Johnson,

1991), reacting against the naturalism of Richard Dawkins. The main complaint of Johnson and his followers was not evolution as such, but the assumption that belief in evolution leads inevitably and inexorably to atheism (Plantinga, 1991). A scientific case for ID has been claimed by a biochemist, Michael Behe (1996, 2007) on the grounds that some biological mechanisms and processes are "irreducibly complex" and incapable of evolution by natural selection. Behe's examples have received short shrift from reviewers; they are in fact nothing more than the dangerous assumption that God can be found in the gaps in knowledge – an assumption that is open to contradiction by further discoveries. An objection to the teaching of ID in biology classes was upheld in an American court on the ground that ID "is not science and cannot uncouple itself from its creationist and thus religious antecedents" (Ayala, 2007). Many Christians are probably sympathetic to ID on the grounds that it finds a place for a God who is a Designer as well as a Creator and Redeemer.

For long, most scientists treated creationist attacks as effectively irrational and ignored them. This has changed, because of their perceived harm to the credibility of science. In recent years there have been a number of authoritative defences of the scientific understanding of evolution – by the US National Academy of Sciences, by the InterAcademy Panel (representing 66 National Academies, including the Royal Society of London), and an increasing number of individual scholars writing from both a secular and a religious basis (*e.g.* Kitcher, 1982; Russell, Stoeger & Ayala, 1998; K.R. Miller, 1999; Berry, 2001; K.B. Miller, 2003; Peters & Hewlett, 2003; Ayala, 2007; Alexander, 2008).

Great Are the Works of the Lord

The problem for the believer about evolution is to understand how God can work in an apparently deterministic universe. This is a bigger problem than that raised by evolution, but evolution can be regarded as a proving bed for it. Probably the most satisfying model is complementarity, building on ideas developed by Niels Bohr to bring together the wave and particle concepts of the electron. Bohr himself suggested that the idea could be extended to other phenomena susceptible to analysis by more than one kind of model: mechanistic and organic models in biology, behavioural and introspective models in psychology, models of free-will and determinism in philosophy, divine justice and divine love in theology (Folse, 1985). Others have edged towards a similar idea for God's action, *e.g.* Austin Farrer (1966) with 'double agency', Michael Polanyi (1969) with 'levels of explanation', but the most robust and satisfying elaboration has been that of a physicist, Donald MacKay (1988, 1991).

For MacKay: "The God in whom the bible invites belief is no 'Cosmic Mechanic'. Rather is he the Cosmic Artist, the creative Upholder, without whose constant activity there would be not even chaos, but just nothing. What we call physical laws are expressions of created events that we study as the physical world. Physically they express the nature of the entities 'held in being' in the pattern. Theologically they express the stability of the great Artist's creative will. Explanations in terms of scientific laws and in terms of divine activity are thus not rival answers to the same question; yet they are not talking about different things. They are (or at any rate purport to be) complementary accounts of different aspects of the same happening, which in its full nature cannot be explained by either alone.. To invoke 'natural processes' is not to escape from divine activity, but only to make hypotheses about its regularity…. (For example, we cannot settle the validity of our ideas in geometry by discussing the embryological origin of the brain!)" (MacKay, 1960: 10, 15; see also MacKay, 1968).

MacKay used a painting to explain his point. This can be described both in terms of the distribution of chemicals on a two-dimensional surface and also as the physical expression of a design in the mind of an artist. In other words, the same material object can have two or more 'causes', which do not contradict or overlap, but are undeniably complementary. MacKay then extended the idea into a dynamic form, using the analogy of a television programme which can be 'explained' in terms of electronics and the physiology of vision, but also as the intention of the programme producer who is telling the story – and who can change the images at will. The idea that the same event can have multiple causes is not new; it is at least as old as Aristotle, who distinguished material and efficient causes (which answer, in general 'how?' questions) from formal and final causes (which answer 'why?' questions) in his *Metaphysics*.

For MacKay and those who accept his approach it is possible to describe and analyse an event in as quantitative and rigorous way as possible, but also to acknowledge God's hand in and control of it. Complementarity has its own rules. It has suffered because it has been sometimes used improperly used to link (or explain away) contrasting explanations, but it is undoubtedly a powerful and satisfying way to bring together scientific and religious explanations (Jeeves, 1969: 70f; Barbour, 1998). In the context of evolution, it is entirely logical to believe in God as creator and sustainer and simultaneously accept a conventional scientific account.

The heading of this section ("Great are the works of the Lord") is the first half of the "Research Scientist's text" (Psalm 111: 2). The second half of the verse complements it: "Studied by all those who delight in them" (Berry, *in press*). The words were carved into the wooden door of the old Cavendish Laboratory in Cambridge at the behest of the first Cavendish Professor, James Clerk Maxwell. They were the doors through which Francis Crick and James Watson rushed to the pub opposite "to tell everyone within hearing that we had found the secret of life". The verse is carved also on the memorial plaque to Darwin's friend and confidant, Joseph Hooker in St Anne's Church Kew. It recalls the tradition that God wrote Two Books – a Book of Words (the bible) and a Book of Works (creation), a tradition that Darwin endorsed when he included opposite the title page of the *Origin* a quotation from Francis Bacon's *Advancement of Learning*: " Let no one think or maintain that they can search too far or be too well studied in the book of God's words or in the book of God's works; rather let all endeavour an endless progress or proficiency in both". Properly understood, there can be no conflict between God's revelation of himself in words or in work. Whatever the causes of the ebbing of faith feared by Matthew Arnold, assaults by science should not be demonised as one of them.

Science is blamed for all sorts of wrong. But as Rowan Williams pointed out in a Holy Week Lecture in Westminster Abbey (17 March 2008), the fact that Darwin was buried in the Abbey "is a very significant witness to the fact that the stand-off between faith and science, even between faith and Darwin, was not always what we might imagine it to be... [rather] it is perhaps a good model for seeing the centrality in our thinking about faith and science". For those of us who profess faith, science should an encouragement to exert ourselves more energetically to understand better both books of God. Neglecting either of them is likely to lead to a distorting of understanding. It was worth remembering that it was Galileo's telescope, not his church, that conclusively refuted the interpretation of Psalm 96: 10 ["The world is fixed immovably"] as a proof-text against the earth's rotation.

As a young man the German astronomer, Johannes Kepler (1571-1630) wrote to a friend, "I wanted to become a theologian; for a long time I was unhappy. Now, behold, God is praised by my work, even in astronomy". For him, the practice of science was "thinking God's thoughts after him". His prayer was:

"If I have been enticed into brashness by the wonderful beauty of thy works, or if I have loved my own glory among men, while advancing in work destined for thy glory, gently and mercifully pardon me; and finally, deign graciously to cause that these demonstrations may lead to thy glory and to the salvation of souls, and nowhere be an obstacle to that. Amen".

Kepler's prayer is a fit and proper one for any scientist.

Notes

[1] Darwin concluded the *Origin*: "It is interesting to contemplate a tangled bank, clothed with many plants of many kinds, with birds singing on the bushes, with various insects flitting about, and with worms crawling through the damp earth, and to reflect that these elaborately constructed forms, so different from each other and dependent upon each other in so complex a manner, have all been produced by laws acting around us... From the war of nature, from famine and death, the most exalted object which we are capable of conceiving, the production of the higher animals, directly follows. There is grandeur in this view of life with its several powers, having been originally breathed by the Creator into a few forms or into one; and that, whilst this planet has gone cycling on according to the fixed law of gravity, from so simple a beginning endless forms most beautiful and most wonderful have been, and are being evolved."

[2] We need to acknowledge that all believers in a Creator are, by definition, creationists. We affirm this every time we say the words of the Apostle's Creed: "I believe in God, creator/maker of heaven and earth..." I put 'creationist' and 'special creationist' in parentheses to indicate those unwilling to accept that the Creator may have used in his creative work mechanisms inaccessible to investigation.

References

Alexander, D.R. (2008). *Creation or Evolution. Do We Have To Choose?* Oxford: Monarch.

Ashton, J.F. (ed.) (1999). *In Six days. Why 50 Scientists Choose to*

Believe in Creation. Sydney: New Holland.

Ayala, F. J. (2007). *Darwin's Gift to Science and Religion.* Washington, DC: Joseph Henry Press.

Barbour, I. (1998). *Religion and Science.* London: SCM.

Barlow, N. (ed.) (1958). *The Autobiography of Charles Darwin, 1809-1882, with original omissions restored.* London: Collins.

Behe, M.J. (1996). *Darwin's Black Box.* New York: Free Press.

Behe, M.J. (2007). *The Edge of Evolution.* New York: Free Press.

Bellon, R. (2006). Joseph Hooker takes a 'fixed post': transmutation and the "present unsatisfactory state of systematic botany", 1844-1860. *Journal of the History of Biology*, 39: 1-39.

Berry, R.J. (1982). *Neo-Darwinism.* London: Edward Arnold.

Berry, R.J. (2001). *God and Evolution*, revised edition. Vancouver, BC: Regent College Publishing.

Berry, R.J. (in the press). The research scientist's psalm. Science & Christian Belief.

Bowler, P.J. (2001). *Reconciling Science and Religion.* Chicago: Chicago University Press.

Bowler, P.J. (2007). *Monkey Trials and Gorilla Sermons.* Boston, MA: Harvard University Press.

Brooke, J.H. (2001). The Wilberforce-Huxley debate: why did it happen? *Science & Christian Belief,* 13: 127-141.

Browne, J. (1995). *Charles Darwin. Voyaging.* London: Jonathan Cape.

Chambers, R. (1844). *Vestiges of the Natural History of Creation.* London: John Churchill.

Cupitt, D. (1984). *The Sea of Faith.* London: BBC.

Dawkins, R. (1986). *The Blind Watchmaker.* London: Longman.

Draper, W. (1875). *History of the Conflict between Religion and Science.* London: Henry King.

Farrer, A. (1966). *A Science of God.* London: Geoffrey Bles.

Folse, H. (1985). *The Philosophy of Neils Bohr: the Framework of Complementarity.* New York: North Holland.

Gillispie, C.C. (1951). *Genesis and Geology.* Cambridge, MA:

Harvard University Press.

Huxley, J.S. (1942). *Evolution: the Modern Synthesis*. London: Allen & Unwin.

Jeeves, M.A. (1969). *The Scientific Enterprise and Christian Truth.* Leicester: IVP.

Johnson, P.E. (1991). *Darwin on Trial*. Washington, DC: Regnery Gateway.

Kellogg, V.L. (1907). *Darwinism Today*. London: George Bell & Sons.

Kitcher, P. (1982). *Abusing Science*. Boston, MA: Baker Booker House.

Larson, E.J. (1997). *Summer for the Gods*. Cambridge, MA: Harvard Universtiy Press.

Lewis, C..E. & Knell, S.J. (2001). *Age of the Earth: from 4004 BC to AD 2002*. *London*: Geological Society of London.

Livingstone, D.N. (1987). *Darwin's Forgotten Defenders. The Encounter Between Evangelical Theology and Evolutionary Thought*. Grand Rapids, MI: Eerdmans.

MacKay, D.M. (1960). *Science and Christian Faith Today*. London: Falcon.

MacKay, D.M. (1968). The sovereignty of God in the natural world. *Scottish Journal of Theology*, 21: 13-26.

MacKay, D.M. (1988). *The Open Mind*. Leicester: IVP.

MacKay, D.M. (1991). *Behind the Eye*. Oxford: Blackwell.

Mayr, E. & Provine, W.B. (eds.) (1980). *The Evolutionary Synthesis*. Cambridge, MA: Harvard University Press.

Miller, K.B. (ed) (2003). *Perspectives on an Evolving Creation*. Grand Rapids, MI: Eerdmans.

Miller, K.R. (1999). *Finding Darwin's God*. New York: HarperCollins.

Moore, A. (1889). The Christian doctrine of God. In *Lux Mundi*: 57-109. Gore, C. (ed.). London: John Murray.

Moore, A. (1892). *Science and the Faith*. London: Kegan Paul, Trench, Trübner.

Moore, J.R. (1979). *The Post-Darwinian Controversies.* Cambridge: Cambridge University Press.

Moore, J.R. (1986). Geologists and interpreters of Genesis in the nineteenth century. In *God and Nature*: 322-350. Lindberg, D.C. & Numbers, R.L. (eds.). Berkeley, CA: University of California Press.

Nitecki, M.H. (ed.)(1988). *Evolutionary Progress.* Chicago: University of Chicago Press.

Numbers, R.L. (1992). *The Creationists.* New York: Alfred Knopf

Ospovat, D. (1979). *The Development of Darwin's Theory.* Cambridge: Cambridge University Press.

Peters, T. & Hewlett, M. (2003). *Evolution from Creation to New Creation.* Nashville, TN: Abingdon Press.

Platinga, A. (1991). Where faith and reason clash: evolution and the Bible. *Christian Scholars' Review,* 21: 8-32.

Plimer, I. (1994). *Telling Lies for God.* Sydney: Random House.

Pollitzer, W.S. (1980). Evolution and special creation. American Journal of Physical Anthropology, 53: 329-31.

Polyani, M. (1969). *Knowing and Believing.* London: Routledge & Kegan Paul.

Porter, R. (2000). *Enlightenment. Britain and the Creation of the Modern World.* London: Allen Lane.

Provine, W.B. (1971). *The Origins of Theoretical Population Genetics.* Chicago: University of Chicago Press.

Ramm, B. (1955). *The Christian View of Science and Scripture.* Grand Rapids, MI: Eerdmanns.

Roberts, M.B. (1997). Darwin's doubts about design – the Darwin-Gray correspondence of 1860. *Science & Christian Belief,* 9: 113-127.

Ruse, M. (1996). *Monad to Man. The Concept of Progress in Evolutionary Biology.* Cambridge, MA: Harvard University Press.

Ruse, M. (2001). *Can a Darwinian be a Christian?* Cambridge: Cambridge University Press.

Russell, R.J., Stoeger, W.R. & Ayala, F.J. (eds) (1998). *Evolutionary and Molecular Biology. Scientific Perspectives on Dvine Action.* Notre Dame, IN: Vatican Observatory Foundation.

Secord, J.A. (2000). *Victorian* Sensation. Chicago: University of Chicago Press.

Stott, R. (2003). *Darwin and the Barnacle.* London: Faber & Faber.

Sulloway, F. (1982). Darwin's Conversion: the *Beagle* voyage and its aftermath. *Journal of the History of Biology,* 15: 325-96.

Temple, F. (1885). *The Relations Between Religion and Science.* London: Macmillan.

Thomas, K. (1983). *Man and the Natural World.* London: Allen Lane.

Whitcomb, J.C. & Morris, H.M. (1961). *The Genesis Flood.* Nutley, NJ: Presybeterian & Reformed Publishing Company.

White, A.D. (1886). *A History of the Warfare of Science with Theology.* New York: Appleton.

Professor R.J. (Sam) Berry, DSc, FRSE was Professor of Genetics at University College London 1978-2000. He is a former President of the Linnean Society, the British Ecological Society, and Christians in Science. In 1996 he received the Templeton UK Award and in 2001 the Marsh Award for Ecology. He was Gifford Lecturer in the University of Glasgow in 1997-8 and Hooker Lecturer of the Linnean Society in 2008.

Cosmology and Faith

Rodney D, Davies

Introduction – setting the scene

"In the beginning ....." is where we start in both in science and the faith. The Genesis world view was born out of the experiences of a tribe leaving the comfort of a civilization on the Euphrates, and then entering a largely nomadic life, on their journey through the "Fertile Crescent" to the margins of the Mediterranean Sea, by way of a sojourn in Egypt.

They lived close to the soil. The stars, the Milky Way, the Sun, the Moon and the planets were ever present. Their daily lives were governed by the Sun's rising and setting; on longer time scales the Moon provided a convenient month. The yearly cycle was established by the pattern of the seasons tied to the movement of the Sun through the stars. These experiences provided the background for the cosmological element of their creation account.

Details of their understanding of nature including the heavens are clearly seen in the Old Testament accounts. They were aware of, and influenced by, the civilizations and the tribal groups in their journey. Most importantly they believed that they were guided by a God who cared for them and also, significantly, the whole of creation. This was not a remote God but one who was a continuous presence, supporting, cajoling and admonishing when necessary. This is the essence of God in the Abrahamic faiths of Judaism, Christianity and Islam. This Old Testament account of creation is attributed to Moses in the 12th to13th century BC.

A more theological statement concerning origins is found in the New Testament of the Christian tradition where John says " In the beginning ...." God (the "logos"- the Spirit, God himself) was in the world, in the whole process of creation, from the very beginning to the present and thence to eternity.

Scientists looking at the panorama of creation see it from a conveniently located planet Earth, circling a minor star, the Sun. This star, our Sun, is itself in orbit in an ordinary spiral galaxy, the Milky Way, which is a member of a cluster of galaxies that are all part of the expansion of the Universe. Modern astronomers find a remarkable sequence of events which stretch in time from the Big Bang to the present day, a time some 13.7 billion years later.

This scientific scenario allows us to follow the development of life from processes in the earliest few minutes after the Big Bang, through the synthesis of the chemical elements in interiors of stars, to the formation of planets around parent stars which provide platforms on which life can emerge. The great diversity of life that has populated the Earth in the 4.6 billion years since its birth is essentially the product of stardust. The great variety of life forms emerging from the chemical elements in this stardust is the consequence of chemistry in the changing environment on the Earth – the birth of the seas, the tectonic movements of the crust and the resulting volcanism. Add to this the competition for the necessities of life that we call "evolution" and are celebrating in this volume.

In the last few million years, hominoids emerged in the maelstrom of life. More recently, Homo sapiens has appeared on the scene with an ability to contemplate the world about him and to ponder where life came from and wonder at its diversity. This wonder and awe are at the root of religion. The relationship between us humans, our fellow creatures and a creating and sustaining God is at the root of faith.

An expanding Universe

A key step in the modern understanding of cosmology was the discovery by Edwin Hubble in 1928 of the recession of the galaxies due to the expansion of the Universe. His remarkable finding was that for each galaxy its recession velocity, its "redshift", was closely proportional to its distance. This implied that the universe was in a state of expansion as would be expected from an explosion at some time in the past and that the fastest moving galaxies had travelled furthest. This picture is at the heart of modern cosmology where each observer (galaxy) sees itself as the centre of the expansion. The tightness of this linear relation between red-shift and distance is of central importance in understanding the evolution of the Universe. Any picture of the Universe which includes gravity would expect to see evidence of slowdown in the expansion velocity due to the self-attraction of the matter of the Universe. Such departures are being found in the most recent ground- and space-based observations of galaxies at the highest red-shifts as I will show later; they have fundamental implications for our view of the Universe and of physics as a whole.

What can physics/cosmology say about the beginnings? Let us now take a quick look back in time from the present to the origin of this expanding Universe. This is the panorama an astronomer sees when looking at more and more distant galaxies. As we first pan back we see the galaxies moving closer together with their constituent stars forming at an earlier phase. The galaxies seen in the deep field of the Hubble space telescope are at a redshift of $z = 1$. The red-shift measures the increase in wavelength as the galaxies recede from us. So at $z = 1$ the wavelength is increased by a factor of $(1 + z)$. This corresponds to a time when the Universe was $1/1+z$ ie one half of its present size. The most distant galaxies seen with the large ground-based telescopes are at a redshift of $z = 7$ when the universe was $1/8$ of its present size, corresponding to a time about 1 billion years after the Big Bang ie some 12 billion years before the present. Clearly the first stars had formed by that time allowing us to see the light from the individual galaxies. It is interesting to note that stars born at this time are also found in nearby galaxies; the oldest stars in our own galaxy, the Milky Way are of comparable age. Before these first stars had collapsed under local gravity their parent galaxies would have been clouds of cool neutral atoms (mainly hydrogen and helium).

Before the first galaxies formed we have no direct evidence for structure in the Universe over most of the first billion years. This is sometimes described as the Dark Age of the Universe. However remarkably at 380,000 years after the Big Bang, we have a snapshot of the structures in the distribution of matter and radiation at this time in the early Universe via the Cosmic Microwave Background (CMB). This occurs when the hot ionized gas of the early Universe cooled enough for the protons and electrons to combine to form neutral hydrogen. These observations provide a unique opportunity for making a comparison with structures in our local Universe and give the strongest constraints on all the cosmological models. In its earlier compressed state this matter would have been hot ionized plasma of hydrogen and helium bathed in a field of radiation. When we move back to the time where the Universe was 1 second old, this plasma would have been have been at a temperature of 1 billion Kelvins and the individual elements we know in our local universe did not exist – only a sea of fundamental particles - principally protons and neutrons - bathed in an intense radiation field which contained most of the energy. At even earlier times the highly dense and hot Universe had the conditions produced in a modern particle physics laboratory. The energies being studied in the Large Hadron Collider at CERN correspond to those in the Universe at an age of 10^{-12} seconds when the temperature was 10^{15} K. We can ask what might happen at even earlier times. A period of inflation is hypothesized to have occurred at 10^{-34} seconds. In the limit physics itself breaks down completely at the Planck time (the Uncertainty Principle) at 10^{-43} seconds after the Big Bang. But more of this later. Physics has nothing to say about what happened before the Big Bang. Time and space are intricately locked together and so they must begin together. There is no concept in physics of time before the Big Bang.

The path to life in the Universe

We will now review the criticalities in the observed properties of the Universe which have allowed life to appear at the present time in at least one place within it, namely our Earth. At the outset it must be emphasized that as far as a physical description is concerned, the universe is extremely uniform. All the evidence is that the average properties of regions of space are the same at the same time. This is called the "cosmological principle". Such properties as the mean matter density, radiation density, chemical composition and indeed all the laws of physics are the same. A natural corollary of this principle is that the conditions for life on the Earth will be repeated in other parts of the universe. Such is the justification for the present day searches for extra-terrestrial intelligence (SETI).

We will begin our exploration of the beginning of the Universe at the earliest time for which there is concrete evidence for an expanding and extremely hot plasma of mixed radiation and matter. This is the famous "first 3 minutes" when the first elements emerged from the primal soup. At the beginning of this period matter had been transformed from quarks to protons and neutrons which in turn were colliding with enough energy to form helium comprising two protons and two neutrons. The fractional mass in helium was 25% and that in hydrogen was 75%, a ratio that is found throughout the Universe (apart from a small additional fraction of helium added in later star-formation. The theoretical prediction of this ratio is the consequence of our understanding of fundamental particle physics in Earth laboratories that has been applied to the situation in the expanding universe at this early time.

Probably the most significant discovery in cosmology after the universal expansion was that of the Cosmic Microwave Background of electromagnetic radiation found by Penzias and Wilson in 1967 with a black body brightness temperature of 3 K. This is precisely the temperature expected for the expanding universe at the time when it had cooled to 3000 K which allowed the charged proton and electron plasma to combine to form neutral hydrogen. The brightness temperature that we register is the 3000 K spectrum redshifted to a temperature of 3000/1+z = 3 K. Before this combination the radiation and charged matter were locked together by the scattering of radiation on charged particles (electrons and ions). But when the plasma became neutral, the radiation could propagate freely through the intervening matter to observers on Earth today. Importantly, the radiation field gives a map of the surface of last scattering which portrays the matter distribution at that early time. The situation is similar to what one sees in a cloudy sky; a map of the structures in the individual clouds is evident from the equivalent surface of last scattering of light by water droplets.

Two important parameters for cosmology emerge from observations of the CMB. The first is the high uniformity of the CMB over the sky. After correction for the motion of the solar system relative to the local Universe, the radiation and matter at z = 1000 is constant over the sky to better than one part in 10^5. This is the strongest demonstration of the uniformity of the universe at any time in its history. The redshift of 1000 where the electrons and protons recombine occurs 380,000 years after the Big Bang.

The second contribution to cosmology from the CMB observations is a map of the structures in the Universe at z = 1000. A most significant pattern is found in the brightness distribution in the sky. Although extremely weak, amounting to 10^{-5} of the 3 K radiation background, features on an angular scale of ~1° are the brightest. This scale corresponds to the distance acoustic waves have travelled between the time of the Big Bang and the last scattering surface at age 380,000 years. It is similar to the ringing of a giant bell which has been struck at the time of the Big Bang. In addition to the fundamental frequency (angle in this case), there are harmonics of decreasing intensity in the pattern on the sky. As the Universe expands this pattern is preserved in the matter distribution seen as a clustering of the galaxies. In the nearby universe the scale of the structure corresponding to the 1° scale in the CMB is 150 Megaparsecs, some 500 million light years. The correspondence between these two scales at epochs when the Universe had expanded by a factor of 1000 is a confirmation of the evolutionary picture of an expanding universe. This scale along with the CMB power spectrum and the recession velocity of galaxies as a function of distance, helps to determine the fundamental parameters of the Universe such as its mass, age and composition.

The origin of the chemical elements necessary for life

In the first 200 seconds after the Big Bang we have seen that hydrogen and helium have been produced; there are also tiny amounts of some of the lighter elements such as deuterium and lithium which are formed in the short period when elements can be synthesized. After this time the temperature of the expanding plasma is too low for the necessary nuclear reactions to produce any of the elements necessary for life. These "heavy" elements can only be formed over long periods of time in regions where temperatures are ~100 million K. Apart from the Big Bang itself, such conditions are only found in the centres of stars. Accordingly, the chemical elements necessary for life will not be available until stars have formed and then have dispersed their synthesis products into the interstellar medium. Although all the heavier elements are produced in stars, we are most interested in those involved in carbon-based life as found on Earth. These are C, H, O and N which are components of such common molecules as H_2O, CO_2, NH_3 and CH_4. Interestingly, these same elements are also involved in one of the chain reactions in stars namely the CNO cycle which converts H to He thereby producing stellar energy.

The nucleosynthesis of all the heavier elements essential to biology depends upon the formation of C^{12} from three He^4 nuclei via the formation of beryllium Be^8. This is a process which is very finely tuned. Fred Hoyle showed that there was a crucial resonance between energy levels in carbon and beryllium which was essential for the production of carbon. This resonance confirms an Anthropic Principle prediction that the Universe is organized to produce life. The statistical unlikelihood of the coincidence of these energy levels was a situation which fascinated Hoyle when he speculated "...we can exist only in parts of the universe where these levels are correctly placed".

A second factor which is critical to the evolution of life in the Universe is its large age. It has to be old enough for stars and galaxies to form under the action of gravity as a first step. Then there needs to be time for the nucleosynthesis of the heavy elements to occur in the central regions of the stars. These complex processes take at least one billion years judging from the highest redshift galaxies detected so far. Then the elements, the products of nucleosynthesis, have to be dispersed into the interstellar medium of their parent galaxies. This occurs through stellar winds and supernova explosions at the end of the star's life. Then the metal-enriched interstellar gas needs to collapse under gravity into second-generation stars along with their attendant planets. Life itself then has to evolve on the planets from the rich mix of atoms and molecules brought to them from the interstellar medium. This latter process appears to have taken rather more than one billion years on the Earth. In fact the best estimate of the age of the Universe from all the data available 13.7 billion years. By comparison, the solar system comprising the Sun with its retinue of planets and cometary debris is 4.6 billion years old. The element abundances in the solar system are similar to those of stars comprised of material that has been enriched through several cycles of stellar nucleosynthesis. Although the Sun is only 4.6 billion years old, there are stars in our Galaxy which are more than twice as old indicating that star-formation began in our Galaxy some 10 billion years ago. It is evident that all the processes described above in the chain of life leading to the emergence of man need timescales of several billion years at least and maybe up to 10 billion years. In an expanding Big Bang model which fits the observational evidence well, the mass of the Universe must be correspondingly large (of the order of $\sim 10^{11}$ galaxies).

Such an age requires a universe that has physical constants closely similar to those that apply in our Universe. For example, a higher value for the gravitational constant would imply a faster collapse of the Universe and insufficient time for nucleosynthesis of the elements critical for life. Similar arguments may be made regarding the other fundamental constants of Nature such as the quark and electron masses. Any changes in these masses would make protons, deuterons and hydrogen atoms unstable. There is only a small region of physical parameter space which allows life to evolve.

What we still do not know about our Universe

One of the great mysteries of cosmology is the origin of the high degree of uniformity of the Universe as evidenced by the CMB. Its brightness which mimics the mass distribution is constant to 1 part in 10^5 in whatever direction one looks. This situation requires an explanation because there is no causal connection between such well-separated parts of the Universe. Electromagnetic radiation and gravity both propagate at the speed of light and cannot guarantee that the properties are the same in both places. A solution to this problem is most likely to lie within the compact phase of the expanding cosmic plasma at times before the first second. A window of opportunity for such a unifying process is at an epoch when the matter/radiation plasma goes through a phase change in analogy with the phase changes of ice/liquid/steam in water which generate sudden changes in volume. This can occur in the cosmic plasma at time 10^{-34} seconds after the Big Bang. This proposed mechanism is called "inflation". During this period the Universe grows exponentially in radius by 60 e-folding times corresponding to a factor of 10^{30}.and ensures that all parts of the Universe are in contact and have the same properties at that time thereby providing the high level of uniformity seen in the CMB and in the Universe today.

Proposals for inflation take many forms. Candidates for the elementary particles which may have suitable phase changes include the scalar Higgs field and the super-massive W and Z bosons. At present all proposals are in the realm of theory. However there is the possibility of testing the inflation scenario. Inflation should leave an imprint on the CMB. It produces tensor fluctuations in the radiation field as well as the normal scalar fluctuations; the former show up as linearly polarized structure in the CMB known as B-modes. Unfortunately B-modes are very weak compared with the scalar signals and are therefore are a significant, but not impossible, challenge to observers. Observing campaigns are currently in progress, one of which is the European Space Agency Planck spacecraft which is designed to make a deep survey of the CMB capable of detecting or setting useful upper limits to the B-mode intensity. Ground-based experiments are in preparation.

A second area where there is a major unknown is in the matter/energy content of the Universe. This arises from the recent CMB power spectrum results and the deep observations of redshift versus magnitude relation of supernovae in distant galaxies. These are complementary data sets which lead to accurate estimates of the important parameters of the Universe such as its age and its matter and energy content. The latter estimates were full of surprises. It turns out that ordinary baryonic matter comprises only ~3% of the matter/energy of the Universe. Dark matter contributes 27 % leaving ~70 % which is in the form of an energy field acting like a repulsive force. The relevant parameters derived in 2006 at the time of the first release of the 3-year data from the WMAP CMB mission are given in Table 1. The dark matter and the dark energy have yet to be identified.

Table 1. PARAMETERS OF THE UNIVERSE

Baryon density (ordinary matter)	2.3 %
Dark matter (has gravity)	25 %
Dark energy (causes expansion)	73 %
Age of the Universe (the Big Bang to the present)	13.7 billion years
Age at recombination (3 K)	380,000 years
CMB brightness temperature	2.725 K

The presence of dark matter has been well-established in the local Universe for the last 40 years or so. It contributes along with the luminous matter to the gravitating matter needed to hold individual galaxies and clusters of galaxies together. There is evidently dark matter distributed more widely in the Universe lying between the galaxies and the galaxy clusters. Various suggestions have been made as to its nature. Black holes have been popular candidates. They are well-established occupants of the centres of galaxies. So far there is no evidence for a population of black holes in galaxies exceeding the mass of normal stars. Other possibilities include exotic members of the zoo of weakly interacting fundamental particles proposed by particle physicists.

The least expected component of the mass/energy of the Universe is the dark energy which acts in opposition to gravity and stops the ultimate collapse of the Universe under gravity alone. Dark energy is 3 times greater than the equivalent energy of dark and normal matter put together. Under the combined influence of inward acting gravity and the outward pressure of dark energy the redshift of the galaxies falls to a minimum of ~0.8c (c is the velocity of light) at z = 0.65 and then accelerates outwards to 1.0c at z ~ 2 and beyond. This dark energy at present has no theoretical explanation. It is the greatest challenge to cosmology and is a central clue to developing a fundamental theory which combines gravity with the other forces of Nature. Ideas include string theory and quantum gravity. This is much debated and is clearly a subject for future development.

Multiple universes

As an alternative to a universe tailor-made to contain life, the idea of multiple universes has been widely discussed. It is argued that among the vast number of possible universes there may be (at least) one which has the properties that have led to the emergence of life. Cosmologists now realize that processes in the early universe may generate an ensemble of universes each having different values of the fundamental physical constants. In this scenario we live in one of those universes which are conducive to life.

The model of inflation allows the possibility of multiple universes. Inflation argues that we live in a patch of the universe that underwent a rapid exponential expansion shortly after the Big Bang. What was a tiny patch of space swelled up to cosmic proportions in a fleeting fraction of a second. The argument goes that there should be infinitely more patches which underwent the same process. Each would be causally separate implying that it is different from every other universe in having its own physical constants and evolutionary history. All these universes would belong to a massive complex of space-time – the "multiverse". Furthermore, the various universes are unable to communicate with one another and accordingly we can never obtain evidence for their existence.

The multiverse theory appears to be highly speculative. It uses statistical arguments to justify the emergence of life in one of the infinite number of universes. It lacks the fundamental requirement of a good scientific theory of being predictable since we can never access the other universes to test whether our predictions are correct. Despite this problem, quantum cosmology is an emerging science. There are many unknowns at this level of understanding. We as yet have no theory of quantum gravity; the dark matter and the dark energy of the Universe have not yet been identified. Further, on the level of fundamental particles the Grand Unified Theory has still to be clarified. Are multiverses in some way a part of this scene?

Science and faith

In our review of the present status of cosmology we have identified many of the issues which are relevant to the emergence of life in the Universe. We now look at the parallels between scientific exploration and religious faith. Both are based on experience. Both are concerned with issues of ultimate reality whether of the physical world or of the moral, ethical and spiritual world of religion. Science and religion are both dependent upon trust. For scientists this trust includes which data and theories to accept; for the religious this trust is in knowing which leaders, rituals and prophets to honour. Trust is at the root of both the scientific and the religious life. There are other similarities between science and religion. In religion a sense of humility is at its heart – an awareness that the way we lead our lives is not perfect. Similarly in science there is a kind of humility in recognizing that we know only fragments about the physical world.

As I have attempted to show in this article, only a small region of the physical parameter space allows life to form in the Universe. The fact that the laws of Nature and the physical constants are such that intelligent life can emerge in the Universe is sometimes attributed to an "Anthropic Principle". One example of such a principle would be that the current age of the Universe cannot be much less than the measured 13.7 billion years otherwise the chemical elements would not have been produced in the centres of stars; on the other hand, in an older universe the stars would have burned out and not exist today. There seem to be special conditions in the make-up of the Universe which also imply such an anthropic principle. A notable example is the resonance (coincidence) of nuclear energy levels which are necessary for the formation of carbon, a crucial constituent of life. It has also been argued that the Moon has a special role in the evolution of life in that it stabilizes the spin axis of the Earth and permits a regulated climate. The multi-universe paradigm may also be considered as another example of the anthropic principle in its attempt to ensure that life would exist in at least one of the infinite assembly of universes

I have touched on some of the issues in cosmology and faith. This continues to be a fertile area of discussion in the fields of science, theology and philosophy. I conclude the survey by posing a question. Is the Anthropic Principle another way of saying the "hand of God"? Those in the faith communities would say yes. They see signs of mind and purpose in the structure of the physical world. For them there is no conflict between science and religious belief; when taken together they make the greatest sense of man and his place in the Universe.

Further reading.

Barrow, J.D. & Tipler F.J. 1988. *The Anthropic Cosmological Principle*. Oxford University Press.

P. C. W. Davies P.C.W. 1992. *The Mind of God*. London: Simon & Schuster.

Hawking S.W. 1988. *A Brief History of Time*. London: Bantam Press

Polkinghorne. J. C. 1998. *Belief in God in an Age of Science*. Yale

University Press

Rees M.J. 2000. *Just Six Numbers*. London: Phoenix

Rodney Davies CBE FRS, Emeritus Professor of Radioastronomy in the University of Manchester. Former Director of the Jodrell Bank Observatory. Past President of the Royal Astronomical Society. Research interests are in the structure of the Galaxy and of the Cosmic Microwave Background. Co-investigator on the ESA Planck mission to study the CMB. Methodist Local Preacher.

Cosmic Evolution

John Quenby

Underneath the 'wrinkles 'of god

Who needs Intelligent Design when Astrophysicists are exploring underneath the wrinkles of the face of God? In this chapter on the beginnings of our Universe, we are going to look at current ideas based on experimental evidence on the very earliest stages in 'creation' of matter as we know it and the speculations about what went on before.

God's 'wrinkles' refers to a headline in the New York Times after the first publication of the satellite mapping of the temperature distribution of the Universe as it was around a few hundred thousand years after the big bang. This map is one of the chief lines of evidence on our 'beginnings' and encourages further experimental and theoretical probing into our 'past'. The boldness, even temerity, of cosmologists in tackling this ultimate question contrasts with the proponents of Intelligent Design who seem to throw up their hands at every puzzling astronomical question and ask for extra, divine intervention to get over the difficult step. Starting back at before the first million years of our history, it seems very possible that we shall be able to understand the course of evolution from this epoch, using known science, down to to-day. By evolution I mean first of all astronomical, next biological and then the emergence of the richness of human experience we know now

By mentioning God in the first sentence we are accepting a theistic view of the universe. It could be possible to start more or less in the same way with the object of removing God completely from the account. On the contrary, I will claim that a viewpoint which looks for a Godly tendency for everything that happens takes both a Christian viewpoint and provides a theological description of evolution as envisaged here which is actually helpful with current puzzles couched in scientific language. In this way, Darwin's *On the Origin of the Species* will be thought of being a profoundly theological book extending revelation more traditionally found in the bible and the Church's teaching.

Let us look at the evidence from the early temperature map and then work back as far as possible into an era where time may not exist. It is worth going into a little detail in this process of projecting back in order to emphasise the evidence-based approach, the rapid progress in the field and the way problems are being resolved. Without some appreciation of the manner cosmology is being pursued, it is all too easy to relapse to a 'we can't understand anything attitude', or alternatively, to go to the extreme of 'we will be able to understand everything' without God.

Apart from all the radio, infra-red, optical and X-ray radiation that we receive from a variety of sources of power located in stars and galaxies, the earth is bathed in a background sea of very low temperature radiation. This microwave background, very like the radio waves used in telecommunication networks, corresponds to a temperature of just 3 degrees above the absolute zero of temperature. It comes from photons, discrete 'particles' of light, scattered when the universe had just cooled down enough to be transparent at a temperature of a few thousand degrees. At this moment, the hot gaseous mixture of ions and electrons started to form atoms which less easily absorbed the energy of the photons. Now a general expansion of the universe has been well established for many years, based on the observed shift to the red of light emitted at particular wavelengths by the motion away from the observer of the light sources, especially energetic, distant galaxies. This expansion effectively greatly cools the photons as they travel, now unhindered, from where they were scattered back at the time when the universe first became transparent, so they become microwaves.

The background radiation is remarkably uniform in intensity, whichever direction it is seen, just showing 'wrinkles' of a few parts in one hundred thousand. The striking implication of this fact is that an era of massive inflation or expansion seems to have occurred, so much that we can only see a small fraction of the total volume arising from the big bang. There must have been large fluctuations in the temperature and density of the 'gaseous' material composing the universe early on, but the massive expansion, by a factor of 10^{60} or so, just picks out a small, rather uniform region where we now exist and all the remainder disappears off the horizon because expansion means that light cannot travel fast enough to tell us about regions with characteristics of density and temperature much different from our own. At the start of inflation, age 10^{-34} seconds, the universe we see was 10 cm across. Expansion after the end of inflation at 10^{-31} seconds is then much less rapid.

Between this inflation era and 200 seconds after the big-bang, a large temperature drop allowed the basic thermonuclear interaction, similar to those happening in the sun today, to start building the nuclei of the elements on a cosmic scale. Initially, only protons and neutrons existed, but helium emerged via intermediate stages where convenient, stable isotopes are available. A gap in the atomic mass range of isotopes in the periodic table above helium meant that making useful heavier elements could no longer proceed. Instead, this element building needed to await the possibility of synthesis by the high pressures which became available in stars, especially in the supernova explosions of massive objects at the end of their lives. Meanwhile, the relative amount of helium and the deuterium and tritium isotopes in-between which were made from hydrogen can now be observed in young stars and gas in space. They provide powerful fossil evidence as to the density of matter in the universe at a time when the hadronic (mainly protons plus neutrons) mass became fixed. Surprisingly, there is much too little matter to explain our existence. A delicate balance is required between the gravitational attraction acting on our galaxy to pull it back into the source of the big-bang and the recession of our galaxy from this source due to the expansion of all space. This expansion is like the movement of an escalator, moving our feet whether we like it or not and gravity due to the whole of matter in the volume inside the bound between us and the centre of the big-bang is counteracting the effect of the escalator's motion. The fact that we can talk about space and gravity in the same breath is due to Einstein's general relativity. Gravity defines space-time in the sense that space as we know it is not just the three dimensions we understand but curved by gravity so that light does not go in 'straight lines' near very massive objects.

Too much matter and the universe would have been pulled back before it got cool enough to do anything. Too little matter and the individual atoms would have disappeared over each other's horizon before essential objects like stars could have had a chance to form. Matter as we know it in the form of protons, neutrons, electrons and so on only gives us about one hundredth of the required amount. Dark matter, made of very weakly interaction particles (WIMPS) postulated by some physicists, is a key to getting the balance nearly right. It is needed to keep large groups of galaxies together as clusters and acts as a template to encourage gravitational collapse of diffuse, gaseous matter to form galaxies. In 1987, when I helped to set up a consortium of UK scientists to search for direct, experimental signatures of this dark matter, it seemed we were getting into a position where we could know the ultimate fate of the universe. Too much dark matter and the big crunch would come. Too little and stars and hospitable planets would ultimately disappear from each other's view due to continuing expansion. Was this experiment, plus astronomical observation of the gravity of clusters, really the ultimate investigation to establish the far future? Was it experimental eschatology? It is certainly linked to the experiments now being done with the CERN Large Hadron Collider where the individual, colliding protons may have enough energy to artificially produce examples of the dark matter WIMPS.

In fact, further observation related to the expansion drastically changed the picture by the year 2000. One type of supernova explosion, due to a sudden nuclear outburst on a common type of dwarf star produces a standard light output which can be used as a measure of distance. Coupled with observation of the red-shift of discrete wavelengths of light from the galaxies containing the supernova, a new result for the total force controlling the expansion has emerged. Galaxies are experiencing a 'negative pressure' as well as a gravitational pull from the rest of the universe to change the initial outward momentum in the expansion from the big bang. This extra force is outwards from the big-bang centre-hence 'negative pressure'-because we think of pressure as being confining or inward. It is related to a mysterious term called the 'cosmological constant' in Einstein's equations describing motion in curved space under General Relativity. The new 'force' is associated with something labelled 'dark energy'. There is no current proper understanding as to what it is. Einstein thought it ought to appear for mathematical reasons in his equations. There are experiments being designed which might relate it to very low temperature fluctuations detectable in laboratory experiments. Dark energy is three times more important than dark matter in controlling galaxy expansion while dark matter is 30 times stronger than ordinary matter in determining gravity force on large scales. Establishing the magnitude of the dark energy effect involved at least two sets of data. Apart from the set of supernova data, the 'wrinkles' in the background provide another measure of distance in the early universe. This is because there is a characteristic, favoured separation in angle seen by the satellite telescope between peaks in the background temperature radiation. Translated into distance, the peaks are related to sound waves travelling across the early universe, a few thousand years after the big-bang when conditions became transparent for photons. Amalgamating the two sets of data, a unique answer for the combined forces was obtained. The net results seems almost certain continued indefinite expansion with the universe ending as a whimper, not a crunch, although we can't be certain that the relative importance of dark energy may decrease later due to unknown physics. A remarkable aspect of the estimates of the energies associated with ordinary matter, dark matter and the negative pressure is that they add up to nearly exactly the amount required to make a flat universe, barely curved by gravity. In other words, the universe is just between expansion and contraction so that galaxies can live in proximity for a very long time. Moreover, this particular amount of total energy must have existed to within one part in 10^{-60} as compared with today's value at a time very close to the time of the big-bang, even at the time pre-inflation.

God's Higgs and other Fundamental Particles

The crude term, gaseous material, was used to describe the contents of the universe around the inflation era. To be more precise it is necessary to look at the behaviour of matter and radiation as we project back towards the beginning, employing the cosmic expansion law found from observation at later times. The temperature of 10^9 K (K is a measure of temperature starting 273 degrees below the centigrade scale) when the universe now visible to us was about 10^{20} cm in radius and when the nuclear building up of elements just started was preceded by a fall from 10^{24} K, a size of 100 cm at only 10^{-35} sec after the big-bang. This was a crucial era that allowed order to appear out of disorder by a process known as symmetry breaking. The disorder consisted of a fluctuating sea of quarks-the constituents of hadrons which are entities like protons and neutrons-electrons and other light particles called muons, the almost mass-less neutrinos and copious photons, together with the 'quanta' of force or bosons which 'carry' the interaction between quarks and between the lighter particles mentioned.

To appreciate conditions in this very simple but crucial era in our cosmic evolution, it is worth giving a few outline ideas about the quantum and elementary particle theory commonly used by physicists. (See Hughes, 1991 for an undergraduate account).To understand the idea of 'quanta' of force which has been mentioned, consider the basic electromagnetic interaction. An electron (with a negative unit of charge) and a proton (with a positive unit of charge) moving towards each other mutually feel an electrostatic attraction. In large scale physics, this is described by an inverse square law of force. One possibility is the electron can circulate the proton like the Earth circulating the Sun. In quantum physics, dealing with the very small dimensions which apply in practice, the position of the particles is uncertain within the product, $\delta(mv) \times \delta(x) \sim h$ where $\delta(mv)$ is uncertainty in momentum (mass times velocity whose change is response to force), $\delta(x)$ is uncertainty in position and the product is approximately equal to a very small number, h. To make use of this uncertainty, atomic and sub-atomic particles are described by probability distributions based on waves. These waves which represent the probability distribution around the atom have 'quantised' or discrete values because the wave must fit to repeat itself after going all the 360 degrees around the atom. This gives the idea of 'quantum numbers' to describe values such as the angular momentum or product of the three quantities '$r \times m \times v$' for the motion around the atom at distance r from the centre. It is a quantisation of energy levels-dependent on the orbital speed at a given distance-that gives rise to the discrete emissions of light wavelengths mentioned previously. Only certain mean distances from the central nucleus can be occupied by the orbiting electron. Elementary particles can be thought of as spinning on their axes with units of angular momentum as multiples of $h/2\pi$. Electrons and protons each have ½ a unit of spin-so their spin quantum number is '1/2'. By having a fractional unit of spin it means that the complete overlapping of the waves describing two identical particles is excluded as a possible state. Bosons are particles which can completely overlap in properties. Particles are most likely to be found where their probability waves are greatest and so have a dual, wave-particle nature. Fields of force also have a probability-particle, dual nature. Forces between particles are described by the exchange of energy carried by 'virtual particles' which just exist in transit between the particle pair and move under some law of probability. The electromagnetic exchange quanta (photons) are mass-less and have a long range and ½ a spin unit. These are the entities which we think of as 'light' and normally describe as 'waves` or rays. The W bosons of the weak force are massive, short range and one spin unit. This is the force involved in radioactive decay, such as the emission of electrons by certain unstable isotopes. The gluons which hold together quarks which make up hadrons are short range, mass-less with one spin unit but work like elastic strings in that they increase their force with increase in the separation between the quarks. Gluons come in colours, r g and b and with 3 more anti-colour pairs. Anti-particles have opposite properties, analogous to an anti-proton which has the same mass but opposite (negative) charge to that of the proton. Hence an anti-red gluon attracts a red gluon for some values of its wave description but repels another anti-red gluon.

Each hadron is composed of 3 quarks of which 6 types exist, each of one third or two thirds electronic charge. They have properties like the spin described previously which is a ½ unit but also other quantum numbers, isotopic spin which will differentiate protons from the very similar mass neutrons and strangeness, which will describe very short lived particles heavier than protons made only in high energy nuclear processes. Defining particles in terms of patterns of quantum numbers has led to discovery of new particles and a very successful standard model for elementary particles. Describing the forces has encountered difficulties in stopping infinitely strong effects when elementary particles approach each other very closely. With electrons, the famous inverse square law has to be modified with something depending on the mathematical behaviour of logarithms when an electron tries to 'enter' a proton and get almost on top of a positively charged quark. Gluons are satisfactory in that a non-stretched piece of elastic, or a gluon from one quark overlapping another quark, is not doing very much. The weak interaction associated with radioactivity, such as an electron and a neutrino coming from an atom, involves the exchange of 'heavy', short lived W^{+-} and Z° particles. Their mass automatically gives a short range which is inversely proportional to mass as they only exist for a time given by their ability to exist, violating energy conservation, as given by the uncertainty principle. These properties we have briefly sketched emerged after a large series of experiments with accelerators of energetic particles and detailed measurement of the products of their interactions.

Not all is sorted in the standard elementary particle model. At the time of writing, September 2008, the physics community is awaiting the results of the switch-on of the CERN Large Hadron Collider and the possible discovery of the Higgs particle-named colloquially as the 'God particle'. Why should the production of this particle, much more massive than proton, without charge and zero spin, be the keystone of our understanding of God sustaining the universe? The reason is that previous theory only easily explained particles without mass. The idea is that laws of force must be consistent in their effects when seen from different view points, moving and stationary. The law of electromagnetism can be formulated in this manner, so that depending on viewpoint-in motion or stationary-the electric or magnetic strengths may vary in importance but the final effects are consistent, once we understand the relativity as Einstein did. For example, doing sums on the output of an electrical generator from the viewpoint of the floor of the power station or from looking as one rotates with the revolving part of the generator still ends up with the same power given to the electricity grid. The exchange force involved here is the mass-less photon. Following this technique, we end up with mass-less exchange bosons for all interactions. To allow massive particles, empty space is believed to be filled with a 'Higgs field' with all other bosons and particles including quarks and leptons (electrons and mesons) interacting with the Higgs particles. This interaction allows the Higgs to slow other particles to less than the speed of light and therefore to have mass because particles with mass cannot attain the speed of light. This treacle effect was notably described by Tom Kibble, one of the first to put forward the theory, as 'like Margaret Thatcher-a massive particle-wandering through a Tory cocktail party and gathering hangers-on as she went.'

Grand unification, the Big bang and before

Having described three fundamental types of forces, electro-magnetic, strong and weak, it is now possible to predict a situation where they are all important and in a continued exchange. Going back in time and up in temperature, before a few 100 seconds into the birth of the universe, electrons could not remain attached to nuclei and copious electromagnetic radiation was produced. Further back, the weak and electromagnetic interactions were in equilibrium and even further towards the big bang, at 10^{27} degrees centigrade, all three types of forces freely exchanged their 'exchange' particles or photons with equal strength. This is known as the GUT or Grand Unification Theory era. At this juncture, a remarkable set of ratios seems to have been set up with the relative numbers of photons to protons and neutrons to anti-matter protons going as $4.10^7:1: (1-10^{-9})$. This means that there are 4 times ten to the power 7 photons as there are baryons, while there are just one part in ten to the power nine less anti-baryons than there are baryons. The almost equality of particles and anti-particles is remarkable.

Although it may seem a very complex situation in terms of even the number of particles and quanta named, we are arguing that the potential for life as we know it today is implicitly contained in this GUT instant of creation. So it turns out that only 28 basic physical properties are needed to define this initial state of material. By this, we mean masses of quarks, leptons, the Higgs and neutrinos, the relative sizes of the various types of forces, and their mutual mixing and the constants of gravity and cosmology. Another 15 are required to specify the amounts of this material which results in the astronomy of our observable universe, the size, age, mass and so on. Photons plus matter define the total energy and hence the gravity and gravitational curvature of the universe. This plus the value of the 'dark energy' pressure determine the expansion of the universe. Most of the matter is also 'dark', apparently made up of 'super-symmetric' particles. These weakly interacting particles, with no charge and heavier than protons are the 'opposites' of the mass-less photons. The theory is that at the end of GUT, symmetry between ordinary and 'dark matter' was broken, like a vertical pencil under pressure falling down or buckling in one of many possible directions. Thus the two types separated out and no longer freely exchanged between each other. We await the results of the Large Hadron Collider to perhaps confirm the existence of 'dark matter' particles. So far, their existence has been indirectly inferred by their gravitational effects or influence on waves deduced from the 3 degree background measurements. At the end of GUT, the massive inflation is believed to have taken place with the long lasting effects of the driving force subsequently showing up in a much reduced negative pressure seeming to continue to push galaxies away from each other.

Having traced back to 10^{-34} seconds with a physics which is increasingly becoming understood, how much further can one probe? At 10^{-42} seconds, the visible universe arose from a size of 0.01 cm. Here gravity forces take over in determining the uncertainty in position, time, energy and momentum. Quantities cannot be determined to better than 10^{-33}cm, known as the Planck scale and the calculation of probabilities based upon providing a quantum theory of gravity based on this uncertainty is proving to be a very difficult problem. Cosmologists have reached a natural observational limit, beyond which we may or may not ever progress. Here I will simply claim that a physics which is rapidly becoming understood points to a universe which we may be able to specify even within 10^{-42} of the big bang which contains all the elements to allow evolution through to humankind to occur.

Before attempting to push the frontiers back even further, let us pause to look at two theological implications of the GUT era. First, I will suggest we have re-written the Genesis 'fall' myth. One can think of the GUT stage when everything turned into everything as a stage where nothing was committed and a harmony where the possibility of 'hurt' because of differences and decay did not exist. The phase transitions where the two types of matter differentiated out and then the forces became distinct enabled the universe to experience the 'groaning and struggling' of creative evolution with all its possibilities, good and bad. Second, is the need for opposites, exemplified by super-symmetry, a hint that in religious language, 'good' and 'evil' are necessary contrasts?

Returning to 'before the big bang', quantum cosmologists struggle to write an equation giving the probability that our universe with its known properties will likely emerge from a 4 dimensional space where time is like any of the three space dimensions and does not exist as we know it. (Isham, 2000)

An attractive alternative way of tackling the problem is to appeal to 'string' theory, popular with those working on the theory of elementary particles but needing some proof that it is valid at all. Elementary particles are suppose to exist in the usual three space and one time dimension but with 6 or 7 other dimensions existing as very compact looped, vibrating strings which define the various 'properties' we mentioned previously. These 10 or 11 dimensions exist and move and interact on membranes, known as BRANES Gravity forces 'leak out' from individual BRANES and are important if reaching across on a Planck scale. This is a 'physics trick' to allow gravity to be as influential as any other force.

Neil Turock, (ex Imperial, now at Cambridge) and colleagues (Khoury, et al., 2001) used the concept of nearby BRANES to propose a mechanism for the origin of our universe which neatly gets over the need for massive inflation at the end of GUT. Our BRANE starts as an uninteresting, cold vacuous state. Nearby, a Planck length away across a 5th, warped dimension is another 3 spatial +1 time dimensional BRANE. A bubble breaks off this second BRANE and moves incredibly slowly across the gap with the edges expanding outwards at the speed of light. The BRANES collide and the energy of collision shrinks all the extra dimensions of our BRANE to the tiny loops giving particle properties in a phase transition. The huge expansion of the oncoming BRANE means the visible universe comes from a very uniform temperature-wise region in the 'bubble' and so satisfies the demands that the inflation theory needed to meet. The only conceivable evidence at the moment for such a theory would be to look at the tiny amplitude waves in the strength of gravity coming from such a collision and this is something which will be done by a space experiment in 10 years or so. However, the results will be clearly ambiguous. The point of choosing one out of several existing ideas is to demonstrate the possibility of plausibly pushing the act of creation a very long time before our big bang and not requiring something very specific to be introduced into creation at what we have been calling 10^{-42} seconds.

There still remains the problem of why a universe got created with the right properties for humankind to evolve (eg Rees 2000). Is it essential that specific design needed to be introduced at the instant of our big bang so that carbon chemistry on an earth-like planet would be very likely? This chemistry depends critically on the charge of the electron and the masses of the electron and three of the quarks. A whole 'landscape' of properties is possible under string theory, so why does the collapse of the extra dimensions select out the correct ones? Is it possible to avoid the need for a direct, design based intervention of God in an otherwise natural process of creation and evolution? From the end of the GUT era at least, it seems plausible to follow cosmic evolution through the stages of element formation and then through the collapse of clouds of these elements under gravity into galaxies, stars and planets. Elsewhere in this volume, the evolution of life is discussed from several viewpoints. To make a satisfying, consistent account of evolution from way back in the colliding BRANE era or from a region where time is imaginary and equivalent to space, there needs to be some overarching principle to achieve a universe with our properties. The concept of the multiverse (Carr, 2007) provides the answer. The idea is that many universes may emerge within the multiverse with a large variety of values for the total energy available, the cosmological constant or outward pressure, the masses of the elementary particles and the strengths of their mutual forces. Infinite expansion from a common origin with large quantum fluctuations in energy in the early universe which favour the more energetic regions could give rise to the emergence of many universes. But only some of this vast array will be suitable for our sort of evolution. We have already seen the critical mass, energy and outward pressure balance necessary. If protons, neutrons and electrons have different properties from the ones we know about, the chemistry of long chains of carbon, oxygen, hydrogen, etc., molecules which are the basis of biology would not arise. To evolve our universe, Smolin (2006) proposes that the 'wrong' types which continually emerge keep collapsing back or expanding off to infinity with new ones emerging from a bounce effect in black holes until we get 'us'. Thus every black hole which forms in our universe due to gravitational attraction collapsing even hadrons to dimensions where quantum gravity applies can be a source of a new universe. As a new universe emerges, the properties of elementary particles change only marginally so a 'natural selection' process can be involved. The idea that physical constants, like the charge on the electron, are not fixed and might even evolve in our universe is a current proposal in theoretical physics. So why not have each try at making a universe involve a different set of fundamental constants? Eventually, the multi-verse will produce 'us' via a natural selection acting cosmically.

Process Theology, the new key?

Having argued that we know enough and can speculate enough to reject the undeniable necessity of specific material intervention by God at crucial stages of the material evolution of our universe, the question now arises 'is incarnation necessary at all?' I would maintain that the ideas of Whitehead's process theology (Cobb and Griffin, 1976) put incarnation firmly into the evolutionary world-view. The concept is that everything that exists, atoms, stones, worms, humans has an awareness of God at some appro-priate level. This awareness will result in a 'Godly' tendency in any process in which the 'thing' gets involved. It is a tremendous claim for properties of anything which can possibly evolve in the multiverse picture just described. Process thought is opposed to the basic Greek philosophical view which describes existence in terms of immutable, therefore static, descriptions of objects with events explained by their purpose. Process thought also opposes Newtonian philosophy which at the most allows change as a rearrangement of unchanging components and events as being completely determined by known mechanical causes. The fundamental Process concept is of transitions from one state of being to another. Quantum and chaos theory chance imply an openness in the future which determinism based on Newton's classical laws of physics would exclude. While looking in from the outside, events might seem to occur all at once, but in practise there is always a finite time for the 'process' to occur. Actually Heisenberg's uncertainty principle in quantum physics requires everything to take some small but finite time to happen. Whitehead gives each unit of 'process' a value which can be enjoyed to a greater or lesser extent. Because process is funda-mental, as looking at the laws of physics which are all about forces and the actions they bring about would suggest, the relat-edness of both inanimate and living things is important. It is a necessity of creation and the evolutionary process which follows. This relatedness means that each event is open to all that happened previously which contributed to it and in this sense, each event is an incarnation of part of the past of the universe. Extend the principle to all events and we see the universe as an incarnation of God. Here we look on God as the 'primordial ground of order'. Going forward, one expects each current activity to influence the whole of the future. 'Incarnation' is passed on and as in Pauline language we enter into each other in one body.

How is determinism avoided in this description of process? It is necessary to require a creative self-determination to cancel out the complete influence of hereditary and previous events. What happens next is partly created by what has previously been given. This will certainly include the influence of the environment. But an additional novelty can also occur, incorpo-rating processes not previously thought of or gone through. This novelty can include self-expression leading to self determination. In the theistic approach, the process is not simply for the benefit of the self but also for the benefit of God. God-relatedness, which we as humans especially appreciate, is our awareness of God as the origin of novelty. Therefore in process thought, God is not only the origin of order but also has an ever continuing presence as the origin of the possibility of novelty.

Let us at this point give two widely different examples of the process principles. First, consider the novelty when it was first possible for an electron to exist in an orbital state around a proton for a long time. This new situation depended on a past history of quarks, gluons and leptons acting 'independently' and the helpful presence of the Higgs field. A potential for a more complex chemistry was released. God's love will ultimately become transparent when humankind can evolve as a result. Second, consider the BBC Symphony orchestra playing Beethoven's Fifth, as it did towards the end of the 2008 PROMS season. Here the object is the 100 or so musicians engaging with Beethoven's score. The preceding events incarnate in this event notably include the training of the musicians and the inspiration of the composer. Novelty includes the quality of the interpretation of this particular performance. The God-relatedness includes the further development of musical expression which many find as a heightened way to God.

There is nothing in our brief account of current cosmology to demonstrate a description of the universe without a God. An atheistic approach to describing the birth of the universe without a 'prime mover' appeals to the uncertainty principle on a grand scale allowing the law of conservation of energy to be violated and energy/matter appear from 'nothing' in the uncertainty time scale of Heisenberg. But why does not this process occur with even probability throughout space and time? Some cross-over of expansion from different origins should be observable (eg Isham, 2000) The version of the multiverse idea with infinite expansion with multiple universes arising, which seems related to creation out of nothing, does have mathematical problems of conservation laws, especially energy, according to Hawking (see Carr, 2007) and must face the problem of the special selection of all the crucial values of physical constants. Even if this approach works, there is still the question of why the physics 'framework' of an uncertainty principle exists. Moreover, why are their specifically four forces of physics plus their associated particles?

Invoking a God of process seems a more satisfying way of explaining the possibilities of elementary particle physics and cosmic evolution. On the other hand, the need for intervention in a miraculous manner at crucial stages in evolution to jump unbridgeable gaps or supply designs for the next stage by an all powerful God again seem unsupported by our discussion. Cosmologists and Astrophysicists can be confidently optimistic that the evolution of the universe from 10^{-42} sec until the present day geology of planet earth emerged can be explained by known or discoverable laws of physics. The God of process thought provides the opportunities without knowing or deciding the outcome. Creation is a tremendous experiment and risk so that God, sharing in the labouring of evolution, could allow a loving, thinking entity to emerge, capable of sharing His ideals and actions.

References

Carr, Bernard, Editor 'Universe or Multiverse' Cambridge, 2007 contains semi-popular style articles without much mathematics by many of the well known workers in cosmological theory

Cobb, J B, Griffin, D R, 'Process Theology, an introductory exposition' Westminster Press Philadelphia, 1976.

Hughes I S., 'Elementary Particles' 3rd edition, Cambridge, 1991 An undergraduate text assuming elements of quantum theory and statistical mechanics.

Isham, C J., 'Quantum Theories of the Creation of the Universe', www.time.and.eternity.org 2000.An approachable elementary description of quantum, relativity and gravitational theory in relation to 'creation'.

Khoury, J K., Ovrut, P J., Steinhardt, T., Turock, N., Phys. Rev D., 12, 3522, 2001. For the specialists, via University Libraries.

Rees, M., 'Just Six Numbers, The Deep Forces That Shape The Universe', New York, Basic Books, Perseus Group, 2000.

Smolin L., a 'popular' article in 'Intelligent Thought', ed John Brockman, Vintage Books New York, 2006 and in more detail at arXiv:hep-th/0407213 and in 'Universe or Multiverse' as cited above.

Prof. John Quenby, Distinguished Research Fellow has taught and carried out research at Imperial College, London throughout his academic career. The research included theoretical work explaining the existence of very energetic, cosmic ray particles and the sources of X-rays and gamma-ray bursts in the universe. Experiments involved participation in several European satellite and spacecraft projects. Currently he is associated with a search for 'dark matter' particles and for gravity waves from the cosmos.

Understanding God's World: Models in Theology and Science

John MacDonald Smith

I once asked a group of ten year old children to draw a picture of God, and I was delighted with the variety of colour and image which they produced. They knew about modelling from plasticene, for they knew their pictures were not like God – not exactly anyway. I think in the wisdom of childhood they knew something that many of their elders have forgotten – that God cannot accurately be imaged. Therefore they were not worried by the fact that they had produced so many different and not entirely compatible pictures, for there was no way they were ever going to identify any of them with their subject. The prohibition of images of Deut. 5, 8 is still necessary to guard against the idolatry which thinks that *this* definition or description of God is correct while *that* one is wrong. It is a warning against regarding any description, model or metaphor as exact. How can one model with accuracy, something which is experienced as a strange, 'other', pervading presence, except by using cultural images which are bound to be less than adequate?

Models

Unlike those children, theologians do tend to identify the image and the reality. Karl Barth insisted that Father, Son and Holy Spirit are the 'names' of God. The American theologian Robert Jenson insists that 'Father, Son and Holy Spirit' is God's proper name and that substitutes such as Creator, Redeemer and Sanctifier are illicit. This means that 'Father, Son and Holy Spirit' applies to God in exactly the same way as Patrick applies to a human being or Uranus to a planet. Recently, the Vatican has insisted that baptism is only validly administered using the 'names' Father, Son and Holy spirit as opposed, for instance, to Creator, Redeemer and Sanctifier.

In Thomas Aquinas' *Summa Theologica* there is a long section 'on the names of God' which makes it clear that in the Angelic Doctor's view the 'most proper' name of God is *He Who Is*. This is because the essence of God is being – itself. Again, the kind of model, or image, of God is revealed in the theological position a person takes up on such matters as women bishops, homosexuality or biological issues such as human fertilisation or cloning. Our models of God lead us along very different paths. Can we, like those children, learn to live with this difference? Sallie McFague differs from this and in her book *Models of God* (SCM, 1987) suggests that Mother, Lover and Friend measure up to the reality of God better than the names or models of patriarchy, in an age beset by the nuclear predicament and the threat of ecological disaster.

Modelling in Science and Theology

God-modelling has become a 'growth industry,' stimulated by cultural change. That is the point: the story must be changed because it no longer quite 'fits'. When the writer to the Hebrews stated (Heb 1,3) that Jesus 'is the effulgence of God's splendour and the stamp of God's very being' he was suggesting that Jesus expressed in a human life, the inadequacy and therefore the end of, all older images such as 'Father' or 'husband' or 'shepherd'. Jesus transcends all of these and is the final fulfilment of such imagery. They can still be used, but used from now on in the context of the new understanding of them which we owe to Jesus. But times change, words change their meanings and new words are developed, as also our understanding of Jesus changes, and all that has to be taken account of in a developing faith. The 'finality' of Jesus is now expressed on a developing understanding of who Jesus is for us. (This does not imply that it will always be an *improved* understanding).

While theology has for centuries been aware that much of what it says is metaphorical – Aquinas worked out how to apply metaphor and analogy to God in some detail – the idea of modelling God is quite recent, and due to rapid cultural change; hence none of its ideas or conclusions can yet be regarded as final. The concept has been borrowed from science, and we turn to science in order to understand more precisely what it involves.

Every sixth form science student very quickly becomes aware of the importance of the imagination. It is not enough to be able to quote the mathematical expressions of physical principles, for one has to be able to give some account of what these mean in terms of what is actually going on. It is necessary to be able to make models which express one's understanding of physics, chemistry or biology. Nobody supposes that the Heath Robinson contraptions of beer froth, cogwheels and elastic which the scientist images, are really there. S/he has only a limited idea what is *really* there, which is why s/he constructs a sort of picture out of ordinary everyday bits and pieces with which s/he is familiar with. They help to develop a measure of understanding of physical processes and therefore to design experiments which ask the next question, or carry out the mathematics involved.

Therefore the student very quickly learns a basic principle: not to identify the model with the reality. The model is what philosophers call the *objectum quo*, the mechanism we invent by means of which we are enabled to know under one or more of its aspects, the *objectum quod*, the phenomenon for which our mind seeks an understanding. Hence the student also learns that what the scientist is really looking for, is not pictures and images at all, but understanding, intelligibility, comprehensibility. This is because science is not about making pretty models of the cosmos, but about gaining some understanding of it. When I was a student of physics my father, who was a professor used to exhort me to 'get the physical picture.' Sometimes I did.

Models in science are therefore aids to the understanding which can be abandoned once their usefulness is exhausted. We are often told in popular accounts of atomic physics that elementary particles sometimes behave like waves and at others like particles.

Wave particle duality is a model derived from cannon balls and waves on water, filtered through nineteenth century 'classical' physics and inherited by modern physics – in some ways rather to the disadvantage of the latter, because it can mislead. But it is the only model we have, so we must make do with it. It is certainly less fundamental to an understanding of the world than the Uncertainty Principle which implies somewhat the same. This states that you cannot say with any certainty where a fundamental particle is, because earlier ideas about causality no longer apply at the subatomic level in quite the same way as they appear to in ordinary life. In order to be able to say where a particle is, it is necessary to act upon it. Because this involves an energetic process it moves the particle, which no longer 'is' where it 'was'. This leads to an invocation of probability and to the idea that a particle cannot be said to be in a single place just like that but is actually to be regarded as everywhere, though with a very high probability of being within a very small volume of space. More accurately, the Uncertainty Principle suggests that the physical universe imposes limits on the uncertainty of position and other parameters in a form which has applications right across physics to the origin of the universe itself. It is a very fruitful expression of the 'meaning', or intelligibility of the cosmos for which the model is wave-particle duality. Physics, like theology, tells a story.

An Evolutionary Model

The year 2009 is the 200th anniversary of the birth of Charles Darwin and the 150th of his book *On the Origin of Species*. This, perhaps more than any publication of the last three centuries has changed the way we understand the world. The reason is that it makes use of a model – evolution – which has a multitude of applications in areas which have very little connection with the biology for which Darwin developed it.

Darwin left his comfortable rooms in Christ's College Cambridge, travelled half way across the world and pondered what he saw. Everybody else took it for granted but Darwin wondered why species differed. He saw how contingent changing circumstances forced the extinction of some characteristics, even the extinction of some species, along with the enhancement of others; and he realised how this process over very long periods of time could, and did, result in speciation. Of course it was necessary that the enhanced characteristics survived for the sake of the species and this meant not only that they 'fitted into' the environment of the time but also that their possessors were able to grow to maturity and reproduce.

More technically, the basis of Darwinism has four parts. Firstly, every organism produces more offspring than will eventually survive to maturity. Secondly, random variations will occur among the offspring. On the other hand, useful traits do tend to be passed on. Finally, traits which make the individual fitter will tend to increase in the population. In addition, evolution by natural selection acts on the individual, one at a time.

Every individual is trying to earn a living by successful adaptation to an environment consisting of other individuals as well as the inanimate world. This involves a complex process of co-evolution between species, symbiosis in which they assist each other's survival, and shaping the environment over periods of time long enough to create fitness – enhancing change and speciation.

The model of evolution has been extended by Lee Smolin and others and used in scientific accounts of creation. The idea that the universe originated in the violent explosion of a black hole (a

'Black hole bounce') is reasonably well known. What may not be so well-known is that throughout the universe we inhabit there are literally billions of black holes distributed among its billions of galaxies, many of which could give rise to a black hole bounce and hence the possibility of generating a universe like ours.

This is where the evolutionary model is appropriate. Again it is known that for a universe to be like ours, that is, life-sustaining, and long-lived, the values of many physical constants must be set within very narrow limits. If say, the velocity of light varied only fractionally from its current value, stars and galaxies would be unable to form and hence there would be no solar system in which life could evolve. Incidentally, this fact forms the basis of a somewhat dubious argument for God known as the Anthropic Argument; it is argued that the constants could not be set with such extreme accuracy as almost to guarantee life, by accident. Well, we shall see.

What Smolin suggests is that each time a black hole explodes into a new universe (he calls them 'offspring' universes) it takes with it in the very first split second of its new and separate life, some of the general characteristics of its 'parent' universe. But in that moment of the birth of a new universe there will be a very slight variation in the values of the constants of nature between the 'parent' and 'offspring' universes. This is consistent with an evolutionary model, for parents and offspring in the animal kingdom carry only small differences, because large differences might make survival more risky – the principle here is 'if it ain't broke, don't fix it'.

In this way it is possible that a very large number of long-lived – long enough to create galaxies – possibly life bearing universes be generated as the characteristics for doing so emerge by small variations from those of the 'parent' universes in the first moment of the creation of 'offspring'. In this way the assembly of black hole bounce originated universes creeps slowly towards an optimum in which each produces a maximum number of 'offspring'. Smolin tests this theory by showing that in many cases a change up or down in a given constant of nature gives rise to a reduction in black hole numbers and invites objectors to find a constant which when varied, gives rise to an increase in black hole population.

Karl Popper: a Short Diversion

The significance of this is that it shows Smolin's theory to be properly scientific: as Karl Popper suggested half a century ago, the characteristic mark of a scientific theory is that it, or one of its consequences, be falsifiable by experiment. Smolin's theory is.

Until Popper's time it was thought that science proceeded by induction: a very large number of very similar events could lead to an undoubted conclusion. But this could not be justified, as Hume pointed out ('Hume's problem'). Popper illustrated Hume's problem with the example 'All swans are white' but for this to be true all the swans in the history of the world would have to be examined. And this is not possible.

Popper's answer was to recognise that science never reaches absolutely final conclusion; that it is a matter, he says like 'pushing piles into a swamp' far enough to support the structure one hopes to build on them. The structure itself, he says, is not built up by any logical, inductive process of what follows from what but more by insight and inspiration. Popper calls it the 'deductive method of testing': ideas come; we hardly know where from except that it looks as if this idea might be useful, and are then subjected to empirical test, conformity with the rest of science and general fruitfulness.

In this way, gradually, a body of knowledge has been built up and through it some understanding of the things – the electron, the galaxies, the genes and so on – which make up the natural world. Thus, knowledge of the individual natures of the various classes of entities can gradually take the place of the idea of generalised law in explaining the behaviour of objects: *this* being behaves in the way it does because it is *that* sort of a thing with *those* characteristics. It is behaving as its nature dictates rather than as some law prescribes. Natural law is then seen as descriptive of the being's nature, as 'what that entity is like'.

Models of God: Muddles

Now to return to theology and talk about God. There is a parallel with the 'classical' account in science, in which the behaviour of each constituent of the cosmos can be precisely determined for ever, assuming one knows all the laws of nature and the initial configuration of the universe. For it used to be thought that the Christian religion offered a complete account of the way things were in the past, the way they are now, and the way they are going to be in the future. Six thousand years ago, it was said, God created the world in a week and put two people in it. One of them, the female, was taken from the man's body. It used to be thought that the Bible provided an accurate account of the history of the Jewish nation. It also used to be believed that God had crated a round number of angels, each one the single member of a distinct species, in nine orders, and that Lucifer their leader rebelled and had to be ejected from heaven along with his supporters, to a place of torment in hell, where evil human beings would also go. It was believed that the reason for the creation of the world was so that God could repopulate heaven with the same number of human beings as there were fallen angels. We can pick out the culturally conditioned bits of this: for instance, Eve as Adam's 'rib' is an obvious piece of patriarchy. But the very fact that it is so culturally conditioned made it very easy for it to be accepted as literal truth in its own culture where no alternative account was on offer. It still is accepted in some quarters.

To our eyes that cosmology is one model, and because we know about other models we can say that it is not very convincing. That story won't do.

But many people still do believe that God has a literal Son, who came into this rebellious world in order that being bloodily done to death he might restore the world's original purity in the eyes of his Father. The original goodness and perfection of the human race, lost at the Fall has now been restored to it by Christ, the Second Adam, in his own flesh. Many people do still believe that the Son proved his claim to be God by working miracles; that he witnessed to himself as Saviour; that his unexpected rising from the dead vindicates his claims, and that his ascension into heaven signifies his kingly rule over all things. They also believe that he will in due time descend to earth in glory to wind up the temporal order and claim as his own those who are to be saved, who had in any case all along been known to and pre-ordained by God the Father. Many more people believe that there is, in a real realm 'outside' this one, an all-powerful, all-knowing and all-seeing being who created and sustains the material order. This is as much of a model and as much of a myth as the story we recounted two paragraphs ago, and is part of the same story.

The muddled thinking which makes it possible for people to reject one part of a single model while retaining the other part which depends on it says something important. It draws attention to the fact that whatever a religious cosmology says, whatever claims are made by a theory of salvation, it is always a model, a story which can never be in one to one correspondence with reality. The analogy with science shows that the model is not an exact description of reality, but a means through which we can gain some understanding of it – though not, of course, of the same kind as we gain through the models of science. Just as models in science require interpretation, so do those of religion. We see through a glass, darkly.

Models of God: Interventionism

There are more or less as many models of God as there are sects and religions which employ the word 'God' and all the stories about God have the same purpose. This is to express an understanding of reality and our place in it; they are stories about us. But in the most general terms only two understandings are possible: interventionism or constant presence. In the former case God does nothing until something goes wrong – a healing is necessary, a planet needs pushing back where it should be or his people are starving in the wilderness. Then he leaps into action to remedy the situation, and what he is believed to have done provides the raw materials for model-building. The eighteenth century physicist Samuel Clarke believed that the order of nature would fall apart unless God occasionally intervened to push it back into shape in a kind of heavenly MOT test. This is interventionism, and is comprehensible in cultural terms, for as a result of Newton's physics a mechanistic account of the cosmos pushed God out of the universe and he became a kind of absentee landlord. This God was needed to create the world, for Newton could not explain that. But he was also needed to account for discrepancies between physical theory and observation or intervene by pushing the Planets back into place.

After its narrow escape from Egyptian slavery in the first recorded 'walk-out' the Israelite community was threatened with extinction many times. It is recorded that a spring gushed out from the desert rocks and saved it, and that strange food appeared on the desert floor to avert starvation. Even its escape from slavery, it is recorded, was a consequence of unusual behaviour on the part of the Red Sea. These events were ascribed to the initiative of Yahweh who was thenceforth modelled or marketed as the saviour of his people with a particular interest in their destiny. It is not surprising that stories about the intervening power of Yahweh developed and in their light an enhanced sense of the peoples' destiny. Eventually this became so deep-rooted that even national tragedy became subsumed into the story. Hence, when on entering the Promised Land, they found there the remains of a once-matriarchal Baalism, toleration was impossible. There was nothing for it but the extermination of the idolaters, and when this was successfully accomplished, that was further proof of the reality of Yahweh and his special concern for his people.

Israel's later growing sense of its own powerlessness in the face of sickness, famine and natural disaster together with a proper sense of its own incompetence and cruelty led in two mutually supportive directions. On the one hand, since this world is so awful, then in fairness there must be a better one to come – another chance. On the other hand, since we can do nothing to improve our lot, somebody else will have to do it for us. Hence the human sense of sin as a blot on the world which God saw was 'very good' (Gen.1, 26) and in which humankind is a fallen creature longing for redemption. God is therefore invested with infinite power, goodness and knowledge together with redemptive love. Out of this arises the hope of salvation through a priest-king who is to put things right. This idea was heavily reinforced by Israelite experience of political oppression, which led to the sense of guilt and unworthiness which thinks that if unpleasant things happen, it must be one's own fault.

All this human despair heaped itself on Jesus. He was soon elevated to cosmic status as the pre-existent Christ 'through whom all things were made' (Jn. 1, 3 & 10 etc.) who had come to claim his own and blaze the trail to a new and eternal 'Promised Land'. Through his suffering he paid the debt owed by humanity to the Father who cannot look on sin. The double identification of Jesus with both humankind and the Father implied that the debt of redemption was paid on behalf of humanity by the Father himself. This itself implies the possession of deep feelings of inferiority, incompetence and unworthiness on the part of humankind. Further, Jesus was the inaugurator of a new relationship with God, the 'New Covenant'. Through his gift of a new law of love he showed Moses as but a temporary precursor, a shadow of the reality to come, and himself as the new Moses.

As second Adam, another ancient image conscripted for Christian use, Jesus was held to have brought about the recreation of the cosmos and the rebirth of the human race, and by his own obedience to have reversed the rebellion of Adam. This is a very beautiful myth but it is essentially interventionist and fixes interventionism firmly into the Christian consciousness: God is a very powerful person who comes into the world in various ways, does things and then goes away. But Jesus promised his constant and unfailing presence.

Models of God: Constant Presence

On the constant-presence understanding, God is never absent; 'God-ness' is discernible in every event. Job's trust in God throughout his sufferings indicates that the origins of this model are not recent, but it has always had to grapple with the popularity of interventionism. The evidence shows that Jesus based his own life on the constant-presence understanding. But the gospel accounts are also full of the interventions by Jesus into the natural order, like the stilling of the storm or the raising of Lazarus. These may have been invented to point to Jesus as a charismatic person but they obscure the truth about his own attitude. It is tempting to wonder whether his crucifixion cry of dereliction marked a breaking-point for him, and the breakdown of his own model of God. There are many people who will know how he felt.

We have seen that religion is culturally conditioned. We have also seen that the beliefs which result very quickly become 'special' as the associated metaphors and analogies harden into realism. In its early days Christianity was a sect within Judaism which made use of Jewish images to support its contention that Jesus was the promised Messiah of Jewish tradition. The Letter to the Hebrews, for instance, makes much play with images of sacrifice drawn from the Temple liturgy. This interpretation of Jesus proved unacceptable to contemporary Judaism and

Christianity became a separate religion, incorporating into itself the more metaphysical thinking of the wider world of its time. This transformed Christianity into something which the early Jewish converts would have had some difficulty in recognising, and turned it into what was to become an explanatory account if the world or what might be described as an early attempt at a complete theory of everything.

The change in cultural environment faced by the new-born church on moving from the Jewish to the Roman world changed the religion. Now, that tradition faces a similarly different cultural environment and a new model of God is required. I have elsewhere suggested cosmic purposive embodiment of an evolutionary nature. This model links God as the 'self' with the cosmos as the 'body' and in the light of this model the tradition can be reinterpreted. 'Incarnation' is generalised to express a sense of the 'God-ness' of all things, of which Jesus is the paradigm case. In the light of self-consciously purposive evolution, 'providence' means human purpose in caring for creation. 'Conversion' involves the adoption of a radically different and more positive perspective, and 'grace' is the ability to treat all things as of value and worth. God *does* become human, and what the tradition thought of as divine intervention becomes human purposive activity in creating a better environment. 'The hereafter' has been transformed into the hope of a potential glorious fulfilment of all creation under the care of sentient life and 'Holy Spirit' expresses the relatedness of all things in the cosmos in this process of fulfilment.

The convictions for which Jesus strove to gain a hearing are consistent with this, though they are differently expressed. They included the absolute, total, permanent commitment of the Father to each and every human being and his utter availability to all, without regard to race, creed, gender or merit. They asserted the absolute value of each and every human being as the equal in worth of every other. The beliefs of Jesus held that the people who find real fulfilment are the reconcilers, the peace-makers, the poor in spirit; they involved an ethic of brotherly love, sharing and equality. A proper study of the New Testament shows that Jesus had no sense that he was in some kind of metaphysical, ontological, eternal relationship with God; this was wished onto him by theologians after his death.

The beliefs of Jesus and Christian history, when disentangled from its cultural confusions, point to a constant-presence model of God. Jesus acted with a freedom which has been described as 'contagious' but his freedom was not a consequence of a special relationship with God denied to the rest of us. It was a human expression of the fullness of humanity, of what it means to be human in emancipation from and independence of other people's dogmas. The tradition points us to Jesus as a unique intervention of God in a fallen world, a mission of rescue from the world into a heavenly hereafter. It is true, as counsellors tell us, that rescuers always become victims, and in a sense this is true of Jesus. But when all is said and done, he points us away from himself to the world as it is, to a perspective which sees it as expressing the 'God-ness' which we first saw in him. This is to take us back to the world, not out of it, as co-creators and co-redeemers of a recreated Planet. This implies a peace-building, ecological and non-threatening ethical perspective.

Conclusion

I end with three quotations about God and one about science. Nicholas Lash protests at 'the fatuous illusion that we could discover of come across God as a fact about the world', comple-menting St John Damascene's observation that in his essence and nature, God is absolutely incomprehensible and totally unknowable. To which my classically educated brother-in-law would add 'good science values questions more than answers. A liberal Christian could not fear questions – for the Christian, honest questions, as with knowledge itself, come from God and will be part of any search for God.'

Further Reading

Two writers well worth attention for the penetrating way they disentangle confused issues are John Dominic Crossan and Marcus Borg. They collaborated to write *The Last Week,* a day-to-day account of Passion Week. Marcus Borg's *Reading the Bible Again for the First Time* offers an effective correction to literalism. Almost anything by Crossan is well worth reading. His titles include *God and Empire, The Birth of Christianity, Who Killed Jesus?*

On Evolutionary studies straightforward accounts are given in Francisco Alaya's *Darwin's Gift,* Michael Rose's *Darwin's Spectre* and the work of Michael Ruse, particularly *Can a Darwinian be a Christian?* More generally Lee Smolin's *The Life of the Cosmos,* and Stuart Kauffman's *At Home in the Universe* apply evolutionary ideas to cosmology and to the order that lies deep at the heart of the cosmos and of life. Karl Popper's work on science and falsification is described in his book *The Logic of Scientific Discovery* finally; *New Scientist* for October 2005 offers worthwhile section on fundamentalism.

John MacDonald Smith is a retired priest and an ex Aldermaston scientist who writes on science and religion.

Evolution and the Problems of Providence

Ruth Page

At what point does Providence become an issue for Christian faith? Most treatments consider it to be a feature of human history, beginning perhaps with homo sapiens sapiens, that is, ourselves, rather than with any earlier humanoid species. In fact these earlier, nearly-human species, in so far as they have been related to God at all, are held to be the last in a providential series leading towards humanity. Anything that has fallen outside this comparatively narrow evolutionary series has not even been considered in providential terms.

But is it still possible to dismiss earlier times and creatures as having one ancillary purpose only within providence, or else as irrelevant? A sense of completeness in the doctrine, so that it embraces all creation, would tell against that exclusivism, but more specifically there are two matters which have immediate bearing on the range of Christian thought on the subject.

The first concerns what we now know about the relative time-scales of life on Earth. There is a well-known version of this which models all such life within the time-span of a year. In that case humans arrive about 10.30pm on December 31st. I like to call us homo-come-lately. It seems to me impossible to believe that God's relationship with evolving creation down all these long aeons of life was virtually on hold until humans appeared.

That belief is strengthened by the second matter which has occasioned very recent rethinking on the part of Christians in general and theologians in particular. That is the ecological crisis in its many forms. Up to then the natural world had been taken as the backdrop to the story of human salvation, or the store-house God had provided for human use, and thus with no value in the Christian scheme of things except utility. But now, alerted by vanishing rainforests and increasing desertification, increased population and pollution pressure, the importance and the fragility of non-human creation is becoming apparent.

Right up until the 1960's Catholic and Protestant theologians alike were describing the human vocation as 'mastering' the world (Page, 1996: 125) Now we are more likely to be called upon to save it, or leave it alone. If we are to save it we have to value it, and believe that God finds it valuable also. The careless loss of any species now seems like a sin against the Creator. The attitude of human mastery has given way at least to one of stewardship, if not to kinship with our fellow creatures.

If today's natural world is seen to be valuable to God, then all creatures in the whole history of life before humans must also be valuable, and may no longer be looked upon as simply a lengthy prologue to the arrival of the one valuable species. If anthropocentricity, that concentration upon the human, is seen to be misguided in relation to ecological concerns, it is equally misguided in relation to providential concerns.

Yet as humans labour to limit greenhouse gases or preserve species and their habitats I am reminded of the story of a visitor from town saying to a farmer: 'What good land God has given you to work with~. To which the farmer replies: 'You should have seen it when God had it to himself'.

To look at the issue of Providence before the evolution of humans with their masterful ways is to ask how it was when 'God had it to him/herself' and there were no issues of sin or moral evil. Does the history of evolution suggest Providence in such matters as God's valuing of species and their habitats? I shall suggest that the history of evolution yields no such positive view. In that case either Christians have to abandon notions of Providence, or the entire relation of God to creation has to be rethought. I shall attempt such re-description at the end of this paper.

The problems of God in the processes of evolution first

became an issue for me when Jurgen Moltmann (1985) was giving the Gifford Lectures in Edinburgh, later published as *God in Creation*. Moltmann was enlarging on the goodness of God in creating an open universe in which creatures had not been fixed from the beginning, but could develop and change. I was sitting next to the then Dean of the Vet School, who told me afterwards that an open world can function only if there are exits as well as entrances. That is, extinctions have to take place for new species to find a niche. He told me that well over 90% of all species that had evolved before humans came on the scene had become extinct. Then he said: 'What God creates, God deletes'. I don't believe that, and everything I have written in ecotheology since, including this paper, has been pitched to find a way out of that conclusion.

But it remains the case that when God, so to speak, had this world to him/herself, over 90% of species died out. Death is certainly part of what it is to be alive and individual death is not at issue here. Individual humans die all the time, as do elephants, but if humanity or the African elephant were to become extinct that would be a very different matter: a whole form of life would no longer be around.

There are three kinds of extinction. Background extinction happens all the time as one group of creatures finds their food, heir habitat, their success at rearing young, steadily diminishing through some change in circumstances. Extinction on a larger scale happens with a climate change. When ice, for example, covers much of the Earth it kills most of what it covers, while ice has advanced and retreated more than once in geological time. Then again extinction occasionally happens catastrophically, as when sixty-five million years ago, it seems that a meteor hit the Earth, sending out dust which blocked the sun and cooled the atmosphere. That either caused or hastened the demise of the dinosaurs and many smaller creatures. I am amazed that I have never seen, except in my own writings, any discussion about what the dinosaurs, living or extinct, have to say about God.

If God was in providential charge of the natural world during these aeons, why the climate changes; why the disasters that periodically struck evolving life; why earthquakes, volcanoes and all the manifestations of natural evil? These are not questions asked by palaeobiologists who are simply happy that every catastrophe was followed by an explosion of new species for them to study as they occupied the vacated niches (Raup, 1991: 1987). But these are certainly questions that have to be asked if God's providence is at issue. Why save the panda or the Siberian tiger now if God let so much go earlier?

Further, as Alvarez and Asaro (1992) conclude:

If whole arrays of well-adapted organisms are wiped out from time to time through the chance disaster of large impact, it means that the history of life is not fore-ordained. There is no inevitable progress leading to intelligent life - leading inevitably to us. The history of life is contingent upon unforeseeable chance events.

If these are not 'unforeseeable chance events' are they part of the plan of God? Surely not if God is the God of love of the Christian tradition. In the end the process of evolution is as opaque in relation to traditional notions of God's providence as human history is.

Again, at the time of the extinction of the dinosaurs our mammal ancestors were the size of shrews, scuttling about out of the way of dinosaur tread. But once these giants had gone the mammals flourished, grew in size, diversified and finally produced homo sapiens. But without the death of the dinosaurs we would not have had the freedom to evolve. If God's providence in evolution was to bring our development about that became possible only after a period of major extinctions. So was God wiping the slate clean with the millions of deaths so that we could evolve? Is God's creation so expendable? Are we worth it?

On the other hand some biologists argue for a notion of progress in evolution, particularly progress in complexity, and theologians have seen God's hand in that. And certainly we are more complex than an amoeba, which itself was quite a development. But to choose complexity as the mark of progress is to choose what we humans are good at; what puts us at the top of the out-of-date ladder image of evolution. (Branching trees with us as a twig are more usual now.) But complexity is an ambiguous development. The more complex a structure is, the more there is to go wrong - from the womb. With our increased brain size we have large heads, and large heads are difficult and painful to deliver at birth. Again we have a capacity for complex harm as well as occasional complex good, so on moral grounds we should not be too ready to celebrate our intellect.

Progress in evolution has also been described as increasing independence from and control over the environment, which creatures like ourselves are supposed to show. And certainly we have been more manipulative of our environment than any other species. But the ecological crisis has exploded that comfortable belief in human independence. In fact humans were never independent of their environment - we breathe and eat and drink apart from anything else; and our control is called into question every time there is a flood or a drought, let alone global warming.

Looking in general at the accounts which would see an upwards and onwards trend in evolution, which might be put down to the providence of God, it seems that all versions are ontological - they are about structure and capacities, and not about relationships or interaction with the environment. If such capacity for interaction became the measuring-rod the prized value would not be complexity or independence, it would be ecological fitness - the way humans fit in with the rest of creation. On that criterion we do not score particularly well, not as well as, for instance, the crocodile which has lasted vastly longer than our species precisely because of ecological fitness. So the notion that God was working steadily up to homo sapiens becomes steadily less tenable.

And finally in this part of the paper, which could be summarized as putting humans in their place literally and metaphorically, there is no assurance, at least no scientific assurance, that we are here for good. Richard Attenborough, at the end of *Life on Earth* gives the perspective:

> This last chapter has been devoted to only one species, ourselves. This may have given the impression that somehow man is the ultimate triumph of evolution that all these millions of years of development have had no purpose other than to put him on earth. There is no scientific evidence whatever to support such a view and no reason to suppose that our stay here will be any more permanent than that of the dinosaur. The processes of evolution are still going on among plants and birds, insects and mammals. So it is more than likely that if men were to disappear from the face of the earth, for whatever reason, there is a modest unobtrusive creature somewhere that would develop into a new form and take our place (Attenborough, 1979: 308).

Would God allow this? The theological opinion might be against the possibility, but it is worth remembering that God has not interfered with multiple extinctions thus far, and if we make our planet uninhabitable for ourselves we should not, perhaps, expect rescue.

Thus, I believe, we have come to the end of vague, untested notions of divinely-directed progress in evolution, for which most creatures are irrelevant, while others laid down their lives so that humans could evolve. And in the matter of God's relationship with creation it appears on the evidence thus far that we have to choose between an uncaring and occasionally violent deity, or one with no connection, no influence on the courses of life.

But that won't do either. We must start from the beginning again, and that means going back to the doctrine of creation, for the way creation is understood will dictate the possible ways of providence.

Whenever God is thought to have a direct connection with a material creation ontologically considered the problem of evil will raise its head and cannot simply be dismissed as mystery. The hope is to conceive of God creating and being connected with creation without attributing to God ultimate responsibility for woe and suffering. That is particularly acute in the matter of evolution, for the non-human is not moral and cannot therefore sin, so their suffering cannot be laid at the door of wrong-doing.

The doctrine of creation and providence I shall sketch here I have described at greater length in *God and the Web of Creation*. I don't believe it answers every last difficulty - the problem of evil is not solved as easily as that - but I do think that the problems that are left are less acute and more liveable-with than those attaching to traditional views.

In a word, what I believe God created was the possibility of possibilities. That was something new, for God is actual. But time and space, or space-time, with 'here' and 'there', 'present' and 'future' is a structure of possibility. I don't believe that God created particular possibilities - the possibilities of your life or mine, for instance - rather God made possibilities possible. What is providential in this way of looking at things is that we have been gifted with possibilities which will continue to our death. It remains possible to do things, for instance to put things right; what the Prayer Book nicely calls 'time for amendment of life'. (You see how time and possibility go together.)

In response to this gift of possibility things came into being - particles, forces, stars, galaxies, Earth and its whole history. Their very existence is a response to the Creator who let possibility be. But possibilities are always and only what is possible for something in its time and place and possibilities once actualised producing an actuality may have better or worse knock-on effects at the time or later. Thus the actualisation of volcanoes, or DNA or the home we were born into will impinge upon the range of later possibilities.

Tillich often uses the phrase 'finite freedom' which I find applies here. Indeed there are multiple finite freedoms jostling in the world as time has gone on and more and more possibilities have been acted on. Everyone's possibilities are constrained by what has gone before and yet possibilities remain before us, including how we react to our constraints. What happens in time and space happens when creatures respond to their possibilities, a response which will lead to both better and worse actualities. (In passing may I say that this is a call to us to use our possibilities in the best way we know as part of our response to God.) But here we are concerned with evil, and if moral and natural evil have been the negative outcomes of possibilities actualised by creatures then God is not responsible. In a sense this is taking the free-will defence for moral evil, extending the freedom involved to the non-human world from the beginning, but insisting that all the actions remain a response to God the Creator and do not exist independently of the original gift of untrammelled possibility.

There remains a difficulty in that point and I shall return to it: but first I wish to say more of God in creation.

The deepest, most comprehensive statement we can make about God is that God is love. Where and how does love fit into this scenario? In the first place the action of creating possibility is the action of letting be, and that in itself is an act of love. The human context in which the action of letting-be has resonance is that of parents with teenage children who have started to explore and experiment with their world themselves. However much parents may worry teenagers have to be allowed more freedom than they had as children. Parental love is still strong, anxious when they go to a rave, less anxious when they help out at an animal sanctuary, but it's a love that lets be. It is with that kind of love God gave creation the freedom of possibility.

What God does is to let be, not to let go. Letting be is not the same as dismissal. Further, precisely because creation has been given this freedom God is not distant, knowing in advance every action of every creature, but rather present, companioning creation through all its pleasures and pains. What God offers in that case is relationship and we should think of God relating to all creation - worms as much as humans - for everything is a response to possibility. Of course humans respond across a much wider range of possibilities than a worm, but we must not think of God looking at a worm as we do from the outside, as a foreign species. God knows as any individual worm knows what a worm's life is and what constitutes a worm-God relationship, just as God knows what any individual human life is and what constitutes a human response to the strong presence of love, companionship and reproach when necessary which God offers us. This description makes it possible to disconnect God from responsibility for natural and moral evil while reconnecting God to the processes of life.

I have said that what God offers is relationship, while the making and maintaining of relationship is what God does, the acts of God. That, I realise, is a far cry from God parting he Red Sea or smiting the Egyptian first-born. Traditionally acts of God have been thought of as divine descent from on high to support his people, sometimes with violence. I used the male pronoun here, for this seems to me to be a very male picture - male of a certain kind, certainly, not true of all males. This is a macho God, and I keep being reminded of films of unruly western towns where a new sheriff rides in to sort out the gunfighters. I suppose that if you see the world as a place of competing violence then you believe in the Lord of the battle-lines of Israel who gives victory over your enemies. But if you see the world rather as a place where possibilities are acted on for better or worse in the freedom of creation, the presence of God, the close relationship of God who knows all possibilities better than any creature does, is a more convincing picture of the acts of God.

I said there remained a difficulty, and it is this. In making it possible for finite freedoms to evolve God could surely have foreseen that the resulting multiple finite freedoms would often be bad for each other, causing the evil that litters evolution and human history. So why gift something with so much potential for pain and suffering?

The only answer I can give to that is that God prizes the good, which is not like divine good for it has been brought about under the conditions of existence. To have that good evil must always be possible too. The metaphor which seems appropriate here is harvest - bearing fruit is a good biblical metaphor. Wherever, whenever such fruit occurs, in human or non-human existence, God, so to speak, harvests it and the whole possibility of creation is justified. The divine project of creation has, in the end, been worth it. I would like to believe that the harvest of creation remains eternal in God's hands, an eternal outcome of temporal possibility, while what is not harvested falls into non-being. Perhaps in the end that harvest is what God wants from creation.

References

Page, R. 1996. *God and the Web of Creation.* London: SCM

Moltmann, J. 1985. *God in Creation.* London: SCM

Raup, D. 1991. *Extinction: Bad Genes or Bad Luck?* New York: W.W. Norton

Alvarez, W. & Asaro, F. 1992. The Extinction of the Dinosaurs in J. Bourriau (ed) *Understanding Catastrophe.* Cambridge University Press

Attenborough, R. 1979. *Life on Earth.* Collins/BBC

Ruth Page, Former Principal, New College, University of Edinburgh. Author of *God and the Web of Creation*. SCM Press 1996.

Biblical and Doctrinal Understanding of Creation

Paul Badham

Fundamentalist Christians and fundamentalist atheists usually share one belief in common; namely that all authentic Christians *ought* to believe in the literal truth of the Genesis Creation story. In the one case such a belief is seen as a litmus test of genuine loyalty to the revealed 'Word of God', and in the other it is seen as exemplifying the willful ignorance of superstitious minds.

Genesis 1 or Genesis 2

It is extraordinary that this situation has come about. The most obvious objection to it is that it is simply false to the Bible itself. It could never have occurred to the priestly author of the beautiful first chapter of Genesis that he was either writing or editing a divinely revealed account of how the creation came about. We know this because in chapter 2 he included an entirely different creation narrative. In this second account creation is not spread over six or even seven days. (For the priestly writer the creation of the Sabbath on the seventh day was an integral part of the created order). In chapter 2 however God's creation all takes place in one sequence. First God made man from the dust of the ground before there were any plants or shrubs (Genesis 2.5). Then God created a garden for the man followed by animals to provide him with some company. Only when it became apparent that no animal was a suitable partner for the man did God anaesthetize Adam, take out one of his ribs and build it up into a woman (Genesis 2.21-2).

The wider range of creation stories

These accounts however by no means exhaust the range of poetic descriptions of divine creation in the Bible. Psalm 104 presents another beautiful account. In this one God spreads out the heavens over the earth like a tent and then fixes the earth on a firm foundation. At this point the waters are high above the mountains so God gets rid of the waters by ordering them to pour down into the valleys (Psalm 104.8). An idyllic picture is presented of the harmony of nature and of God's concern for all living things.

A comparable though different picture is presented in Job chapters 38-41 where God is pictured as laying the foundations of the earth, stretching a measuring line over it and ensuring that it all rests on supportive pillars. God also proclaims the rules that govern the heavens bringing the signs of the zodiac out in their appropriate seasons (Job 38.5 & 32). The Second Isaiah also pictures God 'fashioning the earth and everything that grows on it.' Isaiah likens the creation of Adam as God shaping man from clay as a potter shapes a pot. This was so that the world would not be a formless waste but rather 'a place to be lived in' (Isaiah 49. 9 & 18).

What these and other pictures of creation have in common is that they affirm the goodness of God and the beauty of the Cosmos. And they see the world not simply as a blessing for human beings but for animals and plants as well and even for the great whales created to sport in the water (Psalm 104.26). To attempt to unify these accounts or to see them as in any way scientific is to completely misunderstand them. They are exuberant poetry, marveling at the beauty of nature and they should be read as such.

Biblical echoes of Babylonian mythologies

The poetic character of Biblical creation stories becomes even more apparent when we come across traces of old Babylonian mythology in some of the creation accounts. The books of Job, Psalms and Isaiah all additionally draw on the ancient myth that creation began with the defeat of a great dragon from whose body the earth was formed. So as well as the imagery of the potter and the architect we hear how God 'hacked Rahab in pieces and ran the dragon through' (Isaiah 51.9 cf Job 26.12, Psalm 89.10).

No Christian today would dream of seeking to rehabilitate myths of the great dragon, yet that myth is embedded in at least three biblical creation accounts. More sophisticated accounts using imagery of a potter and a pot, or of an architect with a measuring rod or even accounts of God simply creating by calling into being are all alike human attempts to make sense of the cosmos and of our place in it, and at its best the Christian tradition from the earliest days has recognized this.

Some early Christian understandings

The earliest theological reflections we have on Genesis chapter 1 come from Origen of Alexandria in the third century. He pointed out that it is impossible to take the account as literally true because its ordering of creation simply doesn't make sense:

> What intelligent person would fancy, for instance that a first, second, and third day , evening and morning, took place without sun, moon and stars; and the first, as we call it without even a heaven? Who would be so childish as to suppose that God after the manner of a human gardener planted a garden in Eden towards the east, and made therein a tree, visible and sensible, so one could get the power of living [for ever] by the bodily eating of its fruit with the teeth; or again could partake of good and evil by feeding on what came from that other tree. I fancy that no one will question that these statements are figurative, declaring mysterious truths by the means of a seeming history, not one that took place in bodily form (Gwatkin, 1920: 137-38).

Origen was by no means alone in such an approach. Even St. Augustine, though claiming to defend the *Literal Meaning of Genesis,* acknowledged that one could not and should not seek to defend such details as the creation of light before the creation of the sun. More generally he insisted that we should form our judgments on questions in the natural sciences by reasoning and observation rather than seeking to derive such information from the scriptures.

It frequently happens that there is a question about the earth, or the sky or other elements of this world, the movement, revolutions, or even the size and distance of the stars, the regular eclipses of the sun and the moon, the course of the years in seasons; the nature of animals , vegetables, and minerals , and other things of the same kind, respecting which one who is not a Christian has knowledge derived from most certain reasoning and observation. And it is highly deplorable and mischievous and a thing to be specially guarded against that he should hear a Christian speaking of such matters in accordance with Christian writings and uttering such nonsense that, knowing him to be as wide of the mark as the, to use the common expression, East is from West, the unbeliever can scarcely restrain himself from laughing (Langmead Casserley, 1953: 21-22, citing Augustine *The Literal Meaning of Genesis*, 1,19).

St. Augustine's own understanding of God's creation was that it was a gradual event. In his magisterial summary of early Christian thought Bishop Charles Gore pointed out that St. Augustine himself followed the view of St. Gregory of Nyssa, that God in the beginning created only germs or causes of the forms of life which were afterwards to be developed in gradual course. Gore notes wryly that accommodation between religion and science would have been much easier in the fourth century than it was in the nineteenth (Gore, 1921: 10).

St. Thomas Aquinas

The Christian thinker who expressed most clearly the classic arguments for the existence of God from teleology and cosmology was St. Thomas Aquinas. However it is vital to start the discussion as Aquinas did with an acknowledgement of the strength of the case against such a belief. St. Thomas Aquinas' 'five ways' are preceded by his brilliant summary of why many believe that either God cannot exist , or that God is not a necessary belief. His first argument is that since the concept of God implies 'limitless goodness', evil should not exist at all. 'But evil is encountered in the world, therefore God does not exist'. His second argument was that everything we observe within the world can be fully accounted by natural causes 'therefore there is no need to suppose that God exists' (Aquinas, 1a,2,3). Nothing that Aquinas subsequently wrote takes away the reality of these two observations. Christians have always had to live with the 'problem of evil' and with the fact that belief in God is not a replacement for the search for natural explanations for what we encounter within the world.

If one looks at Aquinas' arguments from causation and design they presuppose that there are natural explanations for the inter-connectedness of all life. Everything we observe in the world is causally related to, and moved by other realities which become the 'natural' or 'efficient cause' of what develops. God, for Aquinas, is not within this natural cycle of 'efficient causation'. Aquinas' five ways are a sustained argument that the discovery of the 'natural' cause of why things happen is insufficient. We need also to think in terms of 'first cause' and 'final cause'. Since God for Aquinas is outside time his understanding of 'first cause ' does not imply temporal priority but simply his belief that the whole created order in the past, present and future is all equally dependent on God.. Likewise his argument from design supplements, but does not compete with his ongoing conviction that there can be a naturalistic explanation for everything that happens within the world which in its own terms is complete.

This is not the place to discuss the validity or otherwise of Aquinas' philosophy but simply to note that for Aquinas belief in God is not some kind of rival explanation to what the sciences disclose to us about how the Universe operates. For Aquinas belief in a creator God goes alongside of and complements what science can discover about the natural order. As a matter of history belief in a Universe created by a single divine mind within which there is a 'natural' explanation for everything waiting to be discovered is why science as we know it began in western Europe rather than elsewhere. Within Britain the founders of the Royal Society acknowledged that they wanted to think God's thoughts after him and discover how God's universe works. In principle therefore there should never be a clash between religion and science since belief in God is not in competition with natural explanations for the way things are.

When the Bible came to be treated as if it were a scientific source of data

With regard to the treatment of the Bible as a source for scientific information it is important to note that as a matter of history belief in the fixity of species was not deduced from the first chapter of Genesis. Christians has read Genesis for seventeen hundred years without drawing such a conclusion from it. Charles Gore, to whom I owe this insight, believes that the idea of the fixity of species was a scientific theory of the seventeenth century derived from observations about the limits within which interbreeding is possible. According to Gore belief in the special creation of each separate species was first taught by John Ray (1628-1705), affirmed as a kind of dogma by Carl Linnaeus in 1751 and made a basis for popular Christian apologetic by William Paley in 1802 (Gore, 1921: 7). Though subsequently the fixity of the species has been proclaimed as 'Biblical' it was a belief read into, rather than out of the Bible.

It is equally interesting that not till the seventeenth century Archbishop Ussher was it demonstrated that if one takes literally the chronological information contained within the Bible one could date the creation to 4004 BCE. Although this and other dates were subsequently included in most English Bibles, this represents seventeenth century literalism rather than the historic Christian approach to the Bible which did not see it as a supposed repository of 'scientific' information of this kind.

The situation was made worse by the influence of the 'Neptunist' school in geology in the first decade of the nineteenth century. In his detailed account of this movement, Charles Gillespie shows that what characterized such scholars was their belief that the best and most recent geological research of their day presented independently a description of the early earth which happened to coincide with the Genesis account of a divine creation followed by a universal flood. Such findings came to be used in Christian apologetic as 'proof' of the veracity of Moses and hence of the revealed character of scripture (Gillispie, 1959: 61-68). It was because of these developments that subsequent geological findings and the theory of evolution were experienced as radical challenges to Christian faith whereas what subsequent geological and evolutionary findings actually challenged were deductions from scripture which were actually of fairly recent origin.

The initial opposition to evolution of Bishop Samuel Wilberforce spelt out in his debate with Huxley in 1860 was not really derived from his theological beliefs but from the scientific world view he had absorbed from his contemporaries. What is more remarkable than that initial opposition was that within a generation Darwin's views were so widely accepted in Christian circles that his burial in Westminster Abbey in 1884 was enthusiastically supported .by all the religious press (cf. the account in

Desmond & Moore, 1991: 671). Though the political establishment had withheld the knighthood or peerage Darwin's
achievements merited, the religious establishment gave him the
public endorsement of an Abbey funeral and a memorial
committee on which both Archbishops and the Bishop of London
sat. By the end of the nineteenth century almost all thoughtful
Christians had come to take evolution for granted. In academic
theology the watershed was in Charles Gore's edited book *Lux
Mundi published* in 1890 which presented Christianity wholly
within an evolutionary framework.

The paradox of the present situation

When we reflect on Origen's belief that no intelligent person
would ever take the Genesis stories literally, or St. Augustine's
belief that building scientific hypotheses out of Biblical texts was
a thing to be 'specially guarded against', or Aquinas' assumption
that there is a natural explanation for everything, then the development of fundamentalist attitudes in the early nineteenth
century and their revival in the 21st is utterly bewildering. It is
false to the Christian tradition itself, let alone to the evidence
from historical and biblical criticism and from the data of the
natural sciences. Yet according to a 1991 Opinion Poll over a
hundred million Americans believe that God directly created
human beings in the recent past in the way that Genesis suggests,
(Jones, 1999: 1) and one firm advocate of this position was chosen
to be the Republican Candidate for Vice-President in the 2008
elections. The tragedy is that this resurgence of belief in a fundamentalist creationism is happening at a time when a number of
philosophers and scientists believe that a stronger case can be
made for Christian theism now than for many centuries.

Diametrically opposed judgements concerning the likelihood of God's existence

According to Anthony Flew who was formerly one of the best

known atheist philosophers of the twentieth century, the case for God 'is now much stronger than it ever was before' and that he 'simply had to go where the evidence leads' and accept that God exists (http://www.biola.edu/antonyflew/flew-interview.pdf). Likewise Keith Ward (2008) , a former atheist who went on to become a Regius Professor of Divinity, now thinks the case for belief has become so strong that he can write a book entitled *Why there almost certainly is a God.*

However at a more populist level a completely different perspective prevails in that Richard Dawkins (2006) and Christopher Hitchens (2007) have both been in the best sellers lists for many months. They both assume that belief in God is incompatible with modern science and that 'there almost certainly isn't a God.' Dawkins' challenge carries great weight not only through his former position as Professor of the Public Understanding of Science at Oxford University but as one whose earlier books of scientific exposition have presented the findings of modern biology to the wider world in a clear and convincing manner. It is evident from the response to Dawkins and Hitchens latest writings that they have struck a chord with the general public in a way that the revival of philosophical arguing for God's existence has clearly failed to do.

The Revival of Philosophy of Religion in the last quarter of the 20th. century.

Professor William Abraham commented recently that when he arrived in Oxford as a graduate student in 1973 he little knew that he was 'at the beginning of a golden period in the philosophy of religion 'in which believers could 'take a lead and create the intellectual space in which Christian belief could be taken seriously once again' (Menssen & Sullivan, 2007: xi). This perspective is endorsed from a different perspective by the atheist philosopher Kai Nielson who laments that

Philosophy of religion in Anglo-American context has taken a curious turn in the past decade... what has come to the forefront... is a group of Christian philosophers who return to the old topics and the old theses of traditional Christian philosophy and natural theology. (Nielsen, 1971: 19)

Similarly Richard Purtill says of the contemporary debate:

All the traditional arguments have able and respected defenders, and if there is not a consensus in favour of philosophical arguments for God's existence it is no longer true that there is a consensus against.

If one examines the arguments being discussed it becomes clear that two key factors in the revival of interest in the cosmological and teleological arguments for the existence of God have been the 'Big Bang' hypothesis concerning the origin of the Universe and the idea that the supposed 'fine tuning of the Universe' indicates that some 'anthropic principle' has affected the way the Universe has evolved. Whether or not these scientific discoveries can carry the weight that has been placed on them is a moot point but that contemporary philosophy of religion (for and against belief in God) has been revived by them is indisputable.

Big Bang Cosmology

From the perspective of St. Thomas Aquinas, Big Bang cosmology is irrelevant because for an eternal and timeless God, the Universe is quite as much dependent on God now, as at any supposed beginning. Popular Christianity however has interpreted 'first cause' as a claim that God created the Universe at some point in the past. If science really has discovered that that the Universe literally did come into being out of nothing then that is far more 'compatible' with this Christian claim than the former scientific consensus that the Universe has always existed.

Since a number of scientists do make precisely the claim that the Universe came into being out of nothing, it is understandable that the cosmological argument has been revived. But of course if talk of an absolute beginning is not scientifically valid, then arguments based on that assumption will fail.

Fine tuning

According to William Craig, who cites Stephen Hawking

> The existence of intelligent life depends on a delicate and complex balance of initial conditions simply given in the Big Bang itself. ... for example Stephen Hawking has calculated that if the rate of the universe's expansion one second after the big bang had been smaller by even one part in a hundred thousand million million, the universe would have re-collapsed into a hot fire-ball' (Hawking, 1988: 123).

There are around fifty such quantities and constants which must be fine-tuned in this way if the universe is to permit life. And it is not just each quantity which must be finely tuned. Their ratio to one another must also be exquisitely fine-tuned. So improbability is multiplied by improbability, until our minds are reeling with incomprehensible numbers (Craig in Wallace, 2003: 20-21).

This argument from the fine-tuning of the universe is described by Robert Jastrow, former Head of NASA's Institute for State Studies as 'the most powerful evidence for the existence of God ever to come out of science' Terry Miethe (1991: 65) notes that as a result of the evidence of fine-tuning, 'The argument from design has very recently gained acceptance among many scientists.' Keith Ward (1986: 45) comments that 'Just when philosophers had thought that the argument from design was gone forever, the physicist brings it back again'.

Some weaknesses in the appeal to the new physics

In making an appeal to Big Bang Cosmology and the Anthropic principle in the way that William Craig and others do, philosophers of religion are taking a risk. The most obvious objection is that both theories derive from current findings in Astronomy yet research into the religious beliefs of American astronomers' show that only 22% of them are prepared to affirm belief in God (Mackenzie Brown, 2003). In the United States context that is a very low percentage. This suggests that one should be cautious indeed in suggesting that astronomical findings are supportive of religious beliefs.

In the case of Big Bang Cosmology there is also the issue of how far one should really speak of the Big Bang as creation out of nothing. It remains a possibility that the Big Bang may after all have been brought about by a previous collapse. It is also argued that talk of 'nothing' is really a misunderstanding of the nature of the 'vacuum' out of which the Universe emerged (cf. Polkinghorne in Ford, 1987). It is also clearly perilous to build theological theories on a scientific foundation which might be wholly undermined by findings published in the next edition of an Astronomical Journal.

In the case of the fine tuning of the Universe there is also a real risk that part of its attraction lies in the fact that currently we lack any scientific hypothesis which would account for it. Indeed William Craig explicitly uses the fact that there is 'no physical reason why these constants and quantities possess the values they do' (Wallace, 2003: 2) as his clinching argument for the existence of God. This is both fallacious and dangerous. Nietzsche was rightly critical of those who place 'into every hole in our knowledge, their stop-gap, their illusion they call "God"' (Nietzsche, 1961: 116). It is axiomatic to Aquinas' position that in studying natural phenomenon we should always seek for the natural or 'efficient cause' for movement and development within the cosmos. Hence physicists should continue to do all in their power to continue to search for the unifying physical principle which draws all the constants of nature together. Belief in God is not a replacement for detailed scientific explanation, it goes alongside it. Our wonder at the 'fine-tuning' of the Universe should only be enhanced when we eventually discover 'how God did it'. As Hawkins (1988) concludes his *Brief History of Time* if and when we discover a unifying principle then we will know more of the 'mind of God'.

The ongoing need for harmony between religion and science

One of the enduring influences of the Enlightenment is the need to reconcile our religious thinking with our scientific understanding. In the end we cannot genuinely believe something in Church on Sunday which we disbelieve for the rest of the week. The heart of the Biblical doctrine of creation is the belief in a mind behind the Universe. It is this that finds expression through the variety of creation myths we find in the Bible. As Origen pointed out no intelligent person should take such myths literally, and as Augustine warned no one should seek to extrapolate scientific facts from scriptural sources. Aquinas rightly insisted that the starting point for thinking of God as creator should be a recognition of the fact that God is not within the cycle of natural causation.

It is interesting that currently many scientists believe that the Universe had an actual beginning. This view harmonizes well with the Judaeo-Christian-Islamic belief that God created the Universe out of nothing. But the theistic vision does not depend on the Universe having a temporal beginning since as Aquinas insisted God is as near now as at any supposed beginning. It is and remains wonderful that the Universe has been so finely tuned for the evolution of life and mind and this wonder should in no way be impaired when we discover the unifying principle behind the physics of the Big Bang, any more than belief in a creator God should be effected by an acknowledgement that evolution was the method he used to develop life on this wonderful planet.

References

Aquinas, St. Thomas. *Summa Theologia*

Dawkins, R. 2006. *The God Delusion.* London: Bantam

Desmond, A. & Moore, J. 1991. *Darwin.* London: Penguin

Flew, A. 'My pilgrimage from Atheism to Theism http://www.biola.edu/antonyflew/flew-interview.pdf

Ford, A. 1987 Video *Whose world? An Exploration of Science and Belief.* CTVC

Gillispie, C. 1959. *Genesis and Geology.* London: Harper Torchbooks

Gore, C. 1921. *Belief in God.* London: Murray

Gwatkin, H.M. 1920. *Selections from Early Christian Writers.* London: Macmillan

Hawking, S. 1988 *A Brief History of Time.* New York, Bantam,

Hitchens, C. 2007. *God is Not Great* London: Atlantic Books

Jones, S. 1999. *Almost like a whale.* Windsor: Black Swan

Langmead Casserley, J.V. 1953. *The Retreat from Christianity.* London: Longmans

Mackenzie Brown, C. The conflict between Religion and Science in Light of the Patterns of Religious Belief among Scientists *Zygon:Journal of Religion and Science* Vol.38 No.3 September 2003

Menssen, S. & Sullivan, T. 2007. *The Agnostic Inquirer.* Michigan: Eerdmans

Miethe, T. & Flew, A. 1991 *Does God Exist?: A Believer and an Atheist Debate.* New York: Harper

Nielsen, K. 1971. *Contemporary Critiques of Religion.* London: Macmillan

Nietzsche, F. 1961. *Thus Spoke Zarathustra.* London: Penguin

Purtill, R. The Current State of Arguments for the Existence of

God *Review and Expositor* Vol. 82.

Wallace, S. 2003. *Does God Exist: the Craig-Flew Debate.* London: Ashgate

Ward, K. 1986. *The Turn of the Tide: Christian Belief in Britain Today.* London: BBC Publications

Ward, K. 2008. *Why there almost certainly is a God.* London: Lion Books

Paul Badham is an Anglican Priest and Professor of Theology and Religious Studies at University of Wales, Lampeter. He is editor of *Modern Believing*, Vice President of The Modern Churchpeoples' Union and Patron of Dignity and Dying. His most relevant publication in this area is *The Contemporary Challenge of Modernist Theology.*

The Genesis Narratives

Anthony Phillips

Introduction

The opening chapters of the Hebrew Scriptures (Genesis 1-3) have been seen as central in any discussion of creation. Yet while these writings do have something to say about man and his responsibility for God's creation, nether the Eden narrative (Genesis 2:4b-3) nor the seven day scheme (Genesis 1-2:4a) strictly speaking are creation accounts. The former concerns the limitations of what it means to be human while the latter proclaims Israel's election come what may.

It has long been accepted by critical scholarship that the Pentateuch, the first five books of the Hebrew Scriptures known as the Torah, is the product of various literary sources written and edited over a considerable period of time, though there is no unanimity about either their identity or dating. That the two so-called creation narratives come from different hands is not difficult to see even in an English translation of the Hebrew text. Genesis 1-2:4a is formal, almost liturgical. The language is dignified and carefully ordered, God remaining distant and transcendent. In total contrast, Genesis 2:4b-3 depicts God in intimate human terms. This is generally regarded as the much older narrative which together with the stories of Cain and Abel (Genesis 4), the birth of the giants (Genesis 6:1-8) leading to the flood (parts of Genesis 7-9), and the Tower of Babel (Genesis 11:1-9), formed the preface to Israel's first literary work.

The Eden Narrative (Genesis 2: 4b – 3)

This first attempt at explaining Israel's origins is still generally dated to the time of the new Davidic-Solomonic Empire that is the tenth century BCE. Made up of diverse peoples both indigenous and foreign, the new state needed a document of title to legitimize its creation in which all could find their origins. The narrative began with the promise to the common ancestor Abraham of both progeny and land (Genesis 12:1-3) and culminated in the establishment of the Davidic-Solomonic state whose boundaries fulfilled that promise (2 Samuel 7:9).

It was however preceded by a preface explaining how it came about that God had to intervene and call Abraham. This described the ever increasing disobedience of humankind as they sought to break the limitations placed on them at creation culminating in their scattering throughout the earth no longer able to communicate with each other (Genesis 11:1-9). Then God had to take action to restore that unity which he had intended in creation of which the new Davidic-Solomonic Empire wielding together such a diverse community was the visible proof of his faithfulness. Israel's election is then of world significance. She could now take her place among the nations of the world with confidence.

But in introducing his work with a preface, the author was not simply recounting ancient traditions and beliefs. Rather he was producing a theological explanation of man's place in the world as it appeared to him. The history of the nation did not in fact begin with the call of Abraham but with the creation of man himself. From the beginning of time, God is seen as acting in history and towards some definite purpose. The ancient stories contained in the preface become part of history itself. So the author produces a coherent narrative in which there are no loose ends. The God who created man, Israel's God, holds the destiny of all men and women in his hands for in his chosen people Israel 'all the families of the earth shall bless themselves' (Genesis 12:3).

The preface begins with the creation of man. The author pictures an arid desert in which neither of the basic necessities for cultivation exists – water and man (Genesis 2:5). In order that vegetation may sprout and flourish, God causes a flood to rise up from beneath the earth and water its surface (Genesis 2:6)[1]. Then like a potter shaping his work, God forms man from clay (Genesis 2:7), a common idea throughout the ancient Near East. The word *adam* = man, mankind is a pun on the Hebrew word for earth, *adamah*. Both words derive from a common root meaning redness – the colour of soil and skin in Palestine[2].

Into his clay model, God breathes vitality. Observation showed that without breath, the body lost its life force. But there is no idea here of man having a separate soul. For the Hebrews man was thought of as a unity. He was either entirely alive or entirely dead. After death he went down into Sheol – the pit of the Psalms – where he spent his time in a state of shadowy non-experience. His personality went on in his children[3].

Somewhere in the east in a place called Eden, God then creates an oasis richly stocked with a variety of delightful trees of which two are named, the tree of life and the tree of the knowledge of good and evil (Genesis 2:8-9). In Hebrew thought the latter phrase does not refer to moral questions, but stands for the knowledge of everything there is to know, the kind of knowledge which God alone can have. Issues of immortality and the limit of man's knowledge are going to dominate the author's preface.

A river flowed out of Eden and watered the garden. Then it divided into four (Genesis 2:10-14). Here the author is clearly drawing on ancient traditions found elsewhere in the Bible (Ezekiel 28; 47) It is though difficult to know where he imagined his garden to be as the identity of all the rivers cannot be ascertained. Indeed the vague description of its location as 'in Eden, in the east' is probably deliberate (Genesis2:8). Eden itself means 'delight'. Here 'history' began, though the author would never have expected anyone to mount an expedition to find its site.

God now places man in Eden 'to till it and keep it' (Genesis 2:15) and so fulfill the purpose for which he was created. As God's tenant, he has the responsibility of maintaining the order of the garden which God has so delightfully created. Though God is regarded as the landlord of the garden, there is no thought of him dwelling there. While man can meet God there after work (Genesis 3:8), he is a visitor and not a resident.

As God's tenant. the man is given instructions as to how he is to manage the garden. He is free to eat any fruit from the trees in the garden but is not to eat from the fruit of the tree of the knowledge of good and evil (Genesis 2:16-17). He is man and not God. An attempt to eat from the tree of the knowledge of good and evil would in effect be a rejection of his creaturely status in an attempt to know as God alone knows.

Man then was created by God to be an agnostic believer. Whether he likes it or not – and mostly he does not - he cannot have an answer to everything, indeed anything outside the created order which is his to explore and order, but in which he must remain both in life and death.

Man is therefore no robot: his co-operation with God is not guaranteed but is up to man himself. He can reject God's provi-dence so richly given him in the garden of delight. But in giving man free will, God also subjects him to the ever-present temptation of rejecting his human limitations in an attempt to grasp at divinity. Giving in to such temptation is the theme of the preface.

God had however created man as a social being. It was therefore necessary that he should have companions. So in the same way in which he had created man himself, God created all animals and birds and brought them to man to name, thereby giving man authority over them. But in spite of man's basic affinity with the animals as being fellow creatures of the earth, they did not provide for him that companionship for which he yearned (Genesis 2:18-20). So from man himself God took a rib and created woman[4]. On seeing the woman, the man immedi-ately recognizes their common affinity resorting to a pun. Out of man *ish*, woman *ishah* was taken. In fact the words have no etymological connection but the author wanted to stress their mutual power over each other. Now at last through sexual fulfillment man can be as God had intended him to be, fully human, a partner with him in the creative process itself. God's work in creation is now complete (Genesis 2:21-25).

But will man be content with his creaturely status? In forbidding him on pain of death from eating of the tree of the knowledge of good and evil, had God denied man what should rightfully be his? It is this doubt which that mysterious creature the snake sows in the woman's mind (Genesis. 3:1-5) and leads her to eat the forbidden fruit and also give it to her husband to eat (Genesis 3:6). In doing so, they do not gain that wisdom which is God's alone, but rather discover their essential creature-liness in a way which was never apparent to them before (Genesis 3:7). This is always the result of man trying to grasp at divinity. Deprived of their idyllic innocence, they seek to cover their shame[5].

The story concludes with God's punishment of the snake, the woman and the man, all of which is used to explain some unpleasant facts of life for each participant. Unlike other animals, the snake is deprived of legs and must wriggle on its belly, clearly imagined as a painful process. Further it is limited to a diet of dust – another faulty observation of contemporary science. In addition perpetual war is ordained between the snake and man, with each set on destroying the other. For woman the joy of child-bearing is now to be accompanied by pain and suffering. And man, created to cultivate the ground, can only do so with consid-erable effort and only partial success (Genesis 3: 14-19).

The effect of man grasping at divinity is the inevitable disorder that results. As part of creation, man cannot act indepen-dently of it. It is only now that the full implications of the author's theological insights are being properly recognized in the clear interaction of man and his environment and man and his body.

The account concludes with the writer reminding man of that

most unpleasant fact of life – death. This is no part of his punishment, but his natural destiny. For nowhere is there any suggestion that man was originally made to be immortal. Death should however remind him that no matter how hard he tries he cannot in the end be like God. *adam* he is and to *adamah* he will return.

Fearing that man may seek to avoid the limitation of death and grasp at immortality by eating of the other tree, the fruit of the tree of life, God expels the man and the woman from the garden (Genesis 3:22-24). So they go out from Eden to do what they were created to do, but no longer in the idyllic situation intended for them in creation. But even though they have disobeyed God by grasping at divinity and suffered punishment, God will not cast them off. They do not die. In this the snake was right, though this does not mean that humankind and the created order can escape the consequences of their actions. But despite their disobedience, *adam* continues to remain the object of God's care and protection, For in the end only through man can God's plan for his creation be realized. So the Eden narrative asserts not only that essential separation between man and God which must for ever remain unbridged, but also their necessary inter-dependence ever to be secured through God's grace alone. It is he who clothes the disobedient pair (Genesis 3:21) It is not always recognised that man matters to God as much as God matters to Man.

It is though a mistake to talk here about 'the Fall' or 'original sin' in the sense that man is no longer constituted as God created him. This is a later Christian doctrine based on Paul's letter to the Romans (5:12-21). It has no part in the theology of the Hebrew Scriptures. The author of the Eden narrative is not concerned with how the tendency to commit sin is passed on – certainly not in tracing it to the sexual act – but rather to recognize that this tendency is a common experience of man in every generation. Humankind is then called to live with the tension of the mystery of evil whose origin only God alone can know though it was not part of the intended paradisal state of Eden. While the snake indicates that the power of evil lies outside man, the story points to that power inevitably finding its expression through man's refusal to accept the limitations of his humanity, his desire to grasp at divinity. No profounder analysis of the human situation has since been offered.

The author is then not concerned with the question whether man descended from a single pair (monogenism) or from multiple origins at various points in the world (polygenism). His purpose is to spell out the nature of what it means to be human in the world which God has created and for which he has made man responsible but both whose knowledge and individual existence he has limited

All this has profound consequences for the exercise of faith as the book of Job confirms. The author makes it clear that Job is suffering unjustly, but despite Job's passionate challenge to God, he receives no explanation for his predicament. Yet unlike his friends, God rewards him for what he has said. He refuses on the one hand to deny his innocence and on the other to reject God. So the book confirms the essential truth of the Eden narrative. Man cannot have the answers for everything. The mystery of unjust suffering remains unexplained. But Job can still know God. And in the end that is what matters. Whether he likes it or not, man can only be an agnostic believer.

The author of the Eden narrative went on in his preface to describe an ever-increasing situation of chaos as man continued to reject the set limitations of his humanity. Abel murders his brother Cain and so gets possession of his blood which properly belongs to God. But lest God's work in creation is brought to naught, the murderer is given divine protection (Genesis 4). Yet disorder so increases that it even goes beyond the confines of the earth to involve the heavens with the birth of monsters, the offspring of the sons of God and the daughters of men (Genesis 6:1-4). Determined to start afresh, God destroys in a gigantic flood all the inhabitants of the earth save Noah and his family (parts of Genesis 7-9). Even this divine purge cannot bring man to heel: his arrogant ambition knows no bounds as with his tower he seeks to penetrate the divine realm itself. So God scatters humankind throughout the earth, chaotically confusing their language to make it impossible for them to organize again such a challenge to his authority (Genesis 11:1-9). Once more God must start again with one man in order to secure what he had intended in creation. God calls Abraham (Genesis 12:1-3). Despite all the horrors of the preface, the author thereby asserts that God and man are on the same side as the emergence of the new Davidic-Solomonic empire confirmed. Israel's election was secure, her future assured.

The Seven Day Creation Account (Genesis, 1 – 2: 4a)

Although the empire divided on Solomon's death into the northern kingdom of Israel and the southern kingdom of Judah, the Davidic monarchy centred on Jerusalem lasted until the Babylonian conquest (587 BCE). The consequent destruction of the temple and the exile of the king and leading citizens led to a radical reassessment of Israel's understanding of her relationship with her God.

On the one hand there were those theologians who explained her defeat as to due to a breach of the covenant which Israel was held to have entered into at Sinai (Exodus 19-24, 32-34). This explicitly spelt out that her election was conditional on her keeping the law, in particular in avoiding other gods. Failure would inevitably result in absolute rejection.

Indeed it is probable that this theological assessment had already been introduced into Israel's thinking to explain the demise of the northern kingdom following the Assyrian conquest (721 BCE) in order to concentrate the minds of southern Judah. She might suffer the same fate. For some, this under-standing of her God was confirmed in the Babylonian conquest and resulted in a new theological work in which the conditions of the covenant were spelt out and then Israel's failure to conform described in an account of her history from entry into Canaan until the exile, namely the books of Deuteronomy, Joshua, Judges, 1 and 2 Samuel and 1 and 2 Kings[6].

But another theologian could not stomach the idea that God's election of his people was conditional[7]. It was this theologian who took the preface to the original account of Israel's origins (Genesis 2:4b-3) and preceded it with his own creation account (Genesis 1-2:4a). His work was to consist of the present books of Genesis, Exodus, Leviticus and Numbers. It would end with Israel on the edge of the promised land. The question he was asking of the exilic generation to whom he wrote was would Israel have sufficient faith to appropriate what God had destined for her. The exiles in their hopeless situation could yet again be restored to their land, re-enter it as of old, if they had sufficient faith. God cannot let Israel go. His grace cannot be limited by man's failure. Only man can let God go. All this he spelt out in the author's new creation account.

Paradoxically the first verse of this account poses considerable difficulties. The issue is whether there already existed a formless waste and primeval sea out of which God created the world, or whether the author held nothing pre-existed God's creative action (*creatio ex nihilo*). The older versions of the Bible[8] take the latter view and translate 'In the beginning God created the heavens and the earth'. But the New English Bible sees the first verse as a temporal clause and the second as describing the situation which existed before God started his activity: 'In the beginning of creation, when God made heaven and earth, the earth was without form and void, with darkness over the face of the abyss'.

This latter understanding corresponds with the Babylonian creation epic *Enuma Elish*[9] and is probably to be preferred. For the author, the alternative to God's creation is not non-existence, but lifeless emptiness amid the watery chaos . Creation was always subject to the possibility of a return to that formless void which was its natural state (Jeremiah 4:23-26). God's creation cannot be taken for granted. It will not endure willy-nilly, but needs man to order it.

Over this formless waste and primeval sea, the wind of God moved. But this was no ordinary wind but God's creative Spirit. The Hebrew word used to describe the movement of the Spirit is used again in Deuteronomy 32:11 of an eagle trying to get her young to fly from the nest. Like the mother bird, God is anxiously flapping over the wasteland as he begins the process of bringing order out of chaos.

It is probable that the author took over an existing Babylonian eight day creation account and adapted it for his own purposes. By squashing two events into both the third and sixth days, he succeeded in completing creation before the seventh day on which he pictures God resting. This is the climax of his account. The Sabbath was a part of the process of creation: there never was a time when it did not exist.

While the author's purposes were then theological rather than scientific, he none the less asserts through his narrative that creation was not due to accident but the deliberate action of God, though inevitably his account reflects the scientific ideas of his time. Thus the earth is envisaged as a disk floating on the primeval waters with over it the firmament thought of as an inverted metal basin, beyond which lay the waters of the heavens. From here God sent rain, and from the waters below the earth came sea, rivers and springs (Genesis 1:6-8). But the earth's existence was precarious: too much water could fall from the heavens or rise from under the earth and engulf it (Genesis 6-9). Indeed scholars have shown that the purpose of the ancient Near Eastern creation accounts was to give threatened man security through their recitation in the cult.

Despite the source of his seven day scheme, the author is

concerned to rule out all foreign religious ideas. So God not only creates all plant and animal life, but provides their means of propagation. This includes even man – created male and female – whose sexual functions far from being ignored or dismissed as a necessary evil to provide for the future of mankind, are not only taken for granted but expected to be luxuriated in. There is no need for Israel to resort to fertility deities. Nor is God himself to be treated as such. In creation itself, in providing seed, seasons and semen, God has done all that was necessary[10].

Further it is God who creates the astral bodies (Genesis 1:14-18), thereby indicating that they are in his control. They are not to be worshipped as was widely done in the ancient Near East, which explains the deliberate avoidance of naming the sun and moon (Genesis 1:16). Nor are they to be held to have independent power to influence men's destinies. Similarly both the sea and sea monsters are God's handiwork and, as subject to him, no longer to be feared (Genesis 1:20-21).

In the Babylonian creation epic man is made out of the blood of a dead god, but the Hebrew author describes man as made like everything else at the direct order of God (Genesis 1:26-27). He is to be made 'in our image, after our likeness'. This Hebrew idiom of saying what appears to be the same thing twice is to emphasize opposite ideas. On the one hand man is near to God, he is made in his image: but at the same time he is distant from God, he is only a likeness. Thus in his relationship with God he is different from all other created beings, but he is not divine. Indeed it is his attempt to grasp at divinity that leads to chaos for him and his world.

This later author is deliberately contrasting his account of creation with the Eden narrative. There man is condemned because he had improperly 'become like one of us' (Genesis 3:22), that is he had attempted to break out of those limitations which constitute the true human state. But in spite of man's repeated acts of arrogance towards God as set out in the earlier narrative culminating in the attempt to enter heaven itself (Genesis 11:1-9), there is a proper sense in which man has been made in the image of God. In other words man properly belongs in intimate relationship with the divine world. Yet he is not one of the divine ones and must for ever remain distinct and separate within the earthly realm.

As a result of this new theology in the seven day creation account, there is now in the combined narrative of Genesis 1-11 a tension between man's intended status as 'like one of us' and his hubris in making himself 'like one of us'. But in bringing out this tension the later author has emphasized man's proper dignity. Unlike the animals he is given the power to communicate with God and so engage in God's ordering activity. But just as a limit is set to the activities of the divine beings (Genesis 6:1-4), so also there is a limit to man's actions, a limit set by his residence on earth and not in the divine realm.

None the less man is commanded to act as the representative of the Creator in his creation, to master and control it. The Hebrew Scriptures thus take a positive view of scientific research and technological achievement. The author of the seven day creation account uses royal language to delineate man's role. But man's kingship over creation is not to be one of exspoilation. His is to be a responsible government in which God's order is maintained. Nor is there any thought of one part of humankind dominating another. All share the same given status and the same responsibility. But whatever new discoveries man may make, he will never be able to know anything outside the created order in which God has set him and which is his to understand and enjoy.

The climax of the narrative is reached with God's blessing of the seventh day on which he rested. The Sabbath thereby becomes part of the creative process itself. It is part of the very fabric of creation, essential to its efficient running as day and night, sun and moon, animals and man. There never was a time when it did not exist.

The actual origin of the Sabbath is not clear. Although etymologically it is now connected with the verb to rest, its proper meaning is probably 'stopping day', that is a day which divides one block of days off from another. We know that there were such stopping days in Babylon, and attempts have been made to find the origin of the Sabbath there. But there is no record anywhere outside Israel of a regular stopping day every seventh day. In view of this is seems preferable to see the Sabbath as a Hebrew creation. It certainly pre-existed the exile (2 Kings 4:23; Isaiah 1:13; Hosea 2:13; Amos 8:5). It is the subject of the fourth commandment (Exodus 20:8-11; Deuteronomy 5:12-15) and mentioned in pre-exilic Hebrew law (Exodus 23:12; 34:21). In view of the tradition of slavery in Egypt, it may have been created as a declaration of political independence. The Hebrews were free under their God to order their own working lives. But whatever its origins, for the author of the seven day creation account it was not to be seen to originate at Sinai, but in creation itself.

What was his purpose in making the Sabbath part of the creation process? Since the only people in the world who kept the Sabbath were the Hebrews, they must have been in God's mind at creation. Their history does not begin with the exodus from Egypt, nor even the call of Abraham. It began at creation in which they too formed part of that ordered fabric brought about by the seven days of God's activity. The Hebrews are then immutably fixed in that order. If they ceased to exist it would be as if the sun or moon ceased to exist, utterly unthinkable.

Now it becomes apparent why the author of the seven day creation account in taking over the Eden narrative had to precede it with his own version. By making the Sabbath the climax of his narrative, he proclaimed to the disillusioned exiles in Babylon that no matter what appearances to the contrary might be, their place in the world was assured. Unlike any other race, the

Hebrews were in God's mind at creation: as long as that existed, they would exist too. Although as a result of the Babylonian conquest Israel had ceased to be an independent nation, her place in God's plan for his world was in no way affected by her political fate. The Hebrews had been chosen at the dawn of time and nothing could cancel their election. Those who interpreted Israel's fate as ultimately determined by obedience to the law were wrong. God's grace can never be limited. While Israel must endure the appropriate punishment for her failure, the Sabbath itself confirmed her future, which only lack of faith on Israel's part could throw into doubt. For the writer of the seven day creation account the only issue was whether despite her parlous state, Israel would appropriate what God had unconditionally provided for her of which the Sabbath was tangible evidence.

Although by his seven day creation account, the author sought to confirm the Hebrews special position in God's scheme of things, none the less he recognized that if God's intended order was to be restored, then Israel must bring all men and women into that relationship for which, as made in his image and after his likeness, they were created. This is why the revised preface still climaxes with the blessing of all peoples in Abraham (Genesis 12:3). In this the author of the seven day creation account was expressing contemporary theology found in other exilic and post-exilic theology (Isaiah 49:6, 55:5, 61:5-7; Zechariah 8:20-23). In the end the importance of the seven day creation account is that although it confirms in the most unlikely political situation the place of Israel in God's salvation plans, it also makes plain God's concern for all peoples. For such a theology to be proclaimed at the moment of apparent total failure is a startling testimony to faith.

Conclusion

The two authors of the so-called creation narratives were then not primarily concerned with either science or history. While they drew on what scientific knowledge they had and certainly saw creation as the first act of God in history, their concern was to convey to their contemporaries their theological understanding of where they stood in relation to their God. Man had been created to order and maintain God's world, but man's knowledge was ever confined to what he could discover within that world where he had complete freedom to act as he willed for good or ill.

Yet no matter how much man failed God, he would not let him go. So he called Abraham, father of his people Israel, a people whom the author of the seven day account saw as in God's mind in the very creation of the world itself. Through Israel God would restore that paradisal state intended from the dawn of time for the first *adam* and all his descendents from the dawn of time. However chaotic the contemporary situation might be, Israel's ultimate destiny was assured provided she had sufficient faith.

Once Hebrew literature is allowed to speak for itself then the assumption that these ancient Scriptures hold only primitive ideas now dispelled by scientific twentieth century man 'come of age' is itself dispelled. Of course there are differences in outlook between ancient Israel and our world. But while science continues to expand man's knowledge and therefore his ability to understand and hopefully order this universe in which he finds himself, there remains no *prima facie* reason why the insights of the ancients into the mystery of God and the equally perplexing mystery of man can not in fact speak to our present condition. Indeed we ignore them at our peril.

Notes

1 This translation which is followed by the New English Bible is preferable to the 'mist' of the older English versions.

2 As with the case of every Hebrew pun, two ideas, in this case man and earth, are understood to be intimately related and exercise power over each other. So man tills the soil to live, yet

in the end is destined to be buried in it. This defines man's essential nature. Whether in life or death, he belongs to the earth.

3   The hope for every Hebrew was that he would die 'full of days' leaving behind him many generations (Job 42:16-17). Infertility was always assumed to be the woman's fault, barrenness being the chief cause for divorce.

4.   Ruth Page, Former Principal, New College, University of Edinburgh. Author of *God and the Web of Creation*. SCM Press 1996.

   It is probable that we are to understand that God took half man's rib cage to make woman, so leaving their lower parts free to engage in sexual intercourse.

5   The Hebrews regarded nakedness with abhorrence associating it with the cultic rites of the Canaanites, the original inhabitants of the land, whose fertility religion constantly provided a temptation to them. As a by-product of his narrative, the author seeks to explain various facts of life, in this case why men and women wear clothes.

6   These theologians are normally called the Deuteronomists responsible for Deuteronomy and the subsequent 'history' books which make up the Deuteronomic Work (Deuteronomy -2 Kings) which reached its final form in the last days of the Davidic monarchy, 2 Kings 25:27-30 being a late appendix.

7   He is usually called the Priestly Writer because his work is dominated by cultic and ritual rules of priestly observance and interest in the temple. The work was probably composed in Babylon, but contains much early material. Its date remains uncertain but it cannot come from a time much after the exiles began to return to Palestine (538 BCE).

8   Authorized Version, Revised Version, Revised Standard Version, Jerusalem Bible.

9   Probably to be dated to the early part of the second millennium BCE.

[10] The division of plants into those such as cereals which scatter their seed, and those like grapes, figs and olives whose seed is hidden in their fruit, reflects current scientific observation (Genesis 1:11-12). Similarly animals are divided into appropriate categories (Genesis 1:24-25). Further both animals and man were created to be vegetarian. Only later would the author recognize the eating of meat as a necessary evil (Genesis 9:3).

Anthony Phillips, formerly Dean of Trinity Hall, Cambridge, Chaplain of St. John's College, Oxford and Headmaster of The King's School, Canterbury

Genesis 1 and the Presuppositions of Science

Jonathan Clatworthy

Introduction

The aim of this chapter is to offer a religious argument against six-day creationists and anti-evolutionists. I shall focus on two principles which are essential presuppositions of all science, namely the order and comprehensibility of the universe, and note how they became accepted parts of Europeans' mental furniture only after millennia of theological debate. Elsewhere in this book Anthony Phillips provides a theological introduction to the beginning of Genesis; I shall examine its first chapter, that jewel in the crown of anti-evolutionist and six-day creationist theory, with the more specific aim of showing how, far from serving their purpose, it played a major role in establishing these science-affirming principles.

I adopt a unified view of knowledge in which science and theology inform each other. This unified view is now controversial. We have inherited a double account of how we came into existence. In one the world is billions of years old and humans evolved out of other primates, while in the other the world is just over six thousand years old and God created all living beings in six days. This double account is a modern development. Before the nineteenth century, when Europeans speculated about the origins of the world and humanity they did so within a unified framework. The information available to them was limited and they put together what there was: the observations of scientists, the speculations of philosophers, biblical texts and church teachings.

Within that older model, when new scientific findings contradicted biblical texts controversy often raged, especially in the twelfth, seventeenth and nineteenth centuries. The main reason why the nineteenth century debates, unlike earlier ones, generated this double account was the rise of positivism. Positivists distinguished between 'facts' – known certainties which cannot be refuted – and 'opinions' or 'beliefs' which can.[1] The dominant nineteenth century view was that facts are derived from scientific methods: empirical observation and the generalization of data into laws. A contrasting positivism claimed that the facts are established by divine revelation through the Bible whereas science is mere human theory.[2] Since then many anti-evolutionist campaigners have sought scientific evidence to justify their case; their view, however, was originally generated, and continues to be motivated, not by empirical evidence but by a distinctive theory about the authority of the Bible. What makes these two positivist theories irreconcilable is the certainty claims; if my 'facts' are irrefutable, anyone who disagrees with me is certainly wrong.

Today scientists are more aware that their rapidly increasing information about the world depends on hypotheses, any one of which may in the future be refuted however unlikely this may seem. Similarly most religious opinion recognizes that the Bible cannot be treated as a collection of certainties about the world. Recently we have witnessed a revival of religious anti-evolutionism, and there remains a lively tradition of atheists denouncing all religion as anti-scientific; but to the twenty-first century ear both these positivisms have an outdated ring to them. The idea that the Bible can refute science seems so old-fashioned as to be bizarre, but so does the claim that science has disproved religious belief.

In the present climate a much more serious threat to science is the non-realism popular among some postmodernists. Their fundamental argument is that all scientific research makes two presuppositions: firstly that the world is ordered, and secondly that the human mind is capable of perceiving and analysing that order. Pointing out that neither of these can be proved by scientific methods, they then argue that scientists, far from describing reality the way it objectively is, are simply finding ways to present chaos as though it were ordered.[3]

Many people today, including many scientists, dismiss these postmodern challenges on the ground that these presuppositions are common sense, but this reveals a lack of historical awareness: however obvious they may now seem, they were only established *after the triumph of one theological tradition* over others.[4] Thus whereas the older, positivist challenges have discredited all religious belief in the eyes of many supporters of science, in the newer challenges science is in trouble precisely because it has forgotten its theological roots.

Order and Comprehensibility

If the world does not function according to ordered regularities, 'laws of nature', there is no role for science. It is not self-evident that it does. We observe some regularities, like the alternation between day and night, but also irregularities: weather patterns, for example, are so unpredictable that forecasts are unreliable. Given our experience of life in general, it is possible either to believe that the world is basically chaotic and seek explanations for the regularities, or to believe that the world is basically ordered and seek explanations for the irregularities.

Many ancient and medieval societies opted for the former. To explain the chaotic nature of reality as a whole they described its creation as the result of interactions between conflicting gods with conflicting agendas. Thus the ancient pantheons could begin their accounts of reality with an original chaos and explain specific regularities as the work of specific gods.

Some of the presocratic Greek philosophers proposed the idea of regular, predictable laws of nature. Characterisitically laws of nature are described in terms of causal sequences: when x is the case, y happens. The traditional Greek gods, far from offering a basis for such a theory, were as good an example as any of a pantheon producing a chaotic world, but the philosophers did not take them at all seriously. In this sense we may think of their theory as a forerunner of modern secular science after the link with religious doctrines has been severed.

For science to be possible the nature of reality also needs to be comprehensible to the human mind. Paradoxically this means that order needs to be limited. If every event is determined by previous events in an unfailing sequence of cause and effect, then even our thoughts must be determined by prior causes. If so it becomes difficult to see how our beliefs can bear any particular relation to their objects. For example, I believe Paris is the capital of France. If this belief of mine is explained by a sequence of physical causes and effects - chemical processes in my brain – it is difficult to see how my belief can bear any relation to whether or not Paris is indeed the capital of France. If it really is, this would seem pure coincidence. In a world entirely governed by a deterministic sequence of cause and effect we have no way to stand outside those causes to check the nature of reality. Currently this is a major theme of debate among philosophers.[5]

For science to be possible, therefore, we need to believe that whereas the world around us operates regularly as a cause-and-effect sequence, our own minds are free to think their own thoughts without physical causation. This was indeed the basis upon which early modern science developed; according to Cartesian dualism its scope was restricted to the physical and observable, while acknowledging the existence of a spiritual and unobservable realm outside the remit of science. It was later, with the rise of positivism, that the existence of the spiritual realm was challenged and the human mind was relocated in the determined physical realm.

If human minds are indeed free to think their own thoughts it still does not follow that we are capable of understanding how the world works. On what basis might we expect to have this capacity? Again theological speculation has explored the options over the millennia. Some religious traditions have argued that the mind, or soul, was created by evil gods who intended to keep us ignorant; such for example seems to have been a common theme in ancient Gnostic teaching.[6] A modern theory with a similar effect argues that since our minds have evolved to maximize our chances of survival, there is no reason why we should expect them to understand deep truths about the nature of reality.[7]

These two presuppositions of science, order and comprehensibility, far from being mere common sense have been proposed by some theologies and rejected by others. The theologies which have been most fruitful in proposing them are the ones which developed out of Jewish monotheism. All the books of the Hebrew Scriptures as we have them were probably edited to make them consistent with the principle that the world was designed by a single benevolent being who intended it for the well-being of all creation and got it right. The Bible expresses it most clearly in the first chapters of Genesis and Second Isaiah. These texts offer an emphatically monotheistic account of the relationship between God, the world and humans in which God intends *shalom* - peace, harmony, well-being and prosperity, for humans, animals and the land.

The Jewish account of order differs from regularity in two respects. Firstly empirical observations establish regularities but not the reasons for them.[8] In the Bible, order means that the regularities are *intended*. On this basis it is possible to speculate about their causes by asking what kinds of intentions the creating mind may have. Secondly, the modern tendency to assume that *everything* in the space-time universe is governed by laws of nature has the effect of presenting these laws not just as real powers but as supreme powers. Monotheism, by describing the supreme power as an intending mind, can affirm regularities as the creation of that mind but also allow for some processes *not* to be governed by regularity.

Among early Christians this was best expressed by the fourth century Basil, Bishop of Caesarea. Basil proposed that the laws of nature described by the Greeks had been established by God as part of the process of creating the world. On this basis he understood regularity to be both reliable where it exists, and limited. If it is the same God who created both the physical world and our minds, and furthermore did so in order to let us understand the world well enough for legitimate purposes, then we have grounds for confidence in our ability to understand the world.[9]

Here then are two essential presuppositions of science: that the world is ordered, and that the human mind can understand that order. The successes of modern science have contributed to their credibility; but precisely because science cannot function without them, it cannot prove them. When good theology triumphed, it made science possible. This was well known to early modern scientists until the middle of the eighteenth century; students of Galileo and Newton, for example, are well aware of the extent to which they drew on theological concepts in the development of their theories.

These theological foundations, however, gradually disappeared from view. From around the middle of the eighteenth century scientific knowledge seemed to many of the European educated classes to be more secure than theological knowledge. A major influence was David Hume, who took for granted that science could establish true knowledge without reference to religious belief, but aired many doubts about the existence of God.[10] Since then the theological foundations of science have been largely forgotten, leaving a situation where order and predictability, and therefore science, still work but science itself cannot explain why.[11] Postmodern challengers seize on this gap to argue that modern science is built on error.

Interpreting Genesis

With these issues at stake I turn to the first chapter of Genesis. My main purpose is to illustrate the connection between its monotheistic theology and the theory that the world is both ordered and comprehensible. A secondary aim is to undermine the claims of six-day creationists and anti-evolutionists.

Readers who have no training in understanding ancient texts often make modern assumptions about how and why they were written, and therefore misunderstand their meaning. Six-day creationists and anti-evolutionists resist scholarly exegesis, usually by appealing to one of two arguments. One is that the true author of the Bible is God. God, they tell us, somehow intervened in the minds of some humans, causing them to write the books regardless of whether they understood what they were writing, so we need not concern ourselves with their intentions. This is a difficult view to defend; it has no empirical support and biblical scholars have pointed out countless texts where God would appear to have been inconsistent, mistaken or incomprehensible. Even the strictest of biblical literalists usually find it necessary to attribute the final wording and intentionality to human authors.[12]

A newer argument, based on reader-response theory and popularized by postmodernism, claims that the authoritative meaning of biblical texts within each Christian church is whatever that church interprets it to be, regardless of the authors' original intentions. Just as we can perceive in Shakespeare's plays insights which Shakespeare himself did not consciously intend, so also with the Bible. This theory can indeed produce the conclusion that Genesis 1 'means' that there was no evolution, but it only 'means' that from the perspective of the churches which decide to make it mean that. Any meaning established in this way has the authority of that church, but cannot claim the authority of the Bible as such. I therefore take the view that whenever we take any biblical text to be authoritative for us, the only meanings we can describe as authoritative-because-they-are-biblical are the meanings the human authors intended to convey.

What they intended to convey is not always easy to establish. When reading texts from a culture very different from our own we need to distinguish what the authors meant to affirm from what they took for granted. We understand literature from our own culture more easily because we take in verbal cues, often without noticing that we are doing so. For example, if I say 'Paris is the capital of France' to a group of educated Europeans, they are likely to anticipate a further statement; after all, on its own it is a well-known piece of information, not worth repeating for its own sake. On the other hand if I say 'Winchester is the capital of France', hearers are likely to focus on the statement. Am I perhaps about to make some claim about medieval kings? If in two thousand years' time archaeologists unearth records containing these two statements they may not appreciate how different they are in intent.

Similarly when we read texts from a very different culture, unless we are steeped in its language and thought forms we are likely to miss the verbal cues, and we may not distinguish successfully between what is being taken for granted and what is being positively affirmed. The idea of treating Genesis 1 as a set of factual statements about how the world was created was an early nineteenth century development. At this time Europeans and Americans were increasingly interested in science and history and interpreted biblical texts accordingly. They did not have other ancient near eastern texts available to them for purposes of comparison. Later in the century they did, but by that time the tradition of rejecting science in the name of the Bible had been established.

Historical background

Today a great many ancient near eastern texts are available to us, and although scholars debate details the main outline with respect to Genesis 1 is clear. Genesis 1:1-2:4a was written, probably in the later sixth or some time in the fifth century BC, by anonymous authors known as 'the Priestly source' or 'P', adapting earlier material to provide a theologically motivated prologue to the Pentateuch, the first five books of the Bible. They are probably responsible for the present form of the Pentateuch and in Genesis 1 as elsewhere they used but adapted pre-existent material.

When Judaea was defeated by the Babylonians in the early sixth century, usual practice would have been to abandon worship of their god – who had failed to protect them - and transfer allegiance to Marduk, the god of the Babylonians. The Judaeans would have been assimilated into Babylonian culture, and no doubt some were. About fifty years later Cyrus the Persian, who had a policy of allowing exiles to return home, marched against Babylon. The author of Isaiah 40-55 looked forward to his victory and interpreted it as part of a plan by Israel's god. Normally gods of small nations were not considered able to influence the faraway events of greater powers, but the prophet identified Israel's god with the supreme God of the whole world, ramming the point home by mocking Babylon's gods as mere pieces of wood. Afterwards P listed the laws applying to the Jewish community, prefixing them with Genesis 1 and the histories describing Israel's role in the divine scheme of things.

The closest literary parallel to Genesis 1 is the *Enuma Elish*, a creation epic recited at the New Year festival at Babylon. This text has been available to scholars since the end of the nineteenth century and has often been called 'the Babylonian Genesis'. It is the older of the two, so it will have been the *Enuma Elish* which influenced Genesis, not the other way round. By comparing them scholars explored which elements of Genesis 1 were borrowed and which were original to P. As more literature has come to light the position has become more complex; some common features were shared throughout the ancient near east, and P may have borrowed from other sources as well. Nevertheless this Babylonian text remains the closest parallel and is likely to have been well known by P's circle since they had been exiled to Babylon.

Ancient creation myths served a purpose which is often misunderstood today. They generally seem to have arisen not from pure speculation but from issues of security. We do the same today. For example, anxiety about global warming motivates societies to bring together their best insights in science, politics, economics, technology and ethics in order to explore how to respond. In the same way the ancients responded to floods, plagues and military defeat by reviewing their theories about what caused these events and what they should do about them. What makes it difficult for us to notice the similarities is that their theories focused on the nature of the gods and their proposed solutions usually involved cultic actions like sacrifices. Nevertheless the point was, then as now, to account for the nature of reality as they experienced it in order to establish what could and should be done about the threats they faced. Once these questions had been answered the explanations were often used for other purposes, like pure speculation about the nature of the world or justifying the prevailing moral norms and cultic practices.[13]

The creator God

The authors of Genesis 1 thus presented their theory about how God has designed humans to live, situating it at the beginning of the Pentateuch to form a prologue to the history of Israel and the lists of laws in later books. They borrowed details of the creation story from the traditions available to them. They affirmed some, took some for granted and rejected others. In addition they seem to have produced new ideas of their own. In order to appreciate their message we need to distinguish what they took for granted from what they were positively affirming.

Genesis 1 is neither narrative nor poetry. It has hymn-like qualities, especially short sentences and repetitions like the choruses of hymns, but the Hebrew is not sufficiently regular for the present text to have been a hymn. It is most likely that P adapted a hymn for the purpose, and this suggests that the irregularities indicate changes P made. The main repetitions are:

God said (i.e. decreed the creation of something)	7 times
God made	5 times
God named	5 times
God saw that the thing created was good	7 times
It was evening and it was morning, the [next] day	6 times.

Listing these repetitions is enough to draw attention to the distinctive character of this text by comparison with other ancient near eastern creation narratives. It is a ringing endorsement of *monotheism*. The *Enuma Elish* is typical of ancient near eastern creation epics by beginning with a long genealogy of the gods. By contrast the first statement in Genesis, 'In the beginning God created the heavens and the earth', is distinctive P; there are no other gods and before God performed this first act of creation there is nothing to report.[14] Centuries later Jews and Christians would elaborate the monotheistic principle by describing God as omnipotent, omniscient and good. P describes what God does rather than what God is, but those later descriptions are in keeping with the theology described here.

The main argument against strict monotheism is the question of why a good God should allow suffering and evil. There are four basic answers, which have remained the same since P's time. Three are that God lacks complete power, or knowledge, or goodness. The fourth is the 'free will defence': that God is indeed perfectly omniscient, omniscient and good, but has withdrawn from complete power so as to allow humans freedom to choose between good and evil. This theory produces the distinction between God's absolute power and God's regular power which the medieval scholastic explored. In the second and subsequent chapters of Genesis P dwells at length on the dangerous implications of God's gift of freedom;[15] our present concern, however, is with Chapter 1's insistence that God is indeed perfectly omnipotent, omniscient and good.

One of the attractions of polytheism is that it can explain disorder and tragedy as the result of interactions between different gods who contributed to creation. In the *Enuma Elish* a great deal happens in heaven before the world is created. This explains why the world was created: Marduk intended to relieve the gods of housework, so our role is to maintain their temples and offer sacrifices; if we do not, a return to the primeval chaos threatens.[16] Though supreme, Marduk had gained power through a historical sequence of heavenly events and could in theory lose it again. In Genesis by contrast there is only one God and there are no restrictions on God's power. The repeated refrain 'God said' followed by 'and it was so' establishes God's omnipotence.

Similarly with God's omniscience. Other ancient near eastern creation myths abound with stories of failed and imperfect creations. In Genesis, after the repeated 'God said' and 'and it was so' comes 'it was very good'. The creating mind not only has complete power to create exactly what was intended, but also gets it right every time.

Together with omnipotence and omniscience God's other main attribute is goodness. In the absence of any rivals or limitations God has no self-concern. Whereas in the *Enuma Elish* humans are created to serve the gods, Genesis 1 tells us that after creating us God *blessed* us, and later books in the Pentateuch, especially Deuteronomy, insist that it is for our own well-being that God has created us and given us laws.

Here then is a text which differs from all other known ancient near eastern texts by its emphatic monotheism. This is qualified only by the absence of a doctrine of creation out of nothing. That idea developed much later, but perhaps is a legitimate development. Claus Westermann describes four main types of ancient near eastern creation myth: creation through word, making, birth and conflict.[17] P of course has no place for creation by conflict; instead he combines creation by word and by making, each of which is monotheistic but open to a polytheistic interpretation: creation by decree denies the influence of other gods but can be taken to imply magic or subordinate deities being commanded, while creation by making avoids any hint of other gods but can be taken to imply pre-existent materials not created by God. P uses the best tools available to express monotheism.[18]

Order

Having established what kind of God Genesis is affirming let us now turn to the acts of creation. The first three constitute, so to speak, the physics of creation. God performs acts of separation: between light and darkness, between the earth and what is above and below it, and between the earth and the waters surrounding it. These describe the dimensions within which ancient Jews and their neighbours believed they lived.

The first is time, expressed by the alternation of day and night. Commentators have noted an inconsistency: P is aware that light comes from the sun and moon, but describes the creation of light first and the heavenly bodies later. This inconsistency suggests theological purpose. The Babylonians were the first to develop astrology, on the basis that the heavenly bodies were gods who could see and influence events on earth.[19] P suppresses the idea; they are created by God, their creation is relegated to a late stage and even their names are not mentioned: the sun and moon are merely referred to as greater and lesser lamps.[20]

The second separation is the vertical one. Here Genesis diverges most strongly from modern science. Throughout the ancient near east it was taken for granted that when one looks up at the sky on a sunny day what one is seeing is a solid inverted bowl, translated into English sometimes as 'dome', sometimes as 'firmament'. The Hebrew word means something that has been hammered out; Homer described it as made of iron.[21] The text tells us that it separated the waters above it from the waters below it. The picture being painted here is the classic ancient near eastern one. The earth is flat. Above it is the sky, topped with its solid firmament; and waters swirl above the firmament and below the earth.[22]

The third separation is the horizontal one. God commanded the waters under the dome to recede, making space for dry land and thus preparing for the creation of animals and humans. In these three acts of separation God establishes time, and the vertical and horizontal dimensions of space, as permanent features of reality at the very beginning.

In other ancient near eastern creation myths what is created is always to some extent relative. The dominant god is usually a young one, has often gained preeminence through battle, and represents the dominant political power. The gods representing earlier empires are not completely forgotten but are kept in the list of gods, demoted to inferior status. Since the current world order has been established by the youngest generation in a succession of gods it is possible that one day things may change again. Such changes are expressed on earth by the rise and fall of empires, and perhaps also by changing natural phenomena – plagues and floods, the appearance and disappearance of giants. In principle *anything* could change if a new supreme god chooses to change it. The monotheism of Genesis tells a radically different story. By breaking the connection between the supremacy of the nation and the supremacy of the national god, and conceiving of the nation as a 'chosen people' in ways which were nothing to do with conquering empires, they were able to envisage a supreme God establishing an order which is independent of the ups and downs of military power. If it is correct to interpret the first act of creation as the creation of time, then not only does the idea of a prehistory before it become meaningless but also the idea of a subsequent history after the rule of this God becomes equally meaningless. These three acts of separation establish *order*, and locate it in *all physical reality and all time*.[23] Polytheists have no theoretical basis for expecting the world to be so ordered, let alone so permanently and reliably; nor, as postmodernists point out, do atheists.

Comprehensibility

Whereas Genesis 1 emphasises order to express a radical difference between monotheism and polytheism, comprehensibility was not under dispute. The surrounding polytheists knew that the world processes they experienced contained many regularities. Crops might be destroyed by floods or droughts because of a god's anger, but they still needed to be planted and harvested at certain times of year. They did not share either the early modern hope of establishing complete knowledge of the universe, or twentieth century non-realism and allied theories of radical ignorance. It was taken for granted that the ways of the world could be understood well enough for everyday purposes while much of it was beyond human comprehension.

Comprehensibility is therefore not asserted so strongly in Genesis 1. It is, though, still part of the story. Two affirmations are worth noting: that God created us 'in his image and likeness' and that God gave us 'dominion' over other living beings. Both have been the objects of extensive discussion.

Image and likeness have often been interpreted to mean that humans have God-like qualities, either mental ones like the ability to reason or physical ones like the ability to stand on two feet. Most Hebrew scholars now believe the text represents a democratized version of imperial practice. It was customary for ancient near eastern emperors to mark their authority over subject regions by erecting statues of themselves in prominent places. These statues were the 'image and likeness' of the emperor and functioned as signs, reminding the people who the supreme ruler was. The ruler, in turn, was the chief representative of the nation's god.[24] P adapted this tradition for the post-exilic situation. Israel no longer had its human emperor; instead, God was its emperor. God was to be represented neither by a human ruler nor, as the Ten Commandments insist, by carved statues; instead the God of the whole world was represented throughout the inhabited world by humans, and more specifically by the Judean community as it obeyed the laws in the Pentateuch.

It appears, then, that calling humans the 'image and likeness' of God is an analogy with the way statues are images and likenesses of emperors. The implication is that humans, while not ourselves the legitimate rulers of the world - because God is – do *symbolize* God to the world. We have a point of connection with God, a *relationship* with God, which other living beings do not have.

God's gift to humanity of 'dominion' over other living beings has been central to western Christian debates about the legitimate use of technology. At their most extreme, supporters of technology argued that it gives us permission to do whatever we wish with everything in the physical world except other humans.[25] Conversely, others have blamed Christianity for its environmentally reckless character. The authors of Genesis, of course, had no idea what scope modern science would give for adapting our environment. They were, however, aware of the latest technologies in their own culture, the domestication of cattle and ploughing the land. Both raised religious questions which have been asked all over the world. We would not find it acceptable for cows to domesticate us; why is it acceptable for us to domesticate them? Does digging the ground cause pain to Mother Earth? Responding to these questions, P tells us that neither animals nor the earth are divine; they have been created by God, and God has intentionally designed us with the capacity to make use of them. This still does not mean we can do whatever we like with them, and later texts in the Pentateuch lay down a great many limits. Nevertheless human technologies are in principle legitimate practices.[26] We are encouraged to make use of the resources God has made available to us.

It is this humanity, created in the divine image and given dominion over other animals, who will be given freedom, law, creativity and desire in Chapter 2, will misuse them in Chapter 3, and whose misuses will cause greater and greater misfortunes in subsequent chapters, setting the scene for the call of Abraham, the creation of Israel and the imposition of law. P describes us as free, capable of reflecting on the consequences of our actions and therefore morally responsible. Although the emphasis here is moral rather than scientific the roles of knowledge and technology are acknowledged. P affirms, and approves of, our ability to observe features of the world's order, understand them, and plan our lives accordingly. It is arguable that the authors intended either the image and likeness text or the dominion text, or both, to convey just this; even if not, the comprehensibility of the world remains essential to their account of humanity's God-given authority to till the earth, domesticate animals and choose between good and evil.

Practical details

By contrast, the practical details which anti-evolutionists and six-day creationists prefer to emphasize are borrowings from the beliefs of the day which are not at all essential to P's theological message. Whether or not they accord with modern science they express how the people of the ancient near east understood the world. The overall order of events for example matches the

Enuma Elish in many ways: chaos at the beginning followed by the creation of the firmament, dry land, the heavenly bodies and people. God's rest corresponds with the Babylonian feast of the gods when the creation is complete. Other scholars have argued for additional correlations.[27] For Christians today to insist that these were divinely inspired truths is to say that the *Babylonians* were inspired and the authors of Genesis copied them.

On these matters there is, though, one significant change, the conversion of an eight-day creation into a six-day creation. Even here it is inconceivable that P would have been motivated by blue skies speculation about the exact number of days it took God to create the world. These authors inherited the eight acts of creation and had no wish to eliminate any of them. However elsewhere in the Pentateuch they emphasize that everybody, including slaves and even cattle, should be protected from over-exploitation by being granted a day of rest every seven days. If we were to be convinced that the text is God's way of telling us the scientific facts about creation, we would have to conclude that, unlike modern scientists, the ancient Babylonians got most of the facts right but were just two days out in the time creation took. Instead of treating Genesis like this we should celebrate its achievement. By describing the creation of the world as a work of six days followed by a day of rest, P presents the Sabbath as an inherent part of a universal established order. Not just Jews but *everyone* should have a regular day of rest. Rarely has an economic innovation met with such widespread and long-lasting success as the Jewish invention of the week.[28]

Conclusion

To summarize, when scholars compare Genesis 1 with other ancient near eastern texts, a pattern emerges. The factual details which modern science considers inaccurate were not the message of Genesis; they were merely the beliefs about the world which were traditional in that time and place, and which the authors of

Genesis accepted. On the other hand when we turn from what these authors inherited and accepted to what they positively affirmed, we find an emphatic message which is theological. Reacting against the polytheism dominant at the time they hammer home a strict monotheism: the world and everything in it have been created by the one and only God who has complete power and knowledge. The basic structure of reality is ordered, and permanently so. Part of God's creative gift is to delegate power to humans, and with it the ability to understand how the world operates.

Where the authors of Genesis made changes to the accounts of creation they had inherited, they did so for theological reasons: to deny other gods and creation by conflict, to present humans not as slaves working to meet divine needs but as free and blessed agents, to establish the Sabbath rest. The descriptive details they retained were the tools they used to express their theology. What they were proclaiming was not that God created the world *flat*, but that the flat world has been created by *this God*; not that the world was created *in six days*, but that the six-day creation tells us *to rest as well as work*; not that God created humans *as a separate species*, but that the separately-created humans are endowed with *understanding, power and freedom, if we so wish, to become holy like God*.

Historically there is no doubt that this is the ground in which the seeds of modern science grew. Because P's successors understood the world to be ordered, intended, and benign it made sense to speculate about the nature of that order. It was not a linear progression: often enough the ubiquitous presence of angels and evil spirits manipulating the environment made it hard to believe the world was ordered, and some medieval scholars argued that the attempt to establish regularities in nature were heretical denials of God's freedom. Nevertheless order, and science, eventually triumphed.

It is most unfortunate that over the last couple of centuries this crucial text has so often been used to oppose the scientific outlook which it had once made possible. Rather than being embarrassed by the errors made by the authors of Genesis, Jews and Christians should celebrate them for their great insights: as far as we know they were the first writers to propose the hypothesis, essential to all science, that the world is ordered and the human mind is able to comprehend its order.

Notes

1 Mandelbaum, Maurice, *History, Man and Reason: A Study in Nineteenth Century Thought*, Baltimore: John Hopkins Press, 1971, provides a good discussion of the development of nineteenth century positivism.

2 I discuss this at greater length in Clatworthy, Jonathan, *Liberal Faith in a Divided Church*: O Books, 2008, Chapter 4.

3 Trigg, R, *Reality at* Risk, Brighton: Harvester, 1980, especially pp. 5, 9, 61-62.

4 Kaiser, Christopher, *Toward a Theology of Scientific Endeavour: The Descent of Science*, Aldershot: Ashgate, 2007, argues that four features are essential in any society capable of generating scientific research: the belief that the universe is lawful, the belief that the human mind is capable of understanding it, a cultural tradition which encourages the investigation of hidden aspects of the world, and a social and technological infrastructure able to support new research. It is the first two, order and comprehensibility, on which I focus here.

5 Honderich, Ted, *How Free Are You?*, Oxford: OUP, 1993, Chapter 2; Trigg, *Reality at Risk*, , p. 49; Kenny, Anthony, *The Metaphysics of Mind*, Oxford: OUP, 1989, p. 4; O'Hear, Anthony, *An Introduction to the Philosophy of Science*, Oxford: OUP, 1991, pp. 207-8.

6 E.g. *The Gospel of Truth* 28-30. Robinson, James M, *The Nag Hammadi Library: The Definitive New Translation of the Gnostic Scriptures, Complete in One Volume*, San Francisco:

HarperCollins, 1990, p. 45; and the Seventh Hermetic Tractate 2.3, Rudolph, *Gnosis*, p. 114 (and see also the discussion on pp. 90-92).

[7] See Patricia Churchland's argument in *Journal of Philosophy* 84 (October 1987), p. 548, quoted in Helm, Paul, Ed, *Faith and Reason*, Oxford: OUP, 1999, p. 265. 'Boiled down to essentials, a nervous system enables the organism to succeed in the four F's: feeding, fleeing, fighting and reproducing... A fancier style of representing is advantageous *so long as it is geared to the organism's way of life and enhances the organism's chances of survival* [Churchland's emphasis]. Truth, whatever that is, definitely takes the hindmost.'

[8] As David Hume pointed out in the eighteenth century, when we say that one event causes another, what we actually observe is only that one event is habitually followed by another. However often we observe the second event following the first, we never perceive the first causing the second; the idea of causation is supplied by our minds. Hume, David, *Enquiries Concerning Human Understanding and Concerning the Principles of Morals*, Oxford: OUP, 11th impression 1990 of 3rd Edition (1975), 7.2.60.

[9] Kaiser, Christopher, *Creation and the History of Science*, London: Marshall Pickering, 1991, pp. 4-34.

[10] Gaskin, J C A, *Hume's Philosophy of Religion*, London: Macmillan, 1978, pp. 17-37 & 94-106.

[11] O'Hear, *Science*, Chapter 2.

[12] Harris, Harriet, *Fundamentalism and Evangelicals*, Oxford: Clarendon, 1998, pp. 161-66.

[13] Westermann, Claus, *Genesis 1-11*, Minneapolis: Fortress, 1994, p. 120.

[14] Westermann, *Genesis 1-11*, pp. 97 & 97.

[15] I have discussed this in my *Good God: Green Theology and the Value of Creation*, Jon Carpenter, 1997, Chapter 2.

[16] Westermann, *Genesis 1-11*, p. 36.

[17] Westermann, *Genesis 1-11*, p. 29.

[18] Westermann, *Genesis 1-11*, pp. 26-47.

[19] Westermann, *Genesis 1-11*, pp. 132-134.

[20] Westermann, *Genesis 1-11*, p. 112.

[21] Westermann, *Genesis 1-11*, p. 117.

[22] Westermann, *Genesis 1-11*, pp. 116-7.

[23] Westermann, *Genesis 1-11*, pp. 80-123.

[24] Westermann, *Genesis 1-11*, pp. 147-158; Barr, James, *Biblical Faith and Natural Theology*, Oxford: Clarendon, 1993, Chapter 8.

[25] In effect the idea has been central to the cult of technology since Francis Bacon's arguments to this effect. See Merchant, Carolyn, *The Death of Nature: Women, Ecology and the Scientific Revolution*, San Francisco: HarperCollins, 1983.

[26] Murray, Robert, *The Cosmic Covenant*, London: Sheed & Ward, 1992, p. 98.

[27] Westermann, *Genesis 1-11*, p. 89.

[28] Westermann, *Genesis 1-11*, pp. 167-173.

Jonathan Clatworthy is the General Secretary of the Modern Churchpeople's Union. Previously he has been a parish priest, university chaplain and tutor in ethics. He is the author of *Liberal Faith in a Divided Church*, (O Books), 2008.

Fundamentalism in a Multicultural Society

Harriet Harris

Multiculturalism

The bombings in London in July 2005, the discovery of further alleged plots by Islamic would-be suicide bombers, and subsequent trials of those arrested, have led to fresh debates about the wisdom or folly of promoting multiculturalism. Multiculturalism offers a model of communities within a community, encouraging people to promote a strong sense of their cultural and religious identities, and, if they like, to develop their own faith schools? But does such a model lead to segregationism and threaten social cohesion and national security? Should the government promote policies of assimilation or cultural integration instead?

The term 'multiculturalism' was coined in 1965 by a Canadian Royal Commission, and was widely used in the 1970s, in both Canada and Australia, to name a government policy of assisting the management of ethnic pluralism within these nations. It is an alternative for policies of assimilation, and one supported by the Chief Rabbi Dr Jonathan Sacks. In Dr Sacks' context, support for multiculturalism partially reflects unresolved Jewish concerns that the Jewish people put themselves at risk when they tried to become assimilated into European culture in the C18, C19 and C20; a culture that then almost eradicated them. Multicultural policies are intended to ensure that 'all citizens can keep their identities, can take pride in their ancestry, and have a sense of belonging' (Government of Canada, 2001). Multiculturalism is associated in principle with values of equality, tolerance and inclusiveness, and with an affirmation of the value of cultural diversity.

By the late C20 most Western liberal democracies described

themselves as multicultural societies, because their national boundaries had become so porous, although few embraced official policies of multiculturalism. In 1998, a Commission on the Future of Multi-ethnic Britain was set up by the Runnymede Trust to propose ways of 'making Britain a confident and vibrant multicultural society at ease with its rich diversity'. Bhikhu Parekh chaired the Commission, and stated famously in the Introduction to the Report (which is sometimes also known as the Parekh Report):

> ...citizens are both individuals and members of particular religious, ethnic, cultural and regional communities. Britain is both a community of citizens and a community of communities, both a liberal and a multicultural society...' (Introduction to the Report on *The Future of Multi-Ethnic Britain*).

Being both liberal and multicultural gives rise to 'conflicting requirements' (Parekh), which are often expressed in terms of how liberal the state should be towards people who are not themselves liberal. But that is a one-sided way of stating the issues. The Parekh Report is in some ways an exercise in exploring what it means to be liberal across diverse people groups. For example, it requires balancing the need to defend and promote human rights and, more broadly, a shared body of values, whilst not defining these so narrowly as to suppress non-dominant, legitimate ways of life. Matters such as the smacking of children, same-gendered unions, types of religious content in school curricula or women wearing veils are examples of moral differences deep enough to raise questions over what counts as a legitimate way of life.

Multiculturalist policies also face the problem of how to promote a sense of belonging and a shared identity, whilst nurturing diversity. This is a key area that exercises educationalists. There is a twofold goal to educate people for citizenship in British society, and to grow in understanding and appreciation of the traditions of their families' culture(s). In the 1980s 'multiculturalism' became a buzzword in the USA in the context of state school curricula. Curricula were criticised for their Eurocentric bias, and their focus on dead, white, middle-class men. It is partly this legacy which leads to the association of multiculturalism with political correctness. Afrocentrism was one multiculturalist response to curriculum reform. It sought to document the centrality of Africa in Western history and the foundation of America. Michael Nazir-Ali, the Bishop of Rochester, wrote an article in *The Telegraph* in August of this year, arguing that 'Multiculturalism is to blame for perverting young Muslims' (Nazir-Ali's article appeared on August 15, 2006). He seems to accuse the government of lack of vigilance, in that 'in the name of multiculturalism, mosque schools were encouraged and Muslim pupils spent up to six hours a day learning the Koran and Islamic tradition, as well as their own regional languages' - although he does not explain what he thinks is wrong with this.

Creation scientists make capital out of multiculturalist sympathies to defend their right to have their view of the world taught in schools. To a leftist critic of multiculturalism, this situation reveals the complacency that multiculturalism within liberal society engenders: it enables diverse groups to exist side-by-side without bothering to engage with one another. To a rightist critic, it is an example of how multiculturalism weakens common, rational and scientific consensus by promoting discrete faith communities.

Rational Debate as an Antidote?

I would like to focus on this particular aspect of rightist criticism: *viz.*, the assumption that if we aim for greater integration, then religious extremism could be met by rational debate. I haven't come across a fully-fleshed out proposal along these lines, but have heard and read many times in the media, the linking of 'Prejudice, Fanaticism, Fundamentalism and a rejection of rational, scientific thinking' (Mike Norris, reply to Nazir Ali's article cited above, posted on the *Telegraph's* website on August 18, 2006).

Salman Rushdie, Yasmin Alibai-Brown, and Tariq Ali, all maintained after September 11th 2001, that Islam needs to experience something equivalent to the Protestant Reformation in order to bring to it the virtue of critical and free enquiry. To quote Tariq Ali: 'We are in desperate need of an Islamic Reformation that sweeps away the crazed conservatism and backwardness of the fundamentalists....This would necessitate a rigid separation of state and mosque; the dissolution of the clergy; the assertion by Muslim intellectuals of their right to interpret the texts...[and] the freedom to think freely and rationally...'. And yet these were precisely the conditions under which fundamentalism took root in Protestant America. There, fundamentalists have always defended the separation of church and state so that the state cannot interfere with their practices. (The Waco massacre has become something of an obsession for the Far Christian Right.) Contrary to Tariq Ali's thinking, it is likely that where Church and state have separated in Western democracies, this has enabled fundamentalism to flourish. Religious historians suggest that Christians are less fundamentalist in Britain than in America precisely because of the modifying effects of church-state links and of keeping religious education and theology as disciplines within public, state-run institutions.

What about Ali's proposal to free scripture from the hands of clergy, and to promote free, rational thought? Protestant fundamentalists stand in a Reformation tradition that frees scripture from the hands of clergy. They uphold the right and ability of everyone to read and understand scripture. This is a key Protestant principle and has been politically and spiritually revolutionary. Few people would wish to go back on it. But it has led to Protestant fundamentalists finding in the pages of scripture justification for segregating the races, for beating wives and children, for murdering doctors in abortion clinics, and for building nuclear weapons in the expectation of an imminent apocalypse. With such examples in mind, it is tempting to agree with the moral theologian Stanley Hauerwas, who says, slightly tongue in cheek but only slightly: 'No task is more important than for the church to take the Bible out of the hands of individual Christians in North America. Let us no longer give the Bible to every child when they enter the third grade... Let us rather tell them and their parents that they are possessed by habits far too corrupt for them...to read the Bible on their own'.

Tariq Ali was specifically interested in Muslim intellectuals asserting their freedom to interpret the Qur'an. This begs the question of who is to count as intellectual. Within even very separatist Protestant fundamentalist Bible-schools there are scholars well trained in the biblical languages who provide intellectual muscle to a fundamentalist apologetic. I expect there are similar figures within Islam. To question whether they really are intellectual opens up the question of what counts as proper rational inquiry, and here is the rub. In the US in the 1920s, J. Gresham Machen railed against a `retrograde, anti-intellectual movement' which `degrades the intellect by excluding it from the sphere of religion' (1925:26, 18). He was a fundamentalist apologist, attacking 'modern liberalism'.

Contrary to the assumption that enlightened, rational, scientific thinking is a good antidote to fundamentalism, fundamentalists are not deterred by rational debate. I will demonstrate this with respect to Protestant fundamentalists, who bear the original and most authentic expression of fundamentalism. Protestant fundamentalists, more than most other Christians, regard faith as a rational and scientific matter. Rationality and hard empirical evidence are deeply important to them. But I have found more parallels than I had expected with Islamist thinking, and with so-called 'fundamentalisms' of other faiths, and I will go on to illustrate some of these parallels.

Fundamentalism

I have used the term 'fundamentalism' without yet explaining what I mean by it. The term 'fundamentalism' was coined in 1920 by a Northern Baptists in the USA who called together a coalition of religious conservatives to 'do battle royale' for the fundamentals of the faith. So the term 'fundamentalism' was originally a self-designation, and still is for many Protestants, especially in the US. It quickly became a contentious term amongst evangelicals, and remains so today[1]

Fundamentalism involves the defence of fundamentals, but is significantly different from traditionalism, in that the fundamentalist impulse is to by-pass tradition in order to get straight back to the Bible. In this respect fundamentalists have an ahistorical, primitivist notion of (biblical) truth. I have found that the most accurate and instructive way to describe fundamentalism is as a way of believing that requires a fundament or fixed foundation upon which to build faith. In the Protestant Christian world, fundamentalists are those who believe that Christian faith stands or falls on the reliability of scripture, by which they usually mean its factual reliability. Not all are politicised. Some withdraw from politics out of a conviction that the world is going to the devil and Christ will come to save his own. But all defend the Bible and are defensive about the Bible as though their faith and lives depend upon it. The philosopher-theologian Francis Schaeffer gave voice to their position from 1960s to the 1980s. He said: 'Unless the Bible is without error, our spiritual and physical children will be left with the ground cut out from under them, with no foundation upon which to build their faith or their lives'.

It is this strong foundationalism that renders fundamentalists so rationally minded. Foundationalism is a particular way of modelling how our various beliefs relate to one another. It portrays a system of beliefs as built upon foundations which are themselves self-justifying. It has been dominant in Western thought, and so is by no means unique to fundamentalists (Murphy 1996; Plantinga and Wolterstorff 1983; Wood 1998). Liberal Protestantism posits universal religious experience as foundational, and places Scripture further up the belief structure, as manifesting the religious experience of its authors. This is why Machen regarded modern liberalism as anti-intellectual, and why fundamentalists today characterise liberalism as subjective, speculative, arbitrary, and overly influenced by experience and feeling.

Fundamentalism treats Scripture as foundational. Hence a fundamentalist theology invariably begins with the doctrine of Scripture, because of the conviction that the Bible must be secured before we can go on to build a theology (from it) (Harris 1998b). Within this tradition, the Bible has frequently been described as the 'textbook' of theology (e.g. Packer 1958: 112; Stott 1982: 188). The dominant method for inferring doctrines from Scripture has been 'Biblical induction', by which the systematician collects relevant texts on a given topic and develops from them general conclusions (Stott 1982:183).

Within this way of thinking, faith is regarded as a matter of rational assent to evidence. BB Warfield, one of the scholars from Princeton Theological Seminary, whose thought provided the main intellectual substance of C20 fundamentalist movement, insisted that although faith is a gift of God, it 'is yet formally conviction passing into confidence; and... all forms of convictions must rest on evidence as their ground, and it is not faith but reason which investigates the nature and validity of this ground' (Warfield [1908]:15). He held that faith and knowledge alike 'rest equally on evidence and are equally the product of evidence' (Warfield [1911b]:330), the only difference being that knowledge is based on perception and faith on testimony, so that faith involves a greater element of trust.

The Princeton theologians, and subsequent fundamentalist apologists defended the absolute trustworthiness of biblical testimony, so that faith could be rationally ground. They were heavily influenced by C18 Scottish Common Sense Philosophy. Thomas Reid (1710-1796), the principal exponent of Common Sense philosophy, was a moderate Presbyterian clergyman who said little about the Bible, and what he did say suggested that he would have endorsed a critical programme of testing scripture by reason.[2] However, his philosophical realism provided intellectual reinforcement for the belief that in scripture we have reliable accounts of actual states of affairs. His views on perception, memory and testimony are all pertinent. He defended the common sense belief that we perceive the outside world directly and not through intermediary ideas (as was the view of Locke and Hume), and therefore that our understanding of the world is not determined by subjective factors. He also argued that memory puts us in relation with the objects remembered, and not with our idea of those objects, and that testimony can be trusted (with certain qualifications) to tell us of actual events in the experience of others, and not simply the reporter's point of view.

The appeal of his realist philosophy for later fundamentalist apologetics was that it could be used to support the conviction that the biblical records inform us not of ideas or interpretations of events, but of events themselves. This was a welcome antidote to the German Idealist influence behind higher-criticism, which named Kant and Hegel in its ancestry. Machen, who was also from Princeton, and the most intellectual apologist for the funda-mentalist cause in the 1920s, insisted that the 'Bible is quite useless unless it is a record of facts' (1936:65). His philosophical differences with modernists became intensely relevant in debates over the nature of Jesus' resurrection. Machen decried the modernist concern with 'the belief of the disciples in the resur-rection' which refused to deal with 'whether the events really took place'[3]. He insisted that the biblical narratives are factual accounts of real events from the past. A number of commentators, including HL Mencken who was no friend of fundamentalism, thought that Machen had the stronger arguments, and that his liberal critics never satisfactorily answered him

Suspicion of interpretation

I hope I have gone some way in illustrating the rationalism of Protestant fundamentalism: a system that bases faith on reason and specifically on the evidence provided in biblical testimony. I will now illustrate some parallels with Islamist thinking.

In order to be sure that scripture is reliable, it is important within Protestant fundamentalism that human agency does not obstruct divine communication. God needs to deliver the words of scripture, it seems, to ensure that the human scribes get the facts right. Within this theology, to say that scripture is the Word of God is to hold that all of the words are God's own words. This renders the Protestant fundamentalist view of scripture very similar, though not identical, to orthodox Islam's view of the Qur'an as revelation given by dictation. Protestant fundamentalists insist that they do not hold a doctrine of dictation, and that the humanity and personality of the scribes is present in their writing. Nevertheless, they do insist that all the words of the Bible, at least in the original autographs, are God's own words.

Given this direct communication from God, it is important that human interpretation does not then undermine scripture's immediacy. The Bible must be perspicuous, readily accessible by everyone. This is where the idea of the 'plain sense' of the text and the ability of the 'plain man' to understand it, comes into play.

This concern is reflected well in an exchange between William Jennings Bryan and Clarence Darrow at the infamous Scopes Trial of 1925 when a school teacher in Tennessee was prosecuted for teaching evolution. Bryan was the prosecuting lawyer, but

Darrow called him as a witness for the defence, and asked him if his readings of Scripture were not in fact interpretations:

Bryan: I would not say interpretations, Mr. Darrow, but comments on the lesson.

Darrow: If you comment to any extent these comments have been interpretations?

Bryan: I presume that any discussion might be to some extent interpretations; but they have not been primarily intended as interpretations.

Darrow: Do you claim that everything in the Bible should be literally interpreted?

Bryan: I believe everything in the Bible should be accepted as it is given there... (Scopes Trial Transcript, 1925:734-35).

More recently, the British creation-scientist David C. C. Watson has argued that Scripture 'no more requires interpretation than the... cricket scores in your morning paper' (1975, 1989: 37). If Scripture needs interpreting, the foundation of faith is shifting rather than fixed.

A number of Muslim and Jewish scholars have regarded such suspicion of the interpretation of Scripture as peculiar to Protestant fundamentalism, as have I (Hassan 1990; Wieseltier 1990. Cf. Barr 1977: 7, 182, 284-86.)

Jewish 'fundamentalists' have allegiances to particular rabbinic traditions, Islamists to particular schools of law. Both consciously reside within traditions of interpretation. For example, Ayatollah Khomeini insisted that the Qur'an and Hadith cannot be understood outside of eleven centuries of Shi'a scholarship.

However, Islamists' disagree amongst themselves over the place of interpretation, partly depending on whether they are Sunni or Shi'a Muslims, and some hold views remarkably similar to those of Protestant fundamentalists.

Shi'i Muslims believe the Qur'an was created and came into existence in the seventh century CE. Therefore they insist on careful exegesis and interpretation, which involves reading the Qur'an with reference to seventh-century Arabia. Sunni Muslims believe that the Qur'an was uncreated, that it is eternally and universally valid in a way that does not require such interpretation. Shi'i Muslims are sometimes described as being more 'catholic', and Sunni more 'Protestant' in their approach to Scripture (Goddard 2002:150). Within Shi'i Islam, *'aql* (reason) came to be considered one of the four legitimate sources of guidance along with the Qur'an, the Hadith (Muslim tradition), and the *ijma* (consensus) of the community. Most Sunni Muslims also recognize sources other than the Qur'an as legitimate for guidance, but in recent centuries a view has emerged that the earliest generation provides the supreme model, and later history is a corruption rather than a legitimate development of the tradition. These Sunni attitudes resemble radical elements of the Protestant Reformation, which regarded Christian history since the days of the Apostles to be a process of corruption (Goddard 2002:154-55). This, then, is the likeliest place to look for similarities between Protestant and Sunni forms of scriptural fundamentalism. Here we find that there are Muslims who are as distrustful as Protestant fundamentalists of the role of interpretation, and as confident about accessing the plain sense of the text.

Within Sunni Islam, the ancestry of this view can be traced back to Ahmad ibn Hanbal in the ninth century. The Hanbali legal school named after him does not accept either *ijma* or *quiyas,* and takes only the Qur'an and Hadith as sufficient authority on which to base conclusions. Descendants of this way of thinking include the eighteenth-century Wahabbi movement in Arabia, and many later groups sometimes collectively known as the Salafiyya – those who base themselves on the *Salaf* (the ancestors), the first generation of Muslims (Goddard 2002:155). They can be said to reveal a primitivism similar to that of Protestant fundamentalists. Indeed, one recent commentator likens the self-taught Salafiyya reformists to fire-breathing Protestant fundamentalists, both of whom abjure traditional scholarship, and who between them are precipitating a clash of civilizations (Ernst 2004). Kureishi describes visiting some mosques in Whitechapel and Shepherd's Bush where: 'There would be passionate orators haranguing a group of people sitting on the floor....there would be diatribes against the west, Jews and – their favourite subject – homosexuals. Men from these mosques, he said 'believed they had access to the Truth, as stated in the Qur'an. There could be no doubt – or even much dispute about moral, social and political problems – because God had the answers. Therefore, to argue with the Truth was like trying to disagree with the facts of geometry' (in *The Guardian* August 4, 2005). Muslims reflecting this Salafist approach are currently involved in separatist or violent responses to the Western world. Fifteen of the nineteen suicide hijackers of September 11, 2001, were Saudi citizens, and therefore influenced by Wahabbism.

Tariq Ramadan, grandson of Hasan al-Banna, who founded the Muslim Brotherhood in Egypt in 1927, has recently criticized his grandfather's Salafist followers. The Muslim Brotherhood called for the establishment of an Islamic state governed by *shar'ia* (divine law), as opposed to the secular Arab states governed by European laws. It today bears an influence over much of the Sunni Muslim world, and has given rise to a number of groups, such s HAMAS in Palestine, which have become separate entities. Ramadan (2004) criticizes al-Banna's present-day followers for teaching Muslims living in the West to keep themselves apart from their host cultures by, for example, adopting distinctive dress-codes. Ramadan himself counteracts these Salafist tendencies by arguing that on social matters (*al-muamalati)* the divine text of the Qur'an 'almost never allows itself, alone, to lay down a universal principle'. Rather, he says: 'it is the human mind that derives both absolute and relative principles, as appropriate, from the Text and from the reality of the context in which it was revealed' (Ramadan, 2004: 21). He emphasises that 'the Revelation was elaborated in time and space, over twenty-three years, in a certain context, expressed in pronouncements affected by circumstance, open to evolution, accessible to reason in a historical setting (Ramadan 2004:21). He reminds Salafists that when they appeal to Scripture they are always interpreting: 'There can be no revealed Text unless there is human intellect up to the task of reading and interpreting it' (Ramadan 2004:20).

If the dynamic in Sunnism is anything like that within Protestantism, Ramadan's argument will be like water off a duck's back to the Salafists. Protestant fundamentalists take no notice of people who argue that all readings of scripture are interpretations, and that the human intellect must be applied responsibly to gain understanding from the scriptures. They believe that human beings reason correctly, or that rationality is only truly itself, when operating in the context of acceptance of (their understanding of) the Bible's authority. Generally they operate under the belief that certain premises are necessary if the study of scripture is to be true to the nature scripture:

> 'scientific', 'objective' study of anything is simply study of it in terms of itself, and... Scripture is studied 'scientifically' and 'objectively' when - and only when - it is studied in full recognition of its character as Scripture, the infallible Word of God (Packer 1958a:157).

We are back to the question of who is behaving most rationally. Fundamentalists believe that they are, and that to make human reason the judge of scripture, is to be polluted by subjectivism. Not surprisingly, attempts at rational debate with fundamentalists drive people to distraction. They do not, as I said at the beginning, deter fundamentalists.

Finding Flaws in the System

That said, it is possible to reveal flaws in the fundamentalist system, and this is one way of educating people out of fundamentalism. It is rather torturous, and less effective than other ways of encouraging trust from fundamentalists, but I can set down some possible moves

The logic of Protestant fundamentalists is tight, but it is not watertight. A key area of leakage in their system is around the question of the relationship of faith to reason. Fundamentalists argue against making reason the judge of scripture, but they build their system of faith on reason being the judge of scripture: on rational and empirical arguments for the authority of the Bible. They attempt more than most other Christians to base faith on reason. They then become doubly inconsistent in that they also place reason within the context of faith and make capital out of the ways in which faith, especially following Michael Polanyi's work, has been identified as an aspect of scientific inquiry.

Creation scientists are interesting in this respect. They waver between arguing that evolution is no less a religion than Christianity, and proposing that creation science is no less scientific than evolution. The point is that in some contexts fundamentalists recognise that something prerational lies at the base of all worldviews. Even then, they do not usually talk about the prior role of faith (perhaps because they are so conditioned to base faith on reason), but rather the prior role of presuppositions. A frustration of arguing with fundamentalists is that they insist that rationality is fundamental to faith, but at the same time they only regard as rational those positions that reflect their own claims about the nature of scripture. If one were to point out that it is a pre-rational move to render claims about scripture a condition of what counts as rational, they would reply that all systems of thought operate with presuppositions, and that they have as much right to their presuppositions as the next person.

By now the fundamentalist system is full of holes, but the

fundamentalist might no longer care. Their interest in presuppositions reveals an important feature of fundamentalism in today's world. Fundamentalist apologists no longer believe in universal reason, as did the Common Sense Philosophers. They use the language of presuppositions in ways that can make them complacent, and compliant with multiculturalism. The Dean of Bob Jones University told me in the 1990s, that he was a pluralist, because he believed that everyone has a right to their beliefs, based on their presuppositions. He was happy for his separatist institution to coexist with all sorts of diverse communities, and saw no particular need to engage with them. His version of pluralism would fuel the left-wing critics of multiculturalism, who see multiculturalism as discouraging engagement. Multiculturalism can foster a lazy form of 'tolerance', in which different parties have stopped having conversations.

Monoculturalism

But if multiculturalism is problematic, monoculturalism is worse. Arguably a form of monoculture has operated at a deep level in the proliferation of fundamentalist movements around the world. Despite these movements existing across very diverse faiths, from Islam to Hinduism, they share many of the same rationalistic and primitivist characteristics.

Almost all of the founders of, what we now call, fundamentalist movements around the world were educated in Western universities. I am thinking specifically of movements founded in the late C19 and early C20 in opposition to Western colonialism, including the Muslim Brotherhood, Hindutva groups and the Sinhalese Buddhists.

Ironically, although these movements all oppose Western cultural imperialism, they betray significant influence from western patterns of thought. For example, attempts to uncover pure Ancient Wisdom are purist in accusing other forms of Buddhism of elevating matters of secondary importance over the primary act of 'Going for Refuge'. The Order claims to develop a Buddhism for people living in the modern world, and has been described as 'Protestant Buddhist' for containing deeply ingrained western assumptions about returning to the essence or fundamentals of faith. The features we have identified in Protestant fundamentalism are part and parcel of this way of thinking: a conviction that the fundamental truth is easily accessible by reason and does not require the filter of tradition or of interpretative communities to help us understand it. found in strains of Hindu and Buddhist thought going back to the Theosophical Society of the nineteenth century. Theosophy was an American and British movement claiming that Asian religions were ethically and metaphysically superior to Christianity. The Western Buddhist Order (est. 1968 by Sangharakshita) is purist in accusing other forms of Buddhism of elevating matters of secondary importance over the primary act of 'Going for Refuge'. The Order claims to develop a Buddhism for people living in the modern world, and has been described as 'Protestant Buddhist' for containing deeply ingrained western assumptions about returning to the essence or fundamentals of faith. The features we have identified in Protestant fundamentalism are part and parcel of this way of thinking: a conviction that the fundamental truth is easily accessible by reason and does not require the filter of tradition or of interpretative communities to help us to understand it.

Effective Responses to Fundamentalism

I have aimed to show that trying to educate people out of fundamentalism by means of rational debate and a kind of rational monoculturalism is not effective, and mimics the conditions under which fundamentalism has flourished.

In terms of what I have experienced as effective responses to fundamentalism, I can speak only from the Protestant context, and would be interested to hear from Muslims and others whether my experience is paralleled in other contexts.

First of all, fundamentalists need to be put in touch with their own experience. Protestant fundamentalists use personal testimony to a great extent in describing conversion experiences and persuading others to join the faith. They also emphasise the importance of knowing Jesus Christ personally as their saviour. But this experiential side to their faith is not integrated into their apologetics, probably because fundamentalist apologists have argued that feelings and experience are dangerous as they can deceive us in ways that facts and reason will not. To enter into rational debate with a fundamentalist, you would be forgiven for thinking that their faith always depended upon rational arguments concerning the authority and teachings of scripture. But if you ask them how they came to faith, most agree that they were not won over by argument, but by friendship with believers, and by a warm experience of God's love and forgiveness.

So they need permission to bring their experience to bear on their concept of faith. They may then start to recognize non-cerebral, sacramental or mystical elements within Christian tradition. They also need permission to be honest about times when their experience feels empty. They may then come to appreciate forms of Christian worship that they had previously rejected as 'going through the motions'. Moving out of funda-mentalist thought-patterns is a huge relief for people, for it is a strain to have sustain belief in matters that seem unlikely or unreal to you, such as the Bible's very high level of factual accuracy, or the need for wives to submit to their husbands. And it is a strain to suspect that you are the only one who often feels nothing when reading the Bible or singing in church. The post-evangelical groups that have arisen since the 1990s are largely reacting against fundamentalist elements within their evangelical experience. Their largest concern is for greater authenticity in both conviction and worship. One group has even called itself Be Real.

People best able to pick up the pieces here, are people who can offer reassurance that a wide variety of feelings and absence of feeling, of arguments and the breakdown of arguments, are represented within the Christian faith, and that to go through such ups and downs is normal to the journey of faith. Those most able to respond effectively to fundamentalism are sufficiently immersed in their faith tradition to be able to show how that tradition is richer than the rationalist and ahistorical version fundamentalists espouse. They are people who can help fundamentalists acknowledge that they did not create or earn their faith (through being rationally persuaded), but received it as a gift. It is true of any of us that if we realize we are receiving something as a gift, we are less anxious about being able to retain it, and we are more humble and grateful in our attitudes. And if we realise that our faith is not fundamentally rational, which is not to say that it is irrational, but rather that its foundation is not characterised or established by reason, but rests in God's own self, then we relax about being able to shore up our faith with reason. Then we are less inclined to think we have the definitive answers, and more inclined to respect the wisdom of other strands of our broader faith tradition, such as apophatic strands. We are also more open to the wisdom of other faiths.

For all this to happen, we need diverse religious communities to be enabled to produce top-rate religious instructors and spiritual guides, who are fully trained in the depth and breadth of their religious traditions. This requires a level of multiculturalism. It is not sufficient, under an assimilationist model, to call for religious moderates to make their voices heard, and to persuade us of the reasonableness of their religion. We need people who can tap the passion of extremists and then persuade them of the richness of their own traditions, who know how to put them in touch with the experiential and mystical sides of their faith, who can show them that promoting an ahistorical understanding of their faith is actually a perversion of their faith, and can help them not to be afraid, defensive or aggressive when faith cannot be portrayed as a simple matter.

Notes

1 Many of whom will say that they are fundamentalists in that they defend the fundamentals of their faith, but that they are not out and out literalists (no fundamentalist is, by the way) or separatists, or premillennialists.

2 'It is no doubt true that Revelation exhibits all the truths of Natural Religion, but it is no less true that reason must be employed to judge of that revelation; whether it comes from God. Both are great lights and we ought not to put out the one in order to use the other .... We acknowledge then that men are indebted to revelation in the matter of Natural Religion but this is no reason why we should not also use our reason here... Tis by reason that we must judge whether that Revelation be really so... [T]hat man is best prepared for the study and practice of the revealed Religion who has previously acquired just Sentiments of the Natural.', *Lectures on Natural Theology*, pp. 1-2, quoted in Wolterstorff, 1983:63

3 'The Relation of Religion to Science and Philosophy', *Princeton Theological Review* XXIV (January, 1926): 38-66, quoted in Marsden 1980: 216-17.

References

Barr, J. 1997. *Fundamentalism*. London: SCM.

Ernst, C.W. 2004. Following Muhammed: Rethinking Islam in the contemporary world. North Carolina University Press; Edinburgh: Edinburgh University Press.

Goddard, H. 2002. 'Is Islam a "Fundamentalist" Religion?' in Percy, M. ed. *Fundamentalism, Church and Society*. London: SPCK: 145- 59.

Government of Canada, 2001. www.pch.gc.ca/muti/what-muti_e.shtml

Harris, Harriet A., 1998a. *Fundamentalism and Evangelicals*, Oxford: Oxford University Press.

Harris, Harriet A., 1998b. 'Fundamentalism and Theology', Farmington Paper, The Farimington Institute.

Hassan, R. 1990. 'The Burgeoning of Islamic Fundamentalism: toward an understanding of the Phenomenon': *The Fundamentalist Phenomenon: A View from Within; A Response from Without* ed. By Norman J. Cohen, Grand Rapids, Mich.: Eerdmans.

Kureishi, Hanif, 2005. 'The Carnival of Culture' *The Guardian* August 4

Machen, John Gresham, 1925. *What is Faith?* London: Hodder & Stoughton

Machen, John Gresham, 1936. *The Christian Faith in the Modern World* London: Hodder & Stoughton.

Marsden, George M. 1980. *Fundamentalism and American Culture: The Shaping of Twentieth Century Evangelicalism 1870-1925*, Oxford: Oxford University Press

Murphy, Nancey, 1996. *Beyond Liberalism and Fundamentalism: How Modern and Postmodern Philosophy Set the Theological Agenda*, Valley Forge: Penn.: Trinity Press International.

Nazir-Ali, Michael, 2006. 'Multiculturalism is to blame for perverting young Muslims', *The Telegraph*, August 15.

Packer, James I. 1958. *'Fundamentalism'and the Word of God*, London: Inter-Varsity Fellowship.

Parekh Report on *The Future of Multi-Ethnic Britain* (Runnymede Trust: 2000)

Plantinga, Alvin and Wolterstorff, Nicholas eds., 1983, *Faith and Rationality: Reason and Belief in God*, Notre Dame: University of Notre Dame Press.

Ramadan, T. 2004. *Western Muslims and the Future of Islam.* Oxford: Oxford University Press.

Scopes Trial Transcript, Billy Graham Center Archives, Collection

244-2, Wheaton College, Illinois.

Stott, John, 1982. *I believe in Preaching*, London: Hodder & Stoughton.

Warfield, B.B. [1908], 'Apologetics', reprinted in *Studies in Theology*, Edinburgh: Banner of Truth, 1932, 1988.

Warfield, B.B. [1911b]. 'On Faith in its Psychological Aspects' reprinted in Studies in Theology, Edinburgh: Banner of Truth, 1932, 1988

Watson, D.C.C. 1975, 1989. *The Great Brain Robbery*, [n.p.]: the author.

Wieseltier, L. 1990. The Jewish Face of Fundamentalism, in *The fundamentalist Phenomenon: A View from Within; A Response from Without* ed. By Norman J. Cohen. Grand Rapids, Mich. :Eerdmans.

Wood, W. Jay, 1998. *Epistemology: Becoming Intellectually Virtuous*, Leicester: Apollos.

Harriet Harries is a member of the Theology Faculty in Oxford, and Chaplain of Wadham College, Oxford. She is author of *Fundamentalism and Evangelicals* (Oxford University Press, 1998, 2008), and co-editor of *Faith and Philosophical Analysis* (Ashgate, 2005). Her chapter in this volume is an adaptation of the Roy Niblett Lecture, 2006, which she delivered to the Severn Forum at the University of Gloucestershire, Cheltenham.

Why Evil, Suffering, and Death?

Russell Stannard

Introduction

God is held to be all-powerful; all-knowing; all-loving; all-good. But does that make sense? If God is like that, why is there evil, suffering, and death in the world he created? This is an age-old problem, dating back to Old Testament times - the biggest stumbling block to people taking religion seriously.

There is no clear-cut, pat answer. We are up against a mystery. By 'mystery' we do not mean a puzzle or a riddle with some neat solution, and all we have to do is be clever enough to find that solution. By 'mystery' we mean something which lies - and will always lie - beyond the complete grasp of the human mind.

That being so, what more is there to be said? Some hold there is nothing more to be said; we are called upon 'to have faith'. And to some extent they are right; we do have to have faith and trust that God knows best. But that surely is not sufficient. To give up that easily is to invite the criticism that religious people are being intellectually dishonest - holding beliefs that plain common sense proves to be false.

While in no way denying the element of mystery, or the need ultimately to have faith, there are certain things that can be said about the problems of evil, suffering, and death, which might be helpful. At the very least, they demonstrate matters to be more subtle and complex than we might at first think. As we shall see, science, and particularly the theory of evolution, has some useful contributions to make to the on-going discussion.

Evil

One solution to the problem of evil is to say that, although God is wholly good, there might be a rival divine power - an evil spirit that challenges the God of goodness. Indeed, we do come across references in the Bible to the Devil. Satan is regarded not as a rival god, but as an angel created by God - one who subsequently rebels against its maker. Some believe the existence of the Devil to be literally true - Satan is as real in the spirit world as God. And it is the Devil who is to blame for the evil in the world. Others see the Devil as nothing more than a useful fiction. By thinking of the power of evil personified, actively seeking to tempt and lure people into sin, one is placed on one's guard against falling into temptation. Does the idea of a Devil solve our problem? Hardly. After all, who created the Devil? Where does the buck stop?

An alternative to thinking of two rival spiritual beings, is to challenge the assumption that God himself is wholly good. Like us, there might be a dark side to God - a 'shadow' side to him, as Carl Jung, the Swiss psychologist, put it. Goodness and evil both originated with God - according to Jung. That might be a possibility. But is that the kind of God one encounters personally in one's prayer life - the kind of God personified for Christians in the perfect life of Jesus?

Yet another alternative is to keep the idea that God is perfect goodness, but lose the other traditional notion that he is all-powerful. He does not want evil, but he is powerless to stop it. There are those who deny God's omnipotence.

A variation of that, is to say that God is all-powerful, but he is somehow placed in the position where he is logically forced into allowing evil to have a place in his created world. Being all-powerful does not mean being able to do logically impossible things - making four-sided triangles, for instance. So, we have to ask whether there might be some logical constraint under which God has to operate - a constraint that forces even an all-powerful God to permit evil, perhaps in the pursuit of some higher aim. If so, what might that be?

If one were allowed just a single word to describe God's most important characteristic, what would that word be? It would have to be *love*. As Christ's two Great Commandments make clear, God's main purpose in creating us was that we might enter into a loving relationship with him and into loving relationships with each other. To make any headway at all with the problem of evil and suffering, one has to start with the recognition of the simple fact that *love* is what it is all about. God makes no promises regarding happiness, comfort, or having an easy time of it. This being so, certain conclusions follow:

In the first place, God must give us freedom. Love is not something that can be forced, or coerced, or programmed into us. By its very nature - in order for it to have any value - it must be freely offered. So God must give us free will.

But if our will is to be really free, then there must be the possibility of our withholding that love and turning our backs on God. It is a risk God has to take. And this cannot be just a theoretical possibility. When dealing with billions upon billions of people, if nobody in practice ever actually did turn their back on God, then there would be strong grounds for doubting that this so-called freedom existed at all - in any real sense. So, for there to be genuine love there must be free will, and for the free will in its turn to be genuine, there must be actual examples of people who do decline to return God's love; they turn their back on God. And in turning their back on God, they turn their back on the source of all goodness; they embrace evil.

It is at this point the theory of evolution by natural selection has something relevant to say. We are evolved animals. Our physical characteristics were shaped through the struggle for survival. And not only our physical characteristics but some of our behaviour patterns too were fashioned in that struggle. Animals who, in the main, had a natural tendency to put their own interests first, grabbing what limited food and shelter were available, for themselves and their offspring - those were the ones most likely to survive - and in surviving, they passed on those same inborn instincts to act selfishly, and if necessary, aggressively towards others. As descendants of those self-centred ancestors, we must in all honesty expect to find in ourselves a built-in genetic tendency orienting us towards being selfish, and self-centred. Self-centred rather than God-centred. We begin at a distance from God. It takes a positive decision on our part to offer our loyalty to him and come over and centre our lives upon him. Some will not take that step; they will turn their backs on him and remain self-centred. Indeed, *all of us* - believers and non-believers alike - from time to time turn our backs on God, doing our own thing, and misusing the freedom he has given us. We are all guilty of this to varying degrees.

This is one of the important spiritual insights we gain from the Adam and Eve story. Recognising this account to be a myth - namely an ancient narration used to convey deep truths of a spiritual rather than a literal nature - we learn that we humans have a tendency to be disobedient to God (Adam's taking of the forbidden fruit). Although we have the potential to be like God (made in God's image), we have from the moment of conception a natural inclination to be selfish. It is called 'original sin'. The theory of evolution provides us for the first time with some insight as to how this comes about.

Not that I want to give the impression that selfishness is the only tendency we get in terms of genetically influenced behaviour patterns. Matters are more complicated than that. Also programmed into us is reciprocal altruism, or more colloquially 'I'll scratch your back if you'll scratch mine'. We see this literally in the case of monkeys grooming each other. There are circumstances where we are prepared to put ourselves out in order to help others. But this is done on the understanding that the favour will be returned. So, although biologists call this 'altruism', it is in truth just enlightened self-interest. Another form of altruism can be seen operating between close kin. A mother bird, for example, might deliberately draw the attention of a predator towards herself and away from the nest, thereby sacrificing herself in order that her young might survive. This behaviour can be understood in terms of the so-called 'selfish gene'. The mother shares the same genetic material with her young, and that material has a better chance of surviving to future generations if it contains a tendency for the mother to behave in this way (she having passed on the genes being to some extent more expendable than the young). But that said, there is no doubt that selfishness is a basic in-born human trait.

But you might say, why does God make it so hard for us? Why build into us a genetic tendency towards self-centredness? Why did God not give us a natural tendency to love him and do his will, rather than the reverse? Just as a hypnotist might place a post-hypnotic suggestion into the subject's mind that on waking she will find herself infatuated with him, could not God have 'programmed' us such that we all had an irresistible tendency to love God and each other and do only what is good. Certainly. But would such a contrived form of 'love' be of value? Would it be genuine? In the case of the hypnotist, would he think he had *won* her love? In the same way, for God to have built into us a tendency, come what may, to love him, would that have been a true love?

In similar vein, one cannot have a God who makes us free - but then is continually overwhelming us with manifestations of his presence and power - through a never-ending succession of spectacular miracles. That would be another form of coercion. No. For our freedom to be genuine, God *must* adopt a manner of approach towards us that is veiled, that is somewhat hands-off, an approach that is clear to those of the faith and have eyes to see and ears to hear, but one that is open to other interpretations for those who exercise their freedom differently.

So, what are we saying? We are saying that it is not God who creates evil; he merely creates the conditions in which *we* have the freedom to create evil. He gives us freedom in order that we might have the potential to pursue the higher good - love. As soon as God elevated love to be the Number 1 priority, he had to give us free will, and in doing so permit evil to enter his world. When evil is actualised, however, it is 100% our responsibility - through the way we misuse our God-given freedom. It is not God's responsibility. This is the so-called 'free will defence' argument. It is the generally preferred argument for tackling the problem of evil.

This, of course, assumes that we do have free will. But is this so? We know that there is some sort of correlation between the activities of the brain and our conscious experiences. But the workings of the brain appear to be deterministic; they are governed by the laws of nature. Given a particular state of the brain at one point in time, it is possible, in principle at least, to predict its future states. If there is an exact correlation between brain states and conscious mental experiences then that would seem to imply that those mental experiences should, in principle, be predictable - including those experiences known as 'making a free will choice'. In other words there is no choice at all; the notion that the future is open is but an illusion. This is the free will/determinism problem.

One approach is to adopt a dualistic approach, according to which the mind and brain are considered to be different entities such that not only can the brain affect mental states, but the mind can influence the brain processes; in other words, the matter that makes up the brain does not slavishly follow the laws of nature; the mind can intervene and over-ride nature's normal course. Another is to invoke quantum theory whereby nature at the atomic level does not follow a strictly deterministic path but is subject to chance according to the Heisenberg uncertainty principle. None of these ideas, however, command universal acceptance. Some conclude that we are not as free as we might wish to think we are. Others side with Dr Samuel Johnson who declared: 'Our will is free, and there's an end on't'. One thing is certain. We cannot opt out of 'making choices' on the grounds that what will be, will be regardless. A decision to opt out is in itself a conscious choice! We are left with no alternative but to live our lives on a daily basis as if we are free.

Suffering

How about the problem of suffering? We begin by noting that evil and suffering go hand in hand. Evil so often leads to suffering. So, if God is logically constrained to allow evil into the world in order that love might have a chance to flourish, God must also permit the suffering that is a consequence of the evil.

But we can't leave it at that: suffering as simply a consequence of human moral evil. Even without anyone perpetrating deliberate evil acts, there is still suffering. Here we are thinking of *natural* disasters - earthquakes, floods - instances where we run foul of nature following her regular pattern of behaviour. We think of disease and disability.

In early times, it was thought that suffering was a punishment for sin. Those who suffered most must have sinned the most. It seemed an obvious way of making sense of why some people suffer more than others. In the Bible, this is what Job was told by his friends: he was having to suffer all the calamities that befell him because he must have been very wicked; God was punishing him for it. But Job would have none of it. He wasn't perfect, but he wasn't *that* bad. This idea that suffering was a punishment for sin was still around at the time of Jesus. But Jesus also would have nothing to do with that as an explanation. And in our own times, it is surely clear that those who suffer most are no more wicked than the rest of us.

So, what is the alternative to suffering being a punishment for sin? We have already established how free will is an essential prerequisite for being able to love God or love each other. But free will can only be exercised in an environment that is predictable. One must be able to anticipate what the likely outcome will be of any course of action one might choose to take. That means the environment must be law-like - it must obey set rules. It must be a neutral environment - one that can be used for good or ill.

Not only that, it must be a *common* medium - one through which we can contact other individuals. We make ourselves known to other people - we interact with them - through the physical world. It is a world that cannot simply bend its rules to meet the passing whim of any individual. The environment has to be even-handed - fair to everyone - the world we all jointly inhabit has to have a *nature of its own*. And that is how we find the world: It has a nature of its own.

But having said that, does it not follow that the inexorable working out of those laws of nature are likely from time to time to lead to some unfortunate consequences for the inhabitants of that world? Is that not likely to be one of the prices we have to pay for our freedom?

Another point to consider is this: Imagine a world where there was no suffering - no suffering of any kind whatsoever - and that includes mental suffering as well as the physical sort. (After all, most people who commit suicide do so because they find mental suffering intolerable - not physical suffering.) In this imaginary world everyone would have everything they could possibly want (otherwise they would suffer feelings of deprivation). It is the sort of world many assume God *ought* to have created. So, why didn't he?

In such a world, how would you demonstrate your love for someone? And it is no good saying you would have good times together, sex, and that sort of thing. Sex is enjoyable, so how is your partner to know that you are doing it out of genuine love for her and not just for the sake of your own enjoyment. Surely, proof of love comes from the way you react to the other person's *needs* - the way you put yourself out for them - the way you *suffer* and *sacrifice* yourself for them. One sees this in little things - like the way a mother will get up in the middle of the night - even though she is desperately tired - in order to feed and change the nappy of the baby. Or you might find it in big things - like the way a husband might devote himself to the care of his house-bound wife suffering from the ravages of multiple sclerosis - rather than going off with another woman. Or you might find it in the way someone gives a big donation to a charity seeking to relieve the miseries of refugees or victims of famine. This is a demonstration of brotherly love for people one does not even know and has never met. In order for love to be manifest, there has to be self-sacrifice and suffering on the part of the giver, in response to the need and the suffering of the person to whom the love is given. In a world without any suffering, there would be no needs to be attended to, no suffering to alleviate, and you yourself would in any case not be allowed to take on any measure of suffering on behalf of the other. So, does that not mean that for love to be the highest principle, there must also be suffering - in order for that love to be given an opportunity of manifesting itself?

Might it not also be true to say that all that is most noble and commendable about a person is born out of trial and tribulation rather than the enjoyment of an easy life. This is not true of everyone, of course. In the face of intense suffering some people become embittered. Suffering can be the making or the breaking of a person - in much the same way as pottery, if it is to be durable and useful, must pass through the fire of the kiln even though the potter knows some of his creations might not be able to survive the test.

The next thing to take on board, is that although we naturally do all we can to avoid suffering, there are circumstances where suffering may not in itself be altogether bad. Take pain, for example. It would be simplistic to think of pain as if it were something *totally* bad. Pain is a vital part of our ability as an evolved animal to live and survive in an environment that can sometimes be hostile. Pain is a warning of danger and injury.

But, one might ask, what about the millions and millions of years of suffering the animal kingdom had to endure before the process of evolution produced us humans. If producing humans is what God had in mind from the beginning, couldn't he have chosen some other way of doing it?

That is all very well, but what might that alternative be? God sits down at a drawing board and designs each one of us individually and fully formed down to the very last detail? If so, would that not yield something indistinguishable from a robot? If such a creature then went on to declare love for God, what would that signify? It would be a mere consequence of the design. For love to be genuine, it has to be freely offered between persons who have a measure of independence from each other. But how is that possible between God and humans when the humans are necessarily dependent for their existence on the one and only creator god? It appears that God solved this problem by calling upon chance. The process of evolution by natural selection relies on chance mutations. God did not design us down to the last detail. It is through the randomness incorporated into the evolutionary process that we gain a measure of independence from God. And it is through that measure of independence we are able to offer meaningful love to our creator.

Of course, when talking about suffering in the animal kingdom, we have to be careful that we are not projecting too much of our own human experience onto the less developed animals. Is a worm in pain when it writhes about having been accidentally cut in two by the gardener's spade? Both halves? They are both writhing about. Does the worm now have *two* minds - both in pain - or is it not mentally experiencing anything at all? Does the wriggling fish on the end of the hook feel pain? If we think that, why isn't angling banned?

How much of pain is in the *anticipation* of it? Is it not curious that a footballer can come off the pitch at the end of a game to discover his leg gashed and bleeding - an injury he cannot remember sustaining - and yet the same person recoils at the prospect of having a needle stuck in him at the doctor's? In one case the attention was distracted, and in the other it was focussed on what was happening. If we ourselves respond so differently to 'injury' depending on our state of mind at the time, can it not be argued that animals - possessing as they do a mental capacity far lower than ours - might feel very little? It is impossible to say. But the problem of suffering in the animal kingdom might not be as pressing as is generally supposed.

In considering whether there is too much suffering in this life, another point to take on board is that all suffering is relative. If it were all to be scaled down - in response to our protests that at present it is too severe - would we not quickly readjust our sense of what was, and was not, 'severe' suffering? We would still end up convinced that the higher levels of suffering, even on this reduced scale, were excessive. Take a small child and the way it yells and screams when it falls down and grazes its knee. To hear it crying one would think it was the end of the world. It is only later, when in adulthood we have been visited with greater pains, that the severity of a grazed knee is viewed in a different perspective.

Is it really true that the suffering of this life is excessive? For some maybe. We have only to think of those driven to commit suicide. But despite all our complaints, very, very few of us would contemplate suicide. Indeed, it is our natural reaction to fight tooth and nail to stay alive. Is this will to live nothing more than a genetic inheritance - part of our evolutionary survival package? Or is it additionally saying something about how we really value this life?

Those are just a few thoughts on how we might make a little sense out of the mystery of suffering. But let me remind you, no matter how hard we strive to come up with answers, we are faced with mystery. This much is made clear in the Bible. We are told the story of Job - a good God-fearing man upon whom there befalls a series of terrifying calamities. At the end of his sufferings, Job comes face to face with God. He has demanded an explanation for his troubles. We are thinking 'At last we are going to get the answer straight from the mouth of God'. But we get none. Instead of an answer, Job is bombarded with a whole succession of questions from God - over 50 of them - all designed to expose how little humans know about anything. Job can do nothing but humbly accept that in the final analysis, suffering is beyond our understanding; it is something we must bear patiently, trusting that the loving all-powerful God will in his own time, and in his own way, ensure that all will be well.

We are like children in the face of God. How often are children bewildered by, and resentful of, the rules laid upon them by their parents? In later life they might be able to look back with the benefit of hindsight and see the good that came out of being required to do homework, being forced to acquire tidy habits, clean one's teeth, not live on a diet of chocolate, take nasty-tasting medicine. It is the fact that we do *not* fully understand God that is the mark of his independence - his independent reality. He is not the sort of God one would have dreamt up out of one's own imagination.

Death

Which brings us finally to the Problem of Death. The knowledge that one has to die concentrates the mind wonderfully. The fact that life is short means that we pay more attention to the way we live it - which we would not if time were unlimited. Without death, the older generation would never get out of the way to make room for the younger. The younger would always live in the shadows of former generations and would not be able to take on responsibility and become mature. Just think what promotion prospects would be like if no-one ever retired. And what of the population explosion? People getting born, but never dying.

Without death there could be no evolution by natural

selection - no survival of the fittest because *all* would survive. There would be no development, and we humans would not be here. Death of the individual is part and parcel of the survival kit of the species as a whole. It could well be that there is some genetic component responsible for our ageing and eventual death. If that is the case, and if as a result of research into genetics scientists were to identify that 'death gene', what ought they to do about it? Should it be regarded as a defective gene - one similar to that which is known to give rise to sickle cell anaemia - and therefore should be eliminated from the gene pool? Or ought we to regard such a death gene as normal and leave well alone?

What about life *beyond* death? What suffering and death - particularly the death of small children - demonstrates is that there is no room for 'half-baked' Christianity. By that one means a belief that is basically Christian - Jesus was the best man who ever lived and we would all do well to follow his example - but Christianity without the resurrection - without a belief in life beyond death. That kind of religious belief does not work. It is manifestly clear that some people in this life have a very rough time of it - children living brutal, short lives. A belief in a loving God - a God of *justice* - can *only* be sustained if there is something more than this life - something infinitely better - as Jesus promised, and himself demonstrated on Easter Day. If God is all he is meant to be, then there *has* to be a Heaven - a means for putting right all that was wrong with this life.

Some will object to this as simply the 'jam tomorrow scenario' - a product of wishful thinking. Psychologist Sigmund Freud claimed that if one wished for something hard enough the unconscious could trick one into believing it to be true. But why shouldn't it be 'jam tomorrow'? What kind of pessimism is it that assumes that happy endings must by their very nature be an illusion? If God is all-powerful, and all-loving, and a God of justice, then this is something he *can* do, and indeed is *bound* to do.

But can a life hereafter possibly compensate for the intense suffering that some individuals have to undergo? Intense their suffering might be, but one thing is certain: it is finite; it comes to an end. The life beyond death is *infinite* - and there is no comparing the finite to the infinite.

We have spoken specifically of Christian belief. Other religions, of course, differ in varying degrees regarding what lies beyond death. Hinduism, for example, speaks of rebirth - coming back to this world in a different form - rather than resurrection. What *is* remarkable is that the major religions - East and West - are agreed that there is something about us that continues on beyond death, and the quality of that extension of life depends to some extent on how we live *this* life. Death marks a transition - not an end - and as such is not to be feared. It is in the life to come that the manifold injustices of this mortal life, in terms of evil and suffering, will be set right.

Summary
Although, as was said at the beginning, there is no easy, pat answer to the problem of evil, suffering, and death, one can perhaps begin to glimpse that it makes some kind of sense once one recognises that (i) God's first priority is love, and from that certain consequences become unavoidable, and (ii) one further accepts that this mortal life is not the whole story - there is eternal life of some form. Of course, there will be those who reject certain aspects of religious belief - eternal life, for instance. Fair enough. That is not the point. The point is that the orthodox religious package, *seen as a whole*, can make sense; it is *not* necessarily self-contradictory as one might erroneously conclude from the existence of evil and suffering. As such, it is an intelligent faith.

Russell Stannard is Emeritus Professor of Physics at the Open University and a Lay Reader in the Church of England.

Climate change, Earth history and the Christian hope

I.N. James

A big species in a finite world

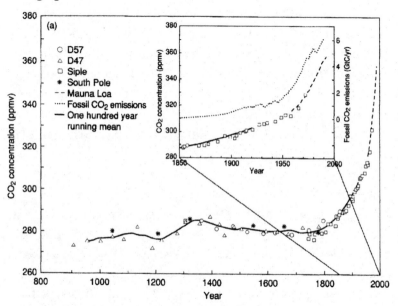

Figure (1): *The concentration of atmospheric carbon dioxide, over the past 1000 years.*

Figure (1) is a suitable preface to what I have to say. It shows the variation of an important constituent of the Earth's atmosphere, namely carbon dioxide, over the last 1000 years. The data are largely derived from bubbles of air trapped in ice from ice cores taken from the Antarctic and Greenland ice sheets. These provide a fossil record of the composition of the atmosphere when the snow fell. They have been supplemented by direct measurements since 1957. For centuries, the level of carbon dioxide has bumped along, with small fluctuations, at around 280 parts per million (ppm). In the early nineteenth century, carbon dioxide concentration began to rise, gently at first, then more and more rapidly. By the end of the twentieth century, it had reached 375ppm; the latest figure for the end of 2007 is 387ppm, and it continues to rise rapidly.

There is no disputing the origin of this extra carbon dioxide. It arises from human activity, principally from the burning of carbon-rich fossil fuels such as coal, oil and natural gas. In the pre-industrial world, photosynthesis by green plants took carbon dioxide out of the atmosphere to make sugars and thence proteins and all the other constituents of living things. A balance was achieved in which carbon was cycled between the biosphere (in the form of organic molecules of living things) and the atmosphere (in the form of carbon dioxide gas), on a timescale of some 15 years. In our present industrial society, vast additional amounts of carbon dioxide are being pumped into the atmosphere as a result of fossil fuel burning, while the capacity of the biosphere to process this carbon is being steadily eroded by deforestation, species loss and the pollution of habitats by human waste.

Although the concentration of carbon dioxide in our atmosphere is small, it plays a very important, if invisible, role. Carbon dioxide is odourless and transparent in visible light; humans are scarcely aware of its presence. However, at the longer wavelengths of infrared radiation, it has strong absorption bands which render the atmosphere nearly opaque at these wavelengths. These infrared wavelengths are precisely the wavelengths at which the warm Earth radiates. So sunlight warms the Earth's surface, which radiates infrared radiation upward. But the carbon dioxide in the atmosphere absorbs this infrared radiation and re-radiates it downward. As a result, the Earth's surface is a great deal warmer than it would be otherwise

– an equable 15°C on average, compared to -18°C without any infrared absorbing components in the atmosphere. This effect is sometimes (misleadingly) called the "greenhouse effect" and without it, life could not survive on Earth. But an uncontrolled greenhouse effect would be just as alarming. A global temperature rise of 2°C would badly disrupt agriculture and would lead to mass migration, famine and great suffering, especially for people of the "third world". A rise of 4°C would be catastrophic, rendering large parts of the Earth uninhabitable and leading to the death of a large fraction of the human population and the extinction of many non-human species.

It is worth noting that carbon dioxide levels have varied in the past without human intervention. The longest ice core records from Antarctica take us back some 800,000 years, and over that time, carbon dioxide levels have fluctuated from levels close to the pre-industrial value of 280 ppm to as little as 200 ppm. Until the last two hundred years, they have never significantly exceeded 280 ppm. These variations correlate well with the fluctuating temperature of the Earth during the recent ice ages. The primary driving for ice ages are the periodic changes in the various elements of the Earth's orbit: its orbital eccentricity, the tilt of the Earth's rotation axis, and the precession of the rotation axis, which mean that, for example, the winter season occurs when the Earth is at slightly different distances from the Sun. The net result is a variation of the amount of sunlight reaching the polar regions of the Earth, with a period of about 100,000 years. During the cold glacial periods, carbon dioxide concentrations were relatively low, and during the inter-glacial periods, much higher. These variations of carbon dioxide mainly arise from changes in the amount of carbon dioxide which can dissolve in seawater; more dissolves when the water is colder, during the glacial periods.

Although these changes in carbon dioxide levels were substantial and undoubtedly contributed to the ice age cycles, they were smaller than the recent human-induced changes of carbon dioxide, and crucially, they were in the opposite sense. Our present situation is already unprecedented in recent Earth history. Yet if fossil fuel consumption continues to increase at its present rate, eventual levels of carbon dioxide will far exceed present levels, and indeed levels that have not been seen for many millions of years.

Humans are of course having other major effects on the Earth. For example, extinctions are taking place at a rate probably greater than at any time in geological history, largely because of habitat destruction and pollution. Other forms of pollution than carbon dioxide emissions have important local effects. But on the large scale, and over the longer period, carbon dioxide pollution is the overwhelming problem humanity is bequeathing to the world.

Climate change has always been taking place. There is no "definitive Earth climate". But our current cause for concern is the speed at which change is taking place, far faster than most species can evolve to adapt to changed conditions, and the magnitude of that change.

The cosmic timeframe

To put our current climate changes into context, I want to illustrate some of the timescales which affect our world. They fall into two broad categories: timescales associated with physical processes, and those associated with biological processes.

Our current picture of the physical Universe is that it had its beginning some 13.7 billion years ago, when all its energy and matter was concentrated in an infinitely tiny volume. We call this a "singularity", and while our physics can take us back to times very soon after that singularity, we can never quite get back to the moment itself. At first, the early Universe was so extremely hot that elementary particles were split into their component parts and so dense that particles were continually colliding with each other and transforming from matter to energy and back again. As the Universe expanded, it cooled, particles began to acquire an identity, and the various forces between particles began to separate. The following story is heavily simplified. The reader is referred to standard texts for fuller and more rigorous accounts. My purpose is largely to emphasise the changing timescales which have characterised the evolution of the largest scale cosmos.

In the very earliest epoch of the Universe, the energy of particles was so large that the four forces which act between particles of matter were indistinguishable. These four forces are (in order of magnitude in the present epoch) the gravitational force, the weak nuclear force, the electromagnetic force and the strong nuclear force. After a brief time, called the Planck time, which has the value 1.4×10^{-43} seconds, the gravitational force separated from the others. Our best physics can unify the electromagnetic force and the two nuclear forces in the "Grand Unified Theory" of Glashow, Georgi, Pati and Salam. No-one has yet succeeded in formulating a "Supergrand Unified Theory" which would bring the gravitational force into a single theory with the other forces. So we may say that the Planck time is the boundary before which our current physics breaks down.

At around 10^{-35} seconds after the Big Bang, modern theory suggests there was a period of inflation, during which the Universe expanded enormously. This coincided with the separation of the strong nuclear force from the electromagnetic and weak nuclear forces. The epoch of inflation lasted until 10^{-32} seconds after the Big Bang, by which time the Universe had expanded by a factor of around 10^{50}. The final separation between the electromagnetic force and the weak nuclear force occurred around 10^{-12} seconds after the Big Bang. Thereafter, the Universe, while still in a very extreme state, began to look more like the Universe of everyday physics. Particle energy levels (or temperature) continued to drop as the Universe expanded, and by 10^{-6} seconds, energies were low enough to permit elementary particles called quarks to stick together as the more familiar protons and neutrons. Free neutrons decay to form protons unless they are bound into a nucleus by the strong force, and so more protons than neutrons were produced. By 3 minutes into the life time of the Universe, the temperature was so low that photons no longer had the energy needed to split up atomic nuclei, and so at that time, the proton/neutron ratio was determined, at about 6 protons per neutron. However, nuclei and particles continued to collide and coalesce to generate heavier elements. This process ceased about 15 minutes after the Big Bang, leaving one helium nucleus per 10 protons (hydrogen nuclei), along with small amounts of lithium and beryllium. All the heavier elements, including carbon, oxygen and nitrogen, were produced much later in the history of the Universe by stars.

At this time, the Universe consisted of hot plasma, that is, a mixture of atomic nuclei and free electrons, together with energy in the form of photons. The photons collided with particles so frequently that they were in thermal equilibrium with the matter. The Universe was filled with intensely hot, incandescent gas: it has been described as a "primordial fireball". The next qualitative change to the Universe took place about 380,000 years after the Big Bang. Temperatures dropped and electrons and nuclei began to stick together to form neutral atoms. The strong coupling between the radiation field and the matter in the Universe broke down, and the Universe became transparent: the sky became dark. The temperature of the radiation field continued to drop, while the temperature of the matter became highly variable, with some cool matter but also some intensely hot matter.

Timescales now become more geological, but they are still extremely short compared to the present age of the Universe. The early Universe was of nearly, but not quite, uniform density. Tiny fluctuations had been smoothed by the inflation epoch, but could be thought of as sound waves following the Big Bang. However, fluctuations there were, and gravity means that a sufficiently extensive density anomaly would start to collapse under its own gravitation influence. "Sufficiently extensive" means larger than a length called the "Jeans length" which would have been about 100 light years at the time the Universe became transparent. The first dense bodies to condense out of the rarefying cosmic gas were probably neither single stars nor galaxies, but assemblies of stars called "globular clusters". Such clusters are tight spherical aggregations of stars; a halo of globular clusters surrounds our own and many neighbouring galaxies, and today they consist of very ancient stars. The first globular clusters probably formed some 60 million years after the Big Bang. Globular clusters may have collided and merged, and the first galaxies probably appeared some 500 million years into the existence of the Universe.

The first stars probably included many very massive, short-lived stars. They would only shine for a few million years before exhausting their nuclear fuel, collapsing and scattering their outer layers through space. It was in the last stages of these massive stars that heavier elements were created: the atoms of life such as carbon and oxygen as well as heavier elements, including metals. So while the earliest stars were almost pure hydrogen and helium, the next generation were relatively enriched with heavier elements. From its composition, our own Sun is thought to be a third generation star, formed 4.6 billion years ago.

Looking into the far future, what will happen to the Universe? There are two possibilities. The first is that it continues to expand indefinitely. The galaxies gradually recede from one another, and the stars which make them up exhaust their hydrogen nuclear fuel and go out. Even the remnants of dead stars – neutron stars and black holes – gradually decay and evaporate. We are left with a cold dark Universe where nothing much happens because without heat flowing from hot to cold places, no energy can be generated. Such a cold, quiescent state is sometimes called the "heat death" of the Universe.

The other possibility is that the expansion might eventually cease, and the Universe then collapses back into itself. As it collapses, galaxies and stars collide with greater frequency, and the Universe approaches something like its initial state – a hot soup of particles and radiation, getting more and more compressed, and hotter and hotter. Eventually, the entire Universe disappears into a singularity. The process is sometimes called the "big crunch".

Whether we end up with a heat death or a big crunch depends on the gravitational forces holding the Universe together and the speed with which it is currently flying apart. If the total mass of the Universe exceeds some critical value, then we will eventually get a big crunch. Less than the critical mass, and gravity can never win; we have a heat death. In principle, by counting the number of galaxies we can see at different distances and measuring their redshift, we can compare the mass of the Universe and the energy of its expansion. The more sophisticated the method, the closer the Universe seems to be to hovering on the transition from big bang and big crunch – that is, the gravitational energy and the expansion energy are apparently almost exactly balanced.

It must be emphasised that we are talking here of immense times in the future, long after our Sun has gone through its life cycle and long after the Earth will have been burnt up and swallowed by its expanding Sun.

Earth history

Earth history follows something of the same pattern as the history of the Universe as a whole, that is, a brief epoch of great violence and rapid evolution to begin with, settling down to a more stable, long lived state subsequently. When the Sun formed

4.6 billion years ago, it was surrounded by an "accretion disk" of gas and dust, representing a small fraction of the mass of the Sun but a large fraction of the angular momentum of the solar system. The hot Sun drove the more volatile material away from the inner part of the accretion disk; the remaining material orbited the Sun in all sorts of erratic, elliptic orbits. As a result, clumps of dust formed by collisions and grew. As they developed a substantial gravitational field, the larger clumps grew preferentially and became sub-planet sized bodies. Those with highly elliptical orbits that crossed the paths of their companions did not last long, but were quickly gobbled up. Those that survived had more circular, regular orbits. It was a short time of tremendous violence; after perhaps 100 million years, something like our present solar system was beginning to emerge. But with decreasing frequency, major and catastrophic events still occurred. One such involved a collision between the proto-Earth and a Mars-sized planetesimal; the resulting concussion probably stripped the Earth of its atmosphere and partially melted the planet. Some of the shattered colliding body re-coalesced to form our present Moon, which is by far the largest satellite in the Solar System, relative to its primary. Some have suggested that tides raised in the early Earth by its giant Moon played a crucial role in the early evolution of life on Earth.

The oldest surfaces in the solar system, such as the surfaces of the moon and Mercury, bear a testimony to this early accretion phase of the Solar System. They are peppered with craters, each the product of a collision with a smaller body. Some craters are tiny, but others cover a large part of the planet and in the case of the Moon were associated with huge floods of molten lava which we now see as the dark markings on the Moon. Even today, that accretion phase has not entirely ceased, although it has drastically slowed down. In 1994, astronomers witnessed the collision of comet Shoemaker-Levy with Jupiter and its subsequent absorption into that planet. Only 65 million years ago, it seems that a collision between the Earth and a 10 km sized body may have set in train the mass extinctions which led to the end of the dinosaurs and gave mammals the break they needed to dominate the earth. The impact has left a crater 80 km in diameter, buried under sediments on the Yukatán Peninsular of Mexico. We have now identified a number of such bodies with orbits such that they have the potential to hit the Earth in the future.

The lighter components of the Earth – the gases making up its atmosphere, the water contained in the oceans - are most likely the result of relatively late accretion events. Any complement of lighter elements would probably have been lost to space in the collision that formed the Moon. But collisions with icy bodies (what we call comets), deflected into the inner solar system by the gravitational perturbations of the outer planets, are the likely source of our atmosphere and oceans. However, the primordial atmosphere was very different from the one we have today. There would have been negligible oxygen, and instead there would have been carbon dioxide and perhaps more fleetingly ammonia and methane: these latter would quickly have been photolysed by sunlight and their hydrogen lost to space, leaving nitrogen and carbon compounds.

The earliest rocks on the Earth's surface have been dated to 3,800 to 4,000 million years old. Although they have been hugely metamorphosed during their long history, they were laid down as sedimentary rocks in water. Even so soon after the formation of the solar system, the Earth had an equable temperature. It was able to support liquid water on its surface, and the sort of geology with which we are familiar today was starting to work.

The biological timeframe

One of the paradigm shifts in our understanding of Earth history is the recognition that the physical environment provided by the Earth and the biota it carries are intimately related. Living things modify the environment, sometimes profoundly, and at the same time, the character of the environment impacts on the survival characteristics of different species, thus driving evolution. There are many expressions of this physical-biological linkage. Figure (2) demonstrates it in the form of the oxygen content of the atmosphere. The primordial atmosphere was very oxygen poor, with tiny amounts of oxygen, some 10^{-4} times the current level, formed by photo dissociation of molecules such as carbon dioxide which contain some oxygen. As photosynthesising organisms developed, levels of oxygen increased, while remaining very small compared to current levels. Around 2000 million years ago, levels reached 1% of the current oxygen concentration. The increases in oxygen may well have proceeded suddenly, in steps, as more effective photosynthesis evolved. But the point to be made is that levels of oxygen only increased very slowly for huge chunks of Earth history. Only very recently in terms of the lifetime of the Earth have they approached current values.

The idea of evolution has generally become part of our

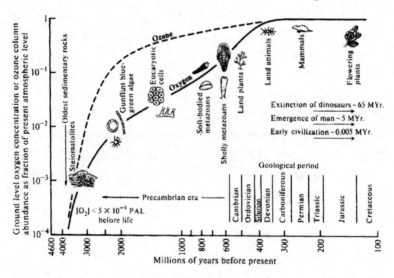

Figure (2): *Variation of atmospheric oxygen and the evolution of life on Earth. From Wayne (2000).*

culture, the myth of our times. What are less generally appreciated are the timescales involved. Most people think of evolution as a set of preliminary experiments from which our modern world emerged and settled down. Indeed, Wayne's graph apparently confirms this. It appears to show oxygen at very low levels before life was established on Earth, rising rapidly as the first photosynthesising organisms evolved, before asymptoting to its modern value.

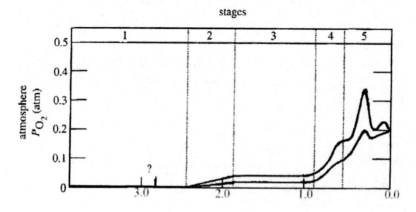

Figure (3): *Oxygen concentration plotted against the age of the Earth. This is similar data as shown in figure (2), but plotted on linear scales. The horizontal scale shows billions of years before present. The "pre-Cambrian explosion" came at the end of stage 4.*

But look more carefully at Wayne's axes. They are logarithmic, and tremendously stretched. The first 2,000 million years of Earth history are given the same space as the last 100 million years. Figure (3) shows similar oxygen data as does Wayne's graph, but on linear scales. Now, the very low levels of oxygen for the first 4,000 million years of the Earth are plain, followed by a dramatic increase around the start of the Cambrian era to values close to those at present. It is our period, the most recent 10% of Earth's history which appears anomalous, not the first part. For those first 4000 million years, life was present but simple, very slowly evolving. The fossil record is extremely sparse since there were no hard-bodied organisms to speak of. But it seems that dominant life forms were stromatolites and blue-green algae.

Three things happened at the end of the pre-Cambrian period. First, the levels of oxygen increased rapidly, to something comparable to their present levels. This was an enormous change, from an unreactive atmosphere to a highly oxidizing atmosphere, indeed, one which was so reactive that it would actually support combustion. Many species found this new environment too toxic and could not survive as it became established. This mass extinction was the second significant impact. But if an oxygen rich atmosphere was toxic to certain lowly species, it made possible a huge range of new species, species which had much faster metabolisms than their predecessors. One can look at the late pre-Cambrian as a major pollution event, which radically altered the biota possible on the Earth. An explosion of high energy consuming creatures, many with hard bodies or skeletons quickly appeared to fill the ecological gaps left by the overwhelmed species.

Since the Cambrian, species have evolved in complexity and in their ability to exploit their environment. Within 200 million years or so, plants and animals began to colonise the land areas of the Earth. A necessary pre-condition for that was the formation of an ozone layer from photochemical reactions involving the newly plentiful oxygen. Without the ozone later in the stratosphere, hard ionising ultra-violet radiation would have effectively kept the Earth's surface sterilized. Life could only have persisted in the oceans. The age of the dinosaurs began some 150 million years ago. Popularly denigrated as the epitome of the ill adapted, unsuccessful species, they were in fact highly successful, dominating the world for nearly a hundred million years. Compare that with the mere 200,000 years in which *homo sapiens* and its immediate precursors have been in existence.

It is interesting to note that if a remote observer in some distant part of our galaxy had turned a telescope onto the Earth, then for 90% of the time between the birth of the sun and now, that alien would have seen a planet with few signs of life. Its atmosphere would have been reducing and unreactive, not dissimilar from the carbon dioxide laden atmospheres of Mars or Venus.

Human and cultural evolution

Until the appearance of humankind, information was passed from one generation to another by the genetic code in an organism's DNA. Occasional beneficial mutations give variants of a species better survival characteristics and so evolution takes. But DNA communication puts a limit on how fast evolution can proceed. It is limited by the time it takes for an organism to pass its DNA onto a new generation.

With humankind, a new mechanism enters the argument. The development of community and language gives the chance for information to pass much more rapidly through a species than the slow process of passing DNA from one generation to another. With the development of language and human culture, so the development of societies was able to accelerate.

The first humans appeared some 2 million years ago, though whether we would have regarded them as more like apes than humans is open to question. *Homo sapiens* or its immediate precursors can be traced back 200,000 or perhaps 250,000 years. They lived in small roaming bands of hunter-gatherers, consisting of perhaps 20-30 individuals. It is worth reminding ourselves that such is the way of life to which we evolved and which has been the norm for most of the history of our species.

The great change came around 9500 BC, when cultivation of crops first began. Necessarily, people settled near the crops, and villages and towns began to develop. The economies of scale meant that not everyone was constrained to spend all their time and energy in the quest for food. As societies became more elaborate, so they developed specialists – artisans, artists, lawyers and philosophers. A pattern of city states, with political and cultural foci in the cities, supported by agricultural hinterlands, became established.

In a way, the industrial revolution simply added scale and impetus to this same tendency. Cities became larger, fewer people worked on the land, and the agricultural resources of whole countries were needed to feed the cities. Industry demanded energy, and the railways supplied it in the form of coal. Almost inadvertently, the railways also demanded rapid communication over large distances, a demand satisfied by the invention of the electrical telegraph. So communications improved to the point where large cities controlled whole countries and supported large populations, few of whom were directly involved in food production. But again, notice the telescoping of timescales. Agricultural humanity was dominant for some 12,000 years of human history. Industrial society began in Europe in around 1830, and so has been in existence for less than 200 years. Along with this increase of pace has come a comparable demand for energy, a demand which can only be met by burning fossil fuels. Thus in fig (1), the level of carbon dioxide in the atmosphere first starts rising appreciably in the early nineteenth century with the start of the Industrial Revolution.

Two trends have characterised human development in the late twentieth and twenty first centuries. First has been the steady rise of industrial activity, of transport and of associated energy consumption. Partly, this is a result increasing *per capita* consumption by industrialised nations. But partly it is also the result of industrialisation spreading to countries which hitherto had still been in their agricultural phase. But secondly, the so-called information revolution, which began only twenty or so years ago, has transformed many societies. The capacity to store, recall and process information electronically has leapt by orders of magnitude over a very short time. While the machinery of the industrial revolution rendered many manual skills redundant, so computers are now rendering the skills of the secretary, the filing clerk, the account keeper, irrelevant. Computers are now monitoring stock markets and able to make decisions about buying and selling shares of greater complexity and more quickly than any human stockbroker could manage.

Perhaps for the first time in human history, the pace of change has shortened to much less than a generation, so that now people have to relearn their function in society, the skills needed to earn their living, several times within a single lifetime. The pace of change is accelerating beyond the point where most people can cope with it. Timescales are collapsing to something like a singularity.

Future of planet Earth

What is the likely future of planet Earth? There are two scenarios, depending on whether or not humanity is able to contain its impact on the Earth. There is a serious prospect that humanity will not be able to control itself. But first, let us consider the future of an Earth without industrial pollution and over-population.

Essential background is to recognise that on geological timescales, the solar output of energy has not been constant. The Sun is a typical "main sequence" star, and during its time on the main sequence, its core has become progressively depleted of hydrogen and enriched with helium. The net result is that the Sun's surface has swollen and warmed gently over its main sequence lifetime. That lifetime is about half gone now; when the Sun first formed, its surface was some 300K cooler than now, its radius was about 6% less and its total energy output was some 40% less than it is now. Yet despite these changes, we know that the climate of Earth has remained roughly constant since its earliest days. The earliest rocks were laid down some 3800 million years ago in water, providing a strong constraint on the temperature of the early Earth. Since then, the Earth has held liquid water somewhere near its surface. This constancy of the Earth's surface temperature has been dubbed the "cold Sun paradox". The implication is that throughout its existence, the physical and chemical states of the Earth's atmosphere and surface have evolved in such a way as to maintain an equable climate. There are many ways in which this might have happened. The concentration of radiatively active gases in the atmosphere such as carbon dioxide would impact on surface temperature. Cloud cover is an important factor in modifying climate since cloud is very effective at reflecting sunlight back to space.

A suggestive comparison is between Earth and Venus, its near identical twin planet. Venus has the same size, mass and density as Earth. However, its atmosphere is dense, with a surface pressure some 90 times that of Earth, and composed largely of carbon dioxide. As a result, a powerful greenhouse effect means that the surface temperature of Venus is over 500°C, compared to a average surface temperature of 15°C for Earth. Yet estimates suggest that if all the sedimentary carbonate rocks in the earth's crust were broken down to release their carbon in the form of carbon dioxide, Earth would end up with an atmosphere more or less as dense as that of Venus. Has Earth maintained its temperature while the sun heats up by sequestering carbon dioxide in limestone rocks, leaving the waterless Venus to suffer a runaway greenhouse effect?

If that is the case, then a curious fact emerges. The capacity for regulating the Earth's surface temperature by sequestering atmospheric carbon dioxide is very nearly exhausted. It has been suggested that the process is sustainable for another 100 million years or so, a long time in terms of human history, but a negligible slice of Earth history. Unless other processes intervene, as temperatures increase, the oceans will evaporate, temperatures will continue to rise, ands we will quickly end up with a lifeless "greenhouse" Earth. On this view, the rise of mammals and humans has come very close to the end of the story of life on Earth.

The evidence of figure (1) is that even this scenario is optimistic. Carbon dioxide emissions by human activities continue to rise at ever increasing rates. Despite the warnings of the scientific community, summarised in some of the most critically written scientific reports ever prepared (the IPCC reports), in sober but dire warnings from an economic perspective (the Stern report in the UK), and despite the widespread public acceptance that global warming is a serious threat, political will and commercial pressure has had virtually no impact at all in moderating carbon emissions. They continue to rise more steeply than ever as less "developed" countries follow the path of western industrialisation. The Stern report suggested that a global warming of 2°C was probably as much as could be sustained while retaining something like our present patterns of population and industry. Scientists are suggesting that peak carbon dioxide concentrations might exceed 650ppm, with a global temperature rise in excess of 4°C. Such a change would be catastrophic, with extensive areas of the Earth rendered uninhabitable, mass movements and starvation of populations, wars, and a devastated biosphere. We are already looking at mass extinction at a faster rate than any in geological history, and every lost species represents a further reduction in the Earth's capacity to adapt to change. Continued unrestrained emissions of carbon dioxide at increasing rates put at risk, not just the continuing existence of human civilisation, but the very survival of much of the life of the Earth.

Lest this seem too pessimistic, I think there are grounds for hope although they may not be very welcome to humanity. As Knoll points out in his book, the dominant life forms on Earth are in fact bacteria, not just because of their numbers, but also because they mediate virtually all the critical chemical path ways which maintain the Earth system. Furthermore, it is to life forms like bacteria that we must look for reproduction rates which give them a chance to evolve in the fast-moving scenario that humans have initiated. It was only with the pre-Cambrian explosion that a surge of "higher" life forms emerged from the primordial bacterial slime. Perhaps the age of humanity will end by handing the torch back to Earth's true heirs, the bacteria.

Kairos time

Finally, let us endeavour to put the ideas discussed in this paper into the context of a Christian understanding of time and history. How does the modern scientific story fit into the Christian account? We have seen two aspects of the scientific account. The physical sciences point to a violent past of extremely fast timescales, leading to a future of lower and lower levels of activity, and finally petering out into the heat death of the cosmos at some unimaginable point in the future. Biological and cultural evolutions point to very long early periods when changes were very slow, moving towards an escalating complexity, diversity and rapidity of change which eventually becomes unsustainable. Our current understanding of the possible futures of our planet suggest that we are poised uncomfortably between the two, and possibly face only a very narrow window in which life as most of us understand it, including human society, remains possible.

The Gospels focus strongly on time, and they especially use the Greek word "*kairos*". This means "time" in the sense of the "right time", the ideal moment. It has something of the same connotation as time in the sense of an actor's or comedian's sense of timing. "*Kairos*" may be embedded within physical time, but it transcends it, it has a continuing significance long after the moment has passed by. Christian mystics speak of moments of insight or perception which are over before one realises they are happening; these too are "*kairos*" events. The message of Jesus and the earliest church was that the kingdom of God is upon us; the moment ("*kairos*") is here. As far as we can tell, the preaching of Jesus and the outlook of the early church was profoundly apocalyptic. Something was about to happen, God was going to do a new thing. As physical time continued, so this eschatological understanding became sublimated. Either it was personalised and became identified with a purely personal event in the life of each individual, or it was seen as an event in the far distant future.

Today, science is obliging us to return to an apocalyptic vision of our world. Wonderful, awe-inspiring and complex as it is, we are compelled to see our living world as a transient state, and a state which conceivably has only a very short time still to run. Humanity has developed a sublime ability to understand, to draw mental pictures. I am in awe of a species that can conceive and discuss and even experiment with the Universe as it was a mere 10^{-43} seconds after its formation. Yet this species is in inexorable thrall to the same imperatives which drive other species, of expansion, domination, and aggression, even when we can see ever more plainly the damage that this is doing to a finite, vulnerable world. The words of St Paul echo in our minds: "I do not do the good I want to do, but the evil I do not want to do - this I keep on doing".

Caught in the hiatus between decaying physical time and frenetic climaxing biological time, as a Christian I hold fast to the promise of *kairos* time, to those unexpected golden moments in our individual and collective lives which offer hope of significance, of beauty and awe. At the heart of the Christian gospel is hope. Yet we must somehow seek for hope that is outside time. I finish by quoting a poem by R.S. Thomas:

I have seen the sun break through
to illuminate a small field
for a while, and gone my way

and forgotten it. But that was the pearl
of great price, the one field that had
the treasure in it. I realise now
that I must give all that I have
to possess it. Life is not hurrying

on to a receding future, nor hankering after
an imagined past. It is the turning
aside like Moses to the miracle
of the lit bush, to a brightness
that seemed as transitory as your youth
once, but is the eternity that awaits you.

Ian James is Emeritus Professor of Geophysical Fluid Dynamics
in the University of Reading. He has published papers on the
fluid dynamics of the Earth and planets. He is ordained priest in
the Church of England and acts as Environment Advisor to the
Diocese of Oxford.

Origins and Stories: Intelligent Faith

John Strain

"God's creation is, if taken seriously, a very mysterious affair... The main point of saying that God did it is ... that we cannot at all think how it was done (as the Book of Job points out)." Mary Midgley (1981) *Heart and Mind*

Introduction: Darwin's story and ours

Darwin's publisher, Robert Murray, thought that putting pictures into the sixth edition of, *On the Origin of Species,* would make a fearsome hole in the profits. His willingness to stand the cost testifies to both the appeal of illustration in 1872 and to its novelty. Today, colour photography has created (not *ex nihilo*) a far more pictorial age for us. Internet and weekly colour supplements inundate us with fauna and flora from every continent. Television enables us to be living witnesses to the morphology of biological systems. Changing the speed of cameras gives us the illusion we are watching natural selection take place before our eyes. We can see pictures of everything from the tiniest changes in insect morphology to the largest of stellar explosions that took place more years ago than could have been imagined by biblical authors.

Knowledge of change has its darker side. It's the survival of species, rather than their origins that matters more today. As we face the threat of extinction not just of our species but our planet, whether or not the fittest will survive is less important than whether any of us will. One consequence of our persistent worries of looming environmental disaster is that we are deeply conscious, individually and communally, about the importance of processes of change, both the avoidable and the inevitable ones. Whatever beliefs we hold about ultimate origins, we no longer need to be convinced of change in the natural world. For Darwin and his readership, it was very different. He addressed an audience for whom the constancy of species and the permanency of creation had been long established. It was change that was new. The transformation of the countryside and the towns by new industries, some only decades old, were the new phenomena in the second half of the nineteenth century, together with the political reform that accompanied them. What is commonplace for us: change, transformation, variation were all new and astonishing phenomena to Darwin's readers, whether frightening, liberating or just exciting.

This was the context in which Darwin demonstrated his commitment to detailed observations and stories of the abundant transformations and variations he witnessed in the natural world. His careful recording of natural phenomena and stories of change in the natural world were exciting in a way that is hard to imagine today. The dynamics of change and their pictorial representation set imaginations aflame - sufficient to calm the nerves of the publisher. Between 1859 and 1872 Darwin's *Origin of Species* went through six editions.

Now that the permanence of change is itself commonplace, new questions set us thinking. In the world that struggles to reconcile particularity and globality, difference and communality, we have a stronger appetite for narratives and stories about origins. In a world obsessed with evidence and utility, questions about faiths, threatening to generate certainties without evidence, occupy us in a way that suggests either appropriate attachments to faiths or fear of them. Two hundred years after his birth, it is striking how little Darwin's work engages directly with the contemporary controversies concerning creation and the nature of our knowledge relating to creation. These were just not the philosophical questions that energised him. Like Dawkins, he was an able biologist, not a philosopher or theologian. He was a committed naturalist and empiricist. Experimenting with the whole of biological history being impossible, Darwin attuned himself to the merits of framing general laws through a process of induction from the material he gathered. He learnt of Paley's version of the argument for God's existence from design (the watchmaker argument) at Cambridge. It failed to convince Darwin as it has continued to fail many. In later life, Darwin admitted to being an agnostic in relation to divine involvement in creation. But these were not the issues at the heart of Darwin's energy. One looks in vain, in Darwin's writing, for epistemology, for philosophy of science and for the scholarly reflection on the hermeneutics of biblical texts.

It is therefore somewhat striking that so much controversy in the wake of Darwin's work has focused on topics that were of relatively little interest to him. The controversies that dominate public debate concerning evolution do not focus very much on the dynamics and processes of biological change that so occupied Darwin's story. They focus on how it all began. What was the process of creation itself? Protagonists of grand evolutionary theory and biblicists of a literalist persuasion clamour to tell us what actually happened. The early chapters of the Book of Genesis and the theory of evolution have at least one thing in common. They both appeal to people's desire to tell the story of our origins. Mary Midgley (1985) observed that "the theory of evolution is, and cannot help being…a powerful folk tale about human origins." We cannot go back there. We cannot re-run the history of the universe in the laboratory and alter some of the variables to see if the story would have been different. It does not follow that either Darwin or whoever wrote the Book of Genesis were wrong in their endeavours. But it does invite us to reflect on the quest for certainty in the stories of our origins. People sometimes get upset about the word story being used of science. But the word history as it used in both human and natural history has its roots in *historia*, the story, the account we give that makes sense.

Faith in Nothing and the Religion of Science

The word 'treasure' is a noun and a verb. You can ask a shopkeeper for bananas, chocolate, jewellery and treasures. The grammar of the sentence is fine but it will surely puzzle the shopkeeper. He will need to know what you treasure (verb). Lash (1996) remarked on how modernity has witnessed a shift in the sense of the word 'god' from what a person sets his heart on to an entity, a thing, a member of class, a noun. For some people, atheists, this is an empty class. The term first appears in 1571 (Buckley, 1987). For others, monotheists, it is a class with one member. Aquinas (Summa Theologiae, Ia, 13.8) was well aware that *Deus* was a proper noun but knew that no distinction can be drawn between divine identity and activity. God is *actus purus*, 'pure act', manifested in God's revelation to Moses in Exodus in the words 'I am who am', the distinction between 'is' and 'does' having no application. The persons of the Trinity are not nouns not verbs, Weinandy (2000) reminds, and the names they are designated by, Father, Son and Holy Spirit designate the acts by which they are defined.

The significance that Lash draws from his reflection on God as activity in relationship is to reject the insistence of modernity in forcing religion into a concern with a certain limited set of super-natural 'things' or entities. Instead, as Lash explains, it is to regard religion as a school in which people learn to relate to God, not worshipping any thing "not the world nor any part, person, dream, event or memory of it" (Lash, 2008).

There is a second step required in Lash's deconstruction of the stranglehold that modernity has imposed on religion. Creation, instantaneous and eternal, the reflection of our entire dependency on the no thing that is the faithfulness of God, is not to produce a change in anything. Creation is not some distant event in which an agent causes some change in some thing. In Carroll's (2000) words: "The Creator does not take nothing and make something out of nothing. Rather any thing left entirely to itself, wholly separated from the cause of its existence, would be absolutely nothing.....Creation, thus, as Aquinas shows, is a subject for metaphysics and theology; it is not a subject for the natural sciences." As Wittgenstein (1961) remarked, "it is not how things are in the world that is [the mystery] but that it exists". Faith in God is to have faith in no thing, faith in nothing. There are, of course, many rival candidates for worship: sex, power, art, scholarship, progress and evolution.

The debate that Ruse (1982) reports as to the scientific status of creation science had no good reason to debate whether evolutionary theory, whatever else it might be, is a religion or not. But Midgley (2002) documents how evolutionary theory can wander far from Darwin's own work, abandoning the methodology of empirical science in explaining change in the natural world and using it instead as an interpretive key to human action. She traces particularly the contrasting stories of how evolution can, on the one hand, guarantee us the best of all possible worlds, through inevitable natural progress; and on the other hand, assure us of the continuing nastiness of human beings on to the other; a sort of theory of counter-ethics. Auguste Compte was an early apostle of the religion of humanity that would guarantee not just material blessings but "a new and more exalted type of human being." The sociobiologist Ghiselin (1974) can stand here for all who would dismiss the possibility of altruism in human behaviour:

Given a full chance to act in his own interest, nothing but expediency will restrain him from brutalizing, from maiming, from murdering – his brother, his mate, his parent, or his child, Scratch an altruist and watch a 'hypocrite bleed'.

Midgley's point is that 'evolutionism' can become a faith with many features of traditional religion about it. It has its own creation myths and it attempts to use them to shape our understanding of ourselves. It has a comprehensive explanation for everything. It has its own theory of morality. It has its own prophecies and its own eschatologies. What appears to be empirical, capable of prediction, falsifiable, is frequently revealed as religious. What is identified as religious can sometimes be seen as idolatrous, inviting faith in – things.

But there is something important in the relationship between science and religion. But to understand this relationship, the different activities and stories that constitute science needs to be recognised.

Stories of Science

The explosion and near disaster that struck the Apollo 13 spacecraft, on its way to the moon in 1970, required an immediate return to earth. The story of Apollo 13's recovery remains an astonishingly graphic illustration of how understanding gravity gives power to predict position and time with exactitude. It was this understanding that enabled the exact amount of thrust required to put the space capsule into an orbit round the moon to enable it to gain sufficient kinetic energy to return to earth over 300,000 kilometres away, exactly as planned. This is science in the mode of using equations to predict the future. It works just as well when calculating the movements of the planets in history or at light years of distance away.

But science is not always like this and in any case such equations only work if you know the start points to put into them. The complex qualitative methodologies that help us understand the efficacy of psychotherapists listening to bereaved children tell their stories of grief are very different. They generate much less exactitude and a very different sort of control. But they are no less serious in their scientific intent and they embrace an enthusiasm for progress, even if the enthusiasm is rooted in caring relationships more than in grand certainties. Darwinian evolutionary theory is rather different again. It presents what

Lonergan (1957:132) called the outstanding instance of the importance of probability as a principle of explanation. It explains why species differ, why they are found as they are, why their numbers vary over time. The explanations are immanent in the data, generating an emergent probability. It is not the isolated individual that matters but the combination of variations that matters over evolutionary time.

In 1871, twelve years after the first edition of *Origin of Species*, Darwin published *The Descent of Man*, a very different story about human evolution, ripe with new hypotheses of human origins and imaginative speculation of the future of mankind, frequently expressed in timorous and honest supposition (the phrase 'we may suppose' occurs 800 times in it).

Despite the differences between the Darwinian *zeitgeist* and ours, there is something else that bonds all these science stories together with Dawkins, intelligent designers and biblical literalists. It is that same combination of awe, imagination, wonder and passion that bonds science and religion together. Sometimes it figures in the gentle concern to find effective remedies for those suffering. Sometimes it is evident in the power of stories that give control across the universe. I have intimated already at the sense of awe in natural history that Darwin conveyed to his readers in both picture and prose. Dawkins has his own evident passions for a rather limited set of activities he would like to call science. Creationists and biblical literalists have their own passions. One of my own earliest intellectual excitements was reading a comparison by Jacob Bronowski (1956) of the work of the astronomer Johannes Kepler and the poet William Blake. One a scientist, one a poet, both had astonishing intellectual imagination in devising new ways of looking at data, fresh hypotheses, exciting metaphors. Both had a capacity to observe, to record with fidelity to what the universe revealed. A key aspect of what we honour in Darwin was his vibrant combination of intellectual imagination and faithfulness in recording what he observed. Imagination and faithfulness to the phenomena remain important shared hallmarks of the scientist, and the theologian in the stories they tell.

Stories of Origins

If the God in whom we are invited to have faith, in the Christian tradition, is no thing, no entity, it follows that our images of God will reflect the shape of our experience. So the people of Israel narrated the stories of God the shepherd and God as king. Narratives of knowledge[1] stand in marked contrast to discussions of a belief in 'a god', a putative member of a class of entities called gods. Stories will encompass origins. What is it to have stories about our origins ? We don't just read stories. We are asked to listen to other people's stories; and in some way or other, to believe in them, intelligently. For many people, narratives are fictions, and grand narratives attempts to impose fictions on others. I contend that faith in our stories should be virtuous. If our faith in them is intellectually virtuous, I shall argue, following a clue in Aristotle, then it is necessarily reasonable. Our faith in stories should be virtuous, whether or not our stories are, in contemporary parlance, scientific. Such would count as intelligent faith. Very often faith is treated as deficient knowledge. Faith suggests something vulnerable, something necessarily less than precise. If we were more intelligent, more knowledgeable at least, faith might be something we could safely discard, something to be left behind in the march of intelligent progress. Faith, it is often alleged, arises where there is no evidence or the conclusion of an argument is accepted but there is a missing premise in the argument. Remedying the deficiency does not justify faith. It enables deductions that enable what John Henry Newman (1844) called a 'notional assent' to formal inferences. My aim is to not to justify faith by turning it into something that is not faith, but rather to point towards faith as a virtue.

Stories of Other's Origins

My wife and I have been together for forty years. We don't argue much about the story of the origin of our marriage. But we tell it differently. Different places, different meetings, different friends, all had different significances and joys for each of us in our stories. My wife is not a Christian and the notion of exactly what it is to 'be married' has different resonances for each of us, so the steps in each of our minds that led to marriage are different. Unsurprisingly, we have different stories of our marriage. But our stories persistently illuminate each other's. Occasionally one of us has a memory sparked off by the telling of the other's story. So a new, rather special revelation emerges as new stories are constructed. Memories can of course play false. We are not relativists imagining that any story goes. It's possible to get stories wrong. We do it all the time. So we try and be truthful.

Stories of origins figure strongly in the bible, but they are all different too. The gospel of Matthew opens with a story of *the genesis* of Jesus Christ, evoking memories of an earlier genesis. This particular one is a rather tedious list that begins with Abraham and proceeds through some surprising omissions and inclusions that Brown (1988) noted. The holy wives of the great Patriarchs, Sarah, Rebekah and Rachel never get a mention. Isaac who, Karen Armstrong (1996) suggests, never quite escaped the trauma of being offered to God on a sacrificial fire by his Dad, is the first to be mentioned after Abraham. Jacob who lied and cheated his way into becoming the eponymous ancestor of Israel also figures but Joseph, that rather egotistical visionary who overcame his enslavement in Egypt with heroism and courage, is not mentioned. The mundane Judah who sold his brother for ready cash and sought out prostitutes, manages to get a mention. The story, Brown suggests, "is faithful to an insight about a God who is not controlled by human merit but manifests his own unpredictable graciousness." It is the genesis story of one who will preach salvation to sinners and tax collectors but not to

299

those who are already religious. It is the story of one who will die for us "while we were still sinners" (Romans 5:8). Clearly, there is considerable sense of design in the story, not quite the meaning of design that some have in mind when speaking of intelligent design of creation, but perhaps a more biblical sense.

The Roman historian Livy, had his own, rather worthier rationale for writing about origins. It too had a strong sense of design and a distinctly ethical flavour, with much less time for human fallibility than the gospel.

> There is this exceptionally beneficial and fruitful advantage to be derived from the study of the past, that you see, set in the clear light of historical truth, examples of every possible type. From these you may select for yourself and your country what to imitate, and also what, as being mischievous in its inception and disastrous in its issues, you are to avoid. *Titus Livius (Livy) Ab Urbe Condita, Praefatio X (translated by Roberts, 1905)*

Carr (1961) described how Leopold von Ranke, that apostle of post Enlightenment 'scientific historiography', had no time for such moralising and turned readers away from using history as source for education in ethics or meaning for the future. Herbert Spencer who coined the phrase "survival of the fittest", encouraged us to see the persistent struggle of biological competition as a model for our social and economic life. Before long, social Darwinism became part of the "science" of capitalist and imperial expansion until the excesses of eugenics in the third *Reich*, caused people to ponder. This was just the sort of imaginative wandering from the evidence Ranke would have no truck with. For Ranke, writing history was "not to judge the past, not to instruct one's contemporaries with an eye to the future, but merely to show how it actually was (wie es eigentlich gewesen)".

Ranke's emphasis on how things actually were suggests a yardstick, a factual benchmark against which any narrative might be judged. Two entities are held together: history and 'what happened'. The truth of the former is measured through correspondence with the second.

Correspondence was a key theme of the early Wittgenstein's *Tractatus Logico Philosophicus*. Wittgenstein was at pains to explain, in somewhat gnomic utterances, what constituted truthful propositions, in history or any other subject. He attempted to define "What every picture.....must have in common with reality in order to be able to represent it." Both Ranke and Wittgenstein encouraged a correspondence theory of truth by which narratives can be seen as morally neutral representations of how things are.

Ranke's and Livy's rationale for writing history and Darwin's for writing natural history, is different from the understanding of the bible that has developed over twenty centuries. Both Ranke, Livy and Darwin, helped us understand their quest by being self conscious about their purposes. They wrote prefaces to their work. But the Bible has no preface. There is no divine author's introduction which explains what it is. In whatever sense God is deemed (or denied) to be its author, there is no foreword, or set of footnotes that form part of the Bible to explain either the author's intention or the approach to be taken to its reading. This is not to suggest there are no distinctively Christian hermeneutics of the Bible. De Lubac (2000) provided an exhaustive summary of how literal and spiritual senses (moral, analogical, and mystical) of the biblical texts have persistently illuminated each other in the Christian tradition in a way that guides the Church as a worshipping community, faithful to the divine covenants revealed in Old and New Testaments. It is easy, but erroneous, to imagine, that 'literal truth' refers to whatever the words represent in the world of historical fact, as Ranke might have described; or as Wittgenstein might have wanted us to understand by his pictorial theory of meaning and his correspondence theory of truth. But this is not how 'literal truth' has been understood in ecclesial exegesis. The *littera* was, above all else, the divine word, not some human construction of it. The literal sense of the text includes such metaphors of six days to describe creation. But the deep dependency of everything that is on the word of God is both instantaneous and eternal. Fidelity to the word and to the story presented by the biblical text is an invitation to apprehend the mystery of its meaning as much as to imagine what it corresponded to in human discourse.

Fidelity to the word and to the story are part of what distinguishes biblical hermeneutics from Livy's account of history. Livy was always open to the charge of picking and choosing whatever examples from the past suited the lessons in ethics and politics that he wanted to preach. Biblical hermeneutics, in contrast to both Wittgenstein's correspondence theory of truth and to Livy's selective use of the past have persistently steered a course between the Scylla of making the truth up for ourselves and the Charybdis of imagining that facts will speak for themselves without our voice.

There are today, 'creationists' who advocate an account of the process of creation from the early chapters of the Book of Genesis and who indeed give primacy to what they might call the 'literal truth' as a historical record. This quest is much closer to an understanding of history that Ranke and Wittgenstein might have shared than it is to the primacy of the divine word, alive in the community that constitutes the Church that has been preserved in the Church over twenty centuries[2]. Literalistic creation science focuses on presenting a factual account of 'what actually happened' It shares common ground with the quest of those evolutionary accounts to tell us the truth of what happened. For all the opposition, conflict even, between creationism and evolutionary theory, there is common bedrock in a correspondence theory of truth across creationist and evolutionary accounts of our origins.

Creationism and intelligent design, whatever the precise

contents of these grand portmanteau concepts, have a strong aroma of clarity about them. They suggest an exactness, a manifestation of intelligence about them (human or divine). Maintaining a strict fidelity to the Genesis account of creation provides a temporal infrastructure of specific days (or at least periods) in which events took place. In so far as the account sets God above the actual events themselves as the author, it is an account with certain similarities with William Paley's argument. This was a notion of God that was energised in the eighteenth century, the God who stands remote from creation having set it all in motion like the cosmic watchmaker, following laws which can be revealed by science. Both biblical literalist and creation science versions of intelligent design have clarity and detail in the processes they allude to. They turn God into entities like "the truth". They are at risk, as Lash would remind us, of being idolatries.

There is another candidate for our intelligent appraisal, a faith that takes leave of the reality of God. Cupitt's (1997) *After God* exhorts us towards a sea of faith as a human creation, a "non realist" view of God, one in which (Cupitt, 1997:83) the "old metaphysics of God" was destroyed by Hume and Kant and will not be revived." This view of faith as a set of customs, rituals, linguistic expressions (games even) was deemed to owe a large debt to Wittgenstein, encouraging us to abandon the "objective" doctrine of God and replace it with a focus on ethics, human rights and "talk of belief in God in terms of the way it leads us to see ourselves." Cupitt's reliance on the later Wittgenstein for this particular version of non-realism is misplaced as will be apparent from my later remarks on basic beliefs.

We have identified three approaches to the story of creation: evolutionary theory, biblical creationism and non-realism. All three approaches share a common reluctance to admit the vital significance of faith. All three depend on an assumption that the quest for certainty in the explanation of creation is to be either established; or in the case of Cupitt, abandoned. I wish to advocate an understanding of faith that steers between the Charybdis of certainty and the Scylla of fairy tales, to return to an approach to faith that is older than the Christian religion but which has been soundly integrated into the Christian tradition of thought. What I have in mind is an approach to faith as a virtue.

Basic Beliefs

In his *University Sermons* Cardinal John Henry Newman (1844) opposed the view that faith is a state of heart or a moral quality or simply a belief based on no evidence. Faith has an intellectual component in which reason had a role. "Faith, considered as an exercise of Reason, has this characteristic, — that it proceeds far more on antecedent grounds than on evidence" The example that Newman provided of a proposition taken on faith, informed by reasons, was the proposition that Great Britain is an island.

> Our reasons for believing that ...[Britain is]... circumnavigable are such as these: first that we have been so taught in our childhood, and it is so in all our maps.....every book we have read, invariably took it for granted; and our whole national history, the routine transactions and current events of the country, our social and commercial system....Numberless facts rest on the truth of it; no received fact rests on its being otherwise.

Kenny (1992) remarked that it was one of Newman's major contributions to philosophy that a claim such as Great Britain is an island is not a claim based on a sufficiently copious stack of evidence. Kenny's point (1992:106) is not that it is based on insufficient evidence: "the reason ... is that it is not based on evidence at all. For evidence has to be better known than that for which it is evidence; and none of the scraps of reasons I could produce for the proposition that Great Britain is an island are better known than that proposition itself."

The belief that Britain is an island belongs to a class of beliefs that Plantinga (1983) and Kenny (1992) called basic beliefs. The belief that Australia exists is a basic belief of mine. I have never been there. I have many reasons to believe Australia exists but none figure in my mental structure quite so firmly as the belief that Australia exists. If it turned out to be the case that Australia does not exist, there would be enormous damage to my mental architecture of beliefs. Far more damage to it would ensue than if any of the reasons I might offer for believing that Australia exists proved false. Even if atlas and geography book fail to mention Australia I would conclude that they are wrong. But if I were to conclude that Australia does not exist, far more violence to my mental architecture of beliefs would ensue than would be done by my realizing that any or all of the reasons I offered proved false. In this sense, my belief that Australia exists and Newman's belief that Great Britain is an island are both basic beliefs. Basic beliefs are not logically necessary truths. They are neither self evident, nor evident to the senses. Scientists too proceed with their own basic beliefs.

Some qualifications are needed. It doesn't follow that people could not believe that Australia exists on the basis of reasons. Children acquire many such beliefs through reasons, particularly the common reason that their teachers say so. But eventually we each form our own mental architecture of beliefs and what is a basic belief for one person may not be a basic belief for others. It is in these respects that I claim that God as my creator and sustainer. I have reasons for this claim. But none of these reasons are such that their abandonment would play such havoc with my mental architecture, were they to prove false, as would the realisation that the basic beliefs are false. Aristotle put essentially the same point when he remarked that the premises of an informative piece of reasoning need to be better known than the conclusion.

I suggest that there is an intimate relationship between our basic beliefs and the stories of our origins. Stories of ourselves, our marriages, our communities and our species will make sense to us in relation to our basic beliefs and, of course, help shape them, particularly as we listen to other stories.

Not every belief can count as basic. If I believe in witches and fairy tales, can I simply tell you that these are my basic beliefs? Is there some sieve to allow through those articles of faith which would count as intelligent faith but which, in Kenny's (1992:20) words are: "not as hospitable to lunacy as an open door policy of laying down no general conditions or restrictions on what can count as basic."

Virtuous Faith

In the *Nichomachean ethics*, Aristotle gave an account of moral virtues in which virtuous conduct stands as a mean between two vicious extremes. Generosity is the mean between meanness and profligacy. Courage is the mean between rashness and cowardice. Aristotle also maintained there are intellectual virtues as well as moral virtues. If these intellectual virtues worked like moral virtues they would lie in a spectrum with a mean. Thus *Sophia*, wisdom, one of Aristotle's five intellectual virtues, might be the virtuous mean between the two vicious extremes of over indulgence in the abstract and refusal to engage with matters beyond the superficial. But Aristotle did not think that intellectual virtues are means in the way that moral virtues are. The reason for this is that mental states associated with theoretical knowledge have truth as their object. Truth is the good which is sought by the intellect. It is not possible to have too much truth. Hence it is wrong to limit knowledge by means of a mean.

Aristotle's concern with the purity of knowledge may have been an unnecessary part of what he inherited from Plato. Once we remove the insistence that what we claim to know has to be in accordance with some external benchmark (*sub-specie aeternitatis* as Plato and perhaps the early Wittgenstein would have it) there is scope, Kenny shows, for a virtue which characterises the appropriate degree of belief. If we believe something too much in relation to its claim upon us we fall into the error of credulity. If we do not believe enough, we fall into scepticism. The intellectual virtue of faith lies between the vicious extremes of credulity and scepticism. Our basic beliefs and our faith in stories associated with them will be intellectually virtuous and reasonable in so far as they honour this mean.

Such intellectually virtuous faith stories of our origins look rather different from biblical literalism and intelligent design which reach out for certainty but err on the side of credulity. It also excludes Cupitt's non-realism which errs on the side of scepticism. But this claim depends on there being some criterion that makes a particular faith or belief virtuous. There needs to be what Aristotle calls an *orthos logos* or 'right idea' to accept some basic beliefs and stories as appropriate objects of faith.

Here we may turn again to Wittgenstein. Whereas the *Tractatus* serves as an ikon for Ranke's objectivity and biblical literalism, the last work of Wittgenstein, *On Certainty*, provides some clues to truthfulness that illuminate the reasonableness of faith. Wittgenstein addressed such foundational propositions in his *On Certainty*. But he rejected the notion of foundation that perhaps suggested a false sense of security. "They do not serve as foundations in the same way as hypotheses which, if they turn out to be false, are replaced by others." Wittgenstein preferred the metaphor of a riverbed to a foundation.

It might be imagined that some propositions, of the form of empirical propositions, were hardened and functioned as channels for such empirical propositions as were not hardened but fluid, and that this altered with time, in that fluid propositions hardened and hard ones became fluid...The same proposition gets treated at one time as something to test by experience and at another as a rule of testing.

Similarities in the approach taken by Newman and Wittgenstein in their approach to the rationality of religious faith are identified by Barrett (1997). Newman distinguished notional and real assent. Formal, logical reasoning, syllogistic in manner, under-pinned notional assent without personal commitment. Informal reason underpinned real assent with moved people to action and commitment. Newman's distinction between what deductive and cumulative reasoning has much in common with Wittgenstein's distinction between what can and cannot be said in ordinary language.

If faith in stories of our origins is intellectually virtuous then it will be reasonable because it will cohere with other beliefs some of which we will share with others and with what deeply matters to us. Such faith may not give us the same sort of certainly promised by intelligent design or biblical literalism. But it is intelligent faith.

Notes

[1] Lash (2008) describes the denarration of knowledge that came with modernity.

[2] Barr (1977) pointed out how biblical literalism was nourished not by the living tradition in which the Bible bore fruit but by modernity.

References

Armstrong, K. 1996. *In the Beginning*. London: Harper Collins.

Barr, J. 1977. *Fundamentalism*. London: SCM Press.

Barrett, C. 1997. *Newman and Wittgenstein on the Rationality of Religious Belief* in Ker, I. (Ed) *Newman and Conversion* Edinburgh: T & T Clark.

Bronowski, J. 1956. *Science and Human Values*. New York: Julian

Messner.

Brown, R. 1988. *An Adult Christ at Christmas*. Collegeville, Minnesota: Liturgical Press.

Buckley, M. J. 1987. *At the Origins of Modern Atheism*. London: Yale University Press.

Carr, E. H. 1961. *What is History*. London: Macmillan.

Carroll, W. E. 2000. *Creation, Evolution and Thomas Aquinas* Revue des Questions Scientifiques 171 (4) 2000 pp 319-317.

Cupitt, D. 1997. *After God*. London:Weidenfeld & Nicolson.

De Lubac, H 2000. *Medieval Exegesis: The Four Senses of Scripture*.

Ghiselin, M. T. 1974. *The Economy of Nature and the Evolution of Sex*. Berkeley California: University of California Press.

Kenny, A. 1992. *What is Faith, Essays in the philosophy of religion*. Oxford: Oxford University Press.

Lash, N 1996. *Theology for Pilgrims*. London:Dartman Longman and Todd.

Livius, *Titus (Livy) Ab Urbe Condita, Praefatio X (translated by Roberts, 1905.)*

Lonergan, B. 1957. *Insight, A Study of Human Understanding*. London:Longmans.

Midgley, M 1981. *Hearts and Minds*. London: Routledge.

Midgley, M 2002. *Evolution as a Religion* Revised edition, London: Routledge.

Newman, J. H. 1844. *University Sermons*.

Plantinga, A 1983. *Reason and Belief in God* in. Plantinga, A and Wolterstorff, N. (Eds) *Faith and Rationality*. Notre Dame, Indiana: University of Notre Dame Press.

Ruse, M 1982. *Creation-Science Is Not Science*, Science Technology and Human Values, vol 7, 40, 72-78.

Weinandy, T. G. 2000. *Does God suffer?* Notre Dame, Indiana: University of Notre Dame Press, cited in Lash, N (2008) *Theology for Pilgrims*, London: Dartman Longman & Todd.

Wittgenstein, L 1961. *Tractatus Logico Philosophicus*, London: Routledge & Kegan Paul.

Wittgenstein, L 1969. *On Certainty*, Oxford: Blackwell.

John Strain is an Anglican Priest and a Chartered Psychologist. He teaches ethics, religion and politics at Surrey University and he is the Advisor in Work, Economy and Business in the Diocese of Guildford. He is also Chaplain to the Supported Housing for retired clergy at Manormead, Hindhead, Surrey. His most recent publication is *Universities, Ethics and Professions,*(2009), London, Routledge, with Ronald Barnett and Peter Jarvis.

Evolution and Christian Faith in the 19th Century

Richard Harries

The intellectual crisis brought about by the theory of evolution was serious. But the one that caused an even bigger furore at the time, and which still causes some Christians great difficulty, was the historical and critical study of the Bible. Of course, how we understand the bible is closely related to how we view evolution, but it was the publication of *Essays and Reviews*_in 1860 that caused the public temperature to rise so sharply. The critical study of the Bible had been carried on in Germany for more than half a century, but although Britain had major controversies over this period, they were mainly to do with issues of Church authority. Rather late in the day the British public was faced with a series of essays by different authors helping readers come to terms with the new approach to the Bible. The Bishops of the Church of England prosecuted the two authors who could be got at in the Church Courts. To the dismay of Churchmen, the decision of the Court of Arches was dismissed on appeal to the Judicial Committee of the Privy Council. The Bishops then decided to condemn the book synodically in Convocation, and only two bishops dissented. Pusey and Lord Shaftsbury (representing Anglo-Catholics and Evangelicals respectively) and *The Record* newspaper persuaded 11, 000 clergymen and 137, 000 laymen to sign an address upholding "without reserve or qualification, the Inspiration and Divine Authority of the whole Canonical Scriptures", including the doctrine of eternal punishment. As with the late 20th century controversy in the church about homosexuality, the issue was primarily one about the nature and authority of the Bible.

The second point that needs to be borne in mind is that

"Around 1850 few scientists of any note had a good word to say for the idea of evolution." (Vidler, 1961:116) This means that in relation to the evolution controversy, those who were determined to refute the idea did not even have to consider the issue of biblical inspiration. They could simply refer to the best known scientific authorities to justify their rejection of an evolutionary view of creation. Fifteen years before the publication of *The Origin of Species* an anonymous author (who 40 years later turned out to be Robert Chambers of Encyclopedia fame) published *The Vestiges of the Natural History of Creation*. This book, which had huge sales, argued that the whole of creation, including the emergence of new species, operates according to scientific laws, laws which God had arranged and in which he trusted. But Chambers was not a professional scientist and the faults in his argument were quickly exposed by those who were.

The result of these two factors, the late arrival of critical approaches to the Bible on the British intellectual scene, and the fact that the majority of well known scientists did not believe in evolution, meant that even a liberally minded person like F.D.Maurice accepted the Biblical account of creation uncritically. Maurice, who was later sacked from his position as Professor at King's College, London, for disbelieving in the eternity of hell, was still talking of the world being only 6000 years old, with all the species being ready made, in the 1850's.

It is against this background that we must see the famous encounter of Samuel Wilberforce and the whole intellectual debate over evolution.

The first challenge to traditional ways of reading the Genesis story came from geologists. In the 1830's Charles Lyell and Dean Buckland established the geological succession of rocks and fossils and showed the world to be much older than the accepted date for the Garden of Eden. However, traditionalists found ways of getting round this, most reputably by interpreting God's day in

Genesis as a great length of time, and less reputably by suggesting that God had planted the fossils to test our faith. It was however Darwin's *Origin of Species* that combined with this new dating from geology to undermine not only a literalist view of creation, but the whole Christian story of a perfect creation, marred by the fall and redeemed by Christ. Darwin's book was no ordinary scientific textbook and it is important to see how and why *The Origin of Species* had such power over people's minds.

First, it consists of a sustained, strongly argued case with enough vivid examples to convince educated readers without overwhelming them with too much technical detail. Ever since his voyage on the *Beagle* in 1831 Darwin had been reflecting on these issues and accumulating data, and the idea of natural selection as the great clue to nature had long been in his mind. But it was not until 1859 that *The Origin* was published. He had written it in 10 months, with few books to hand, as what he called a sketch, spurred into writing by the letter from Wallace outlining a similar thesis. It is this set of circumstances, I think, that gives Darwin's book its force and readability. More than 20 years painstaking research and reflection is distilled into one pure outpouring.

Another reason for its huge influence is that the reader is conscious of listening to an honest man. Time and again Darwin acknowledges the huge gaps in our knowledge. He is fully aware of the difficulties that the reader is likely to feel, and he admits that he feels them himself. He argues that it is only by making a supreme effort of the imagination to think about the vast stretches of time in which tiny changes in form can take place and be passed on, that we can begin to grasp the truth of what has happened. He says that he wants to present the strongest case he can find against the truth of his own position, and does so, grappling in particular with the apparent absence of intermediate species living now and the even more serious difficulty of the patchy geological record. At the same time he is absolutely clear, and determined to show, so far as it can be shown, that the theory of natural selection can account for a huge number of extraordinary features in nature, for which the belief in immutable species has no answer. He is no cheap polemicist trying to win a case with any argument that will serve. But he is ardent for truth.

In addition to this there is something of Darwin's subdued but real sense of intellectual satisfaction at his explanation; not quite "a theory of everything", but nevertheless bringing together a mass of phenomena in a coherent and consistent way. And sometimes the language he uses about this seems to have almost religious overtones in the way that higher beings have emerged over millions of years from a few simple forms. Darwin's theory has been refined since his time, and we now know about genetics in a way that he did not; and in particular how a combination of random genetic mutation together with natural selection ensures lasting change. But the reader still feels a sense of "things coming together" when reading Darwin's book. Something of the effect of the book can be gauged by the letter the distinguished New Testament scholar F.J.A.Hort wrote to his equally distinguished colleague B.F.Wescott in March 1960;

> Have you read Darwin? How I should like to talk to you about it! In spite of the difficulties, I am inclined to think it is unanswerable. In any case it is a treat to read such a book.

It is important to realise that in 1859 all the major palaeontologists except Charles Lyell believed in the immutability of species, and Darwin acknowledges how rash of him it is to depart from the opinion of these experts to whom, he said, he owed so much. William Thompson, later Lord Kelvin, who was not a palaeontologist, but was regarded by Victorians as their pre-eminent man of science, may be taken as an example of an attitude shared by many scientists. Kelvin was a devout Christian who did not take the days in the Book of Genesis literally, who had a moderate opposition to evolution on the grounds that his own calculations of the age of the sun and the solar system did not allow enough time for evolution. In response to this work Darwin subsequently modified his view on the rate of evolution but the irony was that Kelvin had not taken into account the contribution of the heat of radioactivity which was yet to be discovered (Wood, 2008: 83)

So when some religious figures opposed Darwin, on the grounds that his case was not yet proved, it was not simply on the basis of dogma. They could appeal to the best known scientists of the time. Samuel Wilberforce, for example, the Bishop of Oxford, whose encounter with Thomas Huxley at the British Association for the Advancement of Science Meeting in 1860, which is discussed below, and which has gone down in history through a distorted report put about many years later, had a first class degree in maths, was a keen amateur natural scientist and was a Vice President of the National Association for the Advancement of Science. He wrote a 39 page review in *Quarterly Review,* which probed the weaknesses in Darwin's argument in a well informed way. Wilberforce claimed to be swayed by the scientific facts alone and not by what is in scripture, but he is self deceived in this, because it is also clear that he regards some views as honouring to nature and God, and others not, on the basis of the Bible. In short, he brought to the science a particular understanding of what God should be, and what would not be compatible with this. This is a point that is taken up later.

Darwin is patient with those who disagree with him. Only very occasionally does he let his irritation show. To admit one particular view he writes "makes the works of God a mere mockery and deception; I would almost as soon believe... that fossil shells had never lived, but had been created in stone so as to mock the shells now living on the sea- shore."

The encounter between the Bishop of Oxford, Samuel

Wilberforce, and Thomas Huxley at the Royal Association Meeting in the new university museum in Oxford on 30th June 1860 has become one of the most celebrated icons of the alleged clash between science and religion. In the popular mind it is associated with the opposition of the church to Galileo, and the continuing obscurantism of religion in contrast to the truth and progress represented by science. The truth is somewhat different and recent years much good scholarly work has unearthed what really happened (Gould, 1986: 18-33. Brooke, 2001: 127-41). The popular view, the myth that took hold, is well given 40 years after the event in the October 1889 edition of *Macmillan's Magazine* in an article entitled "A grandmother's tale"

> The bishop rose, and in a light scoffing tone, florid and fluent, he assured there was nothing in the idea of evolution; rock pigeons were what rock pigeons had always been. Then turning to his antagonist with smiling insolence, he begged to know, was it through his grandfather or his grandmother that he claimed his descent from a monkey? On this, Mr Huxley slowly and deliberately arose. A slight tall figure, stern and pale, very quiet and very grave, he stood before us, and spoke those tremendous words – words which no one seemed sure of now, nor I think could remember just after they were spoken, for their meaning took our breath, though it left us in no doubt as to what it was. He was not ashamed to have a monkey for his ancestor; but he was ashamed to be connected with a man who used his great gifts to obscure the truth. No one doubted his meaning and the effect was tremendous. One lady fainted and had to be carried out: I for one jumped out of my seat.

John Lucas (1979) in his article "Wilberforce and Huxley: A legendary encounter" argued for a rather different account. First, as mentioned above, Wilberforce was not a scientific ignoramus.

Then, as also stressed, most serious scientists at the time did not believe that the scientific evidence which had then been adduced was strong enough to establish a general theory of evolution. Later Darwin himself said of Wilberforce's argument "It is uncommonly clever; it picks out all the most conjectural parts, and brings forward well all the difficulties" again "The bishop makes a very telling case to me". Secondly, the dominant mind of the conference was neither that of Wilberforce nor Huxley but of Joseph Hooker, who did go some way to answering the scientific points raised by Wilberforce. Thirdly, though it appears to have been very difficult to hear, Wilberforce did make a flippant remark and Huxley, in his response did seem to score over Wilberforce. Fourthly, the judgement of listeners was not that Wilberforce had lost the intellectual battle but that he had a lapse of taste by appealing to Victorian sentiments about the female and that Huxley had emerged as the more gentlemanly of the two. Canon Farrar, friend of Darwin and a pall bearer at his funeral, wrote to Huxley's son to correct the false notions that were beginning to spread even then "The victory of your father, was not the ironical dexterity shown by him but the fact that he had got a victory in respect of *manners* and good *breeding*... the speech that really left its mark *scientifically* on the meeting was the short one of *Hooker*".

More recently we have what I suspect is the most thorough of all examinations of what happened by Professor Frank James (2005), in an essay in a book on science and belief. He very helpfully has a number of tables setting out the dates of the different kinds of evidence. There are some contemporary diaries and letters, that is, dating from 1860. There are some contemporary newspaper periodical reports from 1860, as well as some hearsay reports from that time. Then there are later texts describing their discussion dating from 20 years later, 1880 onwards, as well as later letters and unpublished references from that later period. He is particularly intrigued by how little notice was taken of the event at the time, followed by 20 years virtual silence, and then the raising of it into mythic significance. This is a point made by earlier writers, John Lucas for example, but Professor James develops and emphasises it.

James shows that the encounter was not in fact a great pre-planned set occasion. It arose somewhat spontaneously, or at least was organised rather at the last minute in one of the section discussions, the two antagonists being asked to contribute after other speakers. He also bears out the earlier point made about bad manners because the most thorough contemporary account which appeared in the *Athenaeum* two weeks after the event, a long sober discussion of what occurred presented a sanitised version of the encounter. As James writes:

> Such a neutering must mean that the gentlemen of science at the British Association did not wish to publicise the ungentle-manly behaviour of a bishop and its own savants. This inter-pretation is supported by their being no reference whatsoever to the discussion in the 1860 report of *The British Association*.

He also emphasised the fact that the dominant argument at the conference was in fact of Hooker. Wilberforce thought that he had got the better of the encounter. So of course did Huxley but Hooker wrote about Huxley's response "Huxley answered admirably and turned the tables, but he could not throw his voice over so large an assembly, nor command the audience; and he did not allude to Sam's weak points nor put the matter in a formal way that carried the audience". No doubt because he thought Huxley had not made the best of the case he himself, after one more intervention, rose to speak. As he put it:

> My blood boiled, I felt myself a dastard; now I saw my advantage – I swore to myself I would smite that Amalekite, Sam, hip and thigh if my heart jumped out of my mouth,...

there and then I smashed him amid rounds of applause – I hit him in the wind at the first shot in ten words taken from his own ugly mouth – and then proceeded to demonstrate in a few more one that he could never had read your book and two that he was absolutely ignorant of the rudiments of botanical science... Sam was shut up – had not one word to say in reply and the meeting was dissolved.

Professor James believes that soapy Sam lost the encounter because he was unpopular in Oxford and therefore any sympathy for his arguments was lost. Certainly this is how Huxley viewed Wilberforce. He wrote:

If he had dealt with the subject fairly and worthily I would not have treated him in this way. But the round mouthed, oily, special pleading of the man ignorant of the subject presumed on his position and his lawyer faculty gave me a most unmitigated contempt for him. You can't think how pleased all his contemporaries were; I believe I was the most popular man in Oxford for 4 and 20 hours afterwards.

Nevertheless, the crucial fact is that it was only later in the century that the myth started to emerge. This was partly at Huxley's doing, who was a disbeliever for reasons other than natural science. He was also anti-clerical and strangely reluctant to admit that many clergy were, in fact, adherents of Darwin's view even when faced with one of them who was. It was a time when the Darwinians, though they had become the majority party, had not yet lost the sense of being persecuted. As John Lucas put it "The quarrel between religion and science came about not because of what Wilberforce said, but because it was what Huxley wanted; as Darwin's theory gained supporters, they took over his view of the incident". Professor James also points out that blaming science also in some ways suited churchmen at the time because it enabled them to avoid facing up to the real reasons why people were turning away from Christianity. This is a key point.

The big names of Victorian agnosticism, such as George Eliot, turned away from the Christian faith not because of the rise of science or biblical criticism, but because what the church called upon them to believe with a sense of its own moral superiority, struck them as morally inferior to their own ethical beliefs and standards. As Owen Chadwick has shown, scientists then believed and disbelieved for a whole range of reasons, and it is very difficult to ascertain to what extent, if any, science as such was a factor for those who turned away. As mentioned above, Wilberforce in his long and searching review of Darwin's book, brought a critique to bear that he had derived from the bible, namely that what Darwin described was not honouring to God. But this reaction can work the other way round, leading people to disbelieve in God, precisely because the facts, as revealed in the process of evolution, seem to be incompatible with giving honour to the God described in the Bible.

This raises the question of Darwin's own beliefs and their relation to the theory of evolution by natural selection. What we know from his own account is that on the Voyage on the *Beagle* what unsettled him first was not the evidence of evolution, but the realization that there were many different religions in the world, and doubts about the bible as a unique revelation of God. In *The Origin of Species* he was very cautious in his approach to faith. He wrote that what he has discovered through his researches "accords better with what we know of the laws impressed on matter by the Creator" than the traditional alternative. When he wrote *The Origin* he was still a theist. In fact he lost his faith only gradually, and reluctantly, and for a variety of reasons. He had every reason not to lose his faith, for his great mentor, the Professor of Botany at Cambridge, Henslow, whom Darwin revered, was also a clergyman. His wife, whom he adored, was also a believing Christian. But still his faith became eroded. Perhaps he never lost it entirely, but what is clear is that it was not the theory of evolution as such that he found incompatible with faith. "To the end of his life he believed that Asa Gray and Charles Kingsley were right in denying incompatibility between theism and the doctrine of evolution" (Chadwick, 1972: 20).It was the cruelty of life, as came home to him in the death of his beloved daughter. It was the cruelty in nature, "red in tooth and claw" But in *The Origin,_*Darwin takes a much more accepting view of the struggle of life, indeed seeing something grand and noble in it. "When we reflect on this struggle we may console ourselves with the full belief, that the war of nature is not incessant, that no fear is felt, that death is generally prompt, and that the vigorous , the healthy and the happy survive and multiply".

For reasons which are obvious from above, the encounter of Huxley and Wilberforce was not a happy one, which did Wilberforce no credit at the time and which has cast a shadow on the church ever since Huxley propagated a hostile account of it many years later. Much happier was the sermon at the same *British Association for the Advancement of Science* meeting in Oxford in 1860, delivered by Frederick Temple, later Archbishop of Canterbury. It is an entirely positive sermon, in which he first argued that everything on earth comes about "by the slow working of natural causes". Temple puts a positive gloss on this, saying

> We must find His providence in that perfect adaptation of all the parts of the machine to one another which shall have the effect of tender care, though it proceed by an invariable action.

In short, we have to learn from what scientists discover about nature, as we have to learn from the Bible.

Frederick Temple was not alone. Many Christians, like F.J.A.Hort, quoted above, were open to persuasion. The eminent botanist Asa Gray of Harvard University, a friend of Darwin and his main champion in America was a serious and devout Christian believer. Whereas Wilberforce had brought theological presuppositions to bear that precluded an accurate assessment of the science as science, a brilliant young theologian Aubrey Moore brought to the science a theological perspective that did in fact engender an accurate response to the theory of evolution. Darwin's rival for the first to publish a theory of evolution A.R.Wallace, had similar views of Darwin, except that he believed the emergence of the human brain required a special divine intervention. Moore argued that from a theological perspective it was necessary to assert that the same scientific laws operated throughout the whole process.

Apart from the scientific evidence in favour of evolution, *as a theory*, it is infinitely more Christian than a theory of "special creation"...*A theory of occasional intervention implies as its correlative a theory of ordinary absence.*

He went on to argue that such a view fitted the Deism of the previous century, but not Christian orthodoxy, which saw God present in and through the whole process. Amongst Darwin's best known Christian champions was the novelist Charles Kingsley who argued that God does not just make the world, he makes the world make itself, a theological perspective later developed with great sophistication and depth by the 20th century Oxford theologian Austin Farrer.

Amongst scientists who were also religious believers, the story was the same. Professor Flower of the Natural History Museum told the Dean of Windsor in 1890 that he knew no evidence to suggest more unsettlement of faith among the profession of scientists than among the profession of (say) barristers." Francis Galton, no friend of the churches and a friend of Darwin sent a questionnaire to all persons whom he regarded as established scientists. Of the 126 replies, 88, or seven out of ten, said they were members of one of the established churches, and a number of the others were members of one of the other churches. Lyell, the great geologist whose findings on the age of the earth first got the debate going, was a Christian believer. In 1874 S.P.C.K. an official publishing house of the Church of England published a book on reflecting the new geological findings about the age of the earth. There were some protests, but the book continued to be published. In fact, as Asa Gray told the Bishop of Rochester. "he could not say that there had been any undue or improper delay on the part of the Christian mind and conscience in accepting, in such sense as he deemed they ought to be accepted, Mr Darwin's doctrines". Darwin was buried in Westminster Abbey with a sense of pleasure amongst the churches and the memorial fund committee included the two Archbishops and the Bishop of London. As Owen Chadwick has put it "For two decades before 1896 the acceptance of the doctrine among educated Christians, whole far from universal, was both permissible and respectable" (Chadwick, 1972: 24). Whilst "In 1900 men talked as though the conflict was over. The difficulties in the minds of the young were not scientific." (Chadwick, 1972: 35).

References

Vidler, A. 1961. *The Church in an Age of Revolution.* London: Penguin,

Wood, A. 2008. Fifty-Eight Years of Friendship:Kelvin and Stokes, in *Kelvin, Life, Labours and Legacy,* ed. Raymond Flood, Marck McKcartney and Andrew Whitaker, OUP

Gould, S.J. 1986 Knight takes Bishop? *Natural History* 95(5)

Brooke, J.H. 2001. The Wilberforce-Huxley Debate: Why did it happen? *Science and Christian Belief,* 13, 127-41

Lucas, J.R. 1979. Wilberforce and Huxley: A Legendary Encounter. *Historical Journal* 22, 313-30

James, F.A.J.L. 2005 Open clash between science and the church?: Wilberforce, Huxley and Hooker on Darwin at the British Association, Oxford, 1860 in *Science and Beliefs*, ed David M Knight and Matthew Eddy, Ashgate,

Chadwick, O. 1972. *The Victorian Church, Part Two, 1860-1901.* London: SCM.

Richard Harries was Bishop of Oxford from 1987 – 2006. On his retirement he was made a life peer (Lord Harries of Pentregarth). He is Gresham Professor of Divinity and Hon. Professor of Theology at King's College, London. His latest book is *The Re-enchantment of Morality*, SPCK, 2008. He is a Fellow of the Royal Society of Literature and an Hon. Fellow of The Academy of Medical Sciences.

Postscript

John Quenby

A remarkable unity is apparent in several of the approaches to the relationship between science on the one hand and on the other God, intelligent design, creationism and atheism as discussed in this volume. The outstanding paradox which emerges is that a group of articles setting out to criticise one concept of design in the universe has ended in agreeing on another definition of this concept. On the way, a convincing set of arguments render the atheistic principles, currently popularised by Richard Dawkins, apparently implausible.

Creation of the possibility of possibilities stands out in the account of providence given by Ruth Page. God, in the supreme act of love, created what we know of as the multiverse, described in the chapter 'Cosmic Evolution', allowing everything to happen that actually takes place in this multiverse. All relationships in space and time, especially the one between God and humankind, result. Jonathan Clatworthy interprets the Genesis myth as a realisation that the universe or multiverse is ordered, not controlled by arbitrary Gods but only one. Humankind is blessed with a consciousness to appreciate this creation with all its possibilities, including the enjoyment of rest from endeavour. Discussion of how humankind reacts to the situation in which it exists in light of the underlying message of the biblical creation accounts is also taken up by Anthony Phillips.

Evolution has been the central theme of this collection. The chief issue was the inevitability of evolution, whether it naturally follows from the original creation of possibilities or whether it requires specific intervention by the Deity along the way.

Three concepts of 'design' are defined by Denis Alexander. Bacteria feeding follow a design in nature without individual instruction, bridge builders follow a detailed set of engineering drawings and finally, there is design in the sense of intention or purpose. This purpose is not the Aristotelian purpose that explains natural events and objects by what they achieve, such as rain falls not because of gravity but to grow plants. Rather, it is like the activities of an author setting out with an ending in mind, but on the way subject to inspiration and deviation as the plot develops. No article here finds a need for detailed prescription throughout or detailed intervention at crucial stages within evolution.

At the other extreme, the atheistic, bottom-up approach as defined by Denis Alexander, which attributes creation and evolution to 'accidents', also does not seem to accord with our reading of current scientific research. Instead, design in the sense of purpose fits the many lines of evidence pointing to the seeming inevitability of our emergence. The chapter on Cosmic Evolution reviewing the multiverse indicates how suitable crucial numbers in astronomical and particle physics should appear somewhere in space and time. We use the unproven concept of the multiverse, rather than universe, because we are simply demonstrating that current cosmological thought provides a plausible situation to allow evolution of the universe we experience. If this consistency with known physics could not be demonstrated, the overarching evolutionary picture could not be extended pre-big bang. Ian James takes us through evolution from the beginning of the optically transparent universe to our current climate situation, emphasising the emergence and maintenance of a benign atmosphere. Andrew Robinson and Christopher Southgate tackle the fundamental, chicken and egg problem encountered when considering the joint need for DNA as the genetic information code and catalyst of protein construction and RNA as the transfer mechanism allowing the building to take place. Self replicating, purely RNA sequences or early history, simpler coding methods are put forward to avoid the need for the insertion of developed RNA and DNA sequences at a crucial stage in evolution Denis Alexander points to an arrow of evolution, for example the sharing of genetic code in all living things with protein sequences limited to a surprisingly small number and also obvious constraints on the variety of evolutionary paths. Clearly the eye must evolve and it has done so in 20 different ways. In the same vein Simon Conway Morris points out that a level of intelligence equivalent to that in general in primates has evolved independently in crows and dolphins. It is interesting that the general concept of evolution dependent on a 'landscape' appears in widely different scientific areas. For string theorists, (see chapter on Cosmic Evolution) the problem is to show an enhanced probability of useful values of the numbers describing the properties of the particles of physics emerging from a vast landscape of possibilities. For Simon Conway Morris, there is a landscape which predetermines the inevitable outcome of evolution.

While there seems some convergence on design in the sense of creation serving God's purpose and the multiverse being intelligent in that order comes out of chaos under rational, physical laws, there are differences in emphasis when philosophical and theological languages are used. Simon Conway Morris attributes the shape of his 'landscape' to underlying principles like 'language' and 'music' which unify species and their properties and constitute a bed-rock of existence. Andrew Robinson and Christopher Southgate introduce the concept of interpretation, clearly linked to the role of RNA. They consider an object, the sign for the object and the 'interpretation' of the sign, for example the awareness of the environment by a living organism. The idea is akin to the Trinitarian 'relationship'. Communion ultimately becomes a making of meaning which contributes to the Divine life. It could be that these views are related to a development of the teleological (purposeful) influence of Plato and Aristotle on biblical ideas. Moving to those who emphasise the dynamic and emergent, Sam Berry advocates the approach of Donald MacKay who appeals to the complementary nature of the dual wave and particle models in quantum mechanics. While physical laws express relationships in the physical world of our experience, theologically we may talk of God's hand and control of an event without contradiction between the respective 'causes'. John MacDonald Smith uses the life of Jesus to model God as continual presence, especially in events. Incarnation is generalised to express a sense of God-ness in all things with Jesus as the paradigm. Divine intervention in humankind becomes purposive activity in our environmental creativity. Process theology as described by Whitehead has also been invoked in this volume to explain the whole sweep of evolution, astronomical and biological. It is based on a God-ward tendency in all events as influencing the self expression of the 'object' involved. Although there maybe differences of emphasis when expressed in philosophical language, there is clear agreement in seeing purposive evolution in some sense as compelling evidence for the underlying presence of God. Turing's non-infallible intelligence with which we started this book could be a helpful picture of this presence.

It should be clear from what has just been written that scientists, confronted by evolution as described, do not have a difficulty in finding God within the process.

In the context of the well known problem that Galileo had with the church, it comes as a surprise to read about how some early Christian Fathers viewed Genesis. Paul Badham points out the mainstream theology down to the start of the 17th century which accepted the Genesis view of God as creator while in parallel also regarding developing science as a valid description of this creation. Harriett Harris, however documents the rising trends in branches of Christianity and Islam which use the presupposition of infallibility of the sacred text as a starting point for a rational set of ideas which conflict with the evolutionary and cosmological world view we have just advocated. The free-flowering of divergent presuppositions in a multi-cultural setting, can lead to extremes, a worry of Bishop Michael Nazir-Ali, especially if the internal logics of the different idea sets stop any rational argument between the proponents.

Several authors take up the wastefulness of our relationship with creation as found on our planet. Solutions of many problems can be proposed. What is difficult is confrontation with personal disaster. Richard Harries recounts Darwin's slow loss of faith, especially due to the death of his daughter and not as a result of writing '*On The Origin of Species*'. Russell Stannard takes up the problem of why there are evil, suffering and death. He points out that 'love' can only work in the context of these problematic events. Evil is of course partly humankind's fault and therefore partly avoidable. Death must be necessary to make way for new life, especially new humans. Natural disasters are consequences of the process of evolution. It is the thrust of this whole collection that evolution is the expression of God's creative love. However unless we take on board an acceptance and understanding of evil, suffering and death, it is difficult to see a true acceptance of evolution as a proper description of God's underlying presence.

John Strain's stated aim in philosophical contribution is to justify faith in stories of origins, not by transforming faith into something that is not faith; but instead by returning to an older insight of faith as a virtue. He wishes to break down barriers between science and theology, restoring the importance of narrative; to invoke basic beliefs and to appeal to Aristotle's notion of intellectual virtue as developed by Kenny.

A stimulating piece by R.I. Vane-Wright looks at the remarkable navigational skills of the North American Monarch butterflies in an extended comment on a remark by Kalevi Kull that 'organisms can be proud to have been their own designers' which put one reader in mind of a remark attributed to Frederick

Temple about a God who makes a universe make itself. This has echoes of the arrow of evolution and the workings of Process Thought mentioned by others in the volume.

Perhaps the last word should embody a quotation from our climatologist, Ian James.

He notes we are in a period of frenetic climaxing of biological time with a very uncertain future, incidentally compounded at the time of writing by a world economic crisis which many believe to be an example of misuse of our given resources! Ian takes us into God's real time where we experience unexpected, golden moments in our lives which offer hope of significance, of beauty and of awe. Appreciation of the power and universality of Darwin's evolutionary idea surely provides such a moment.

BOOKS

O is a symbol of the world, of oneness and unity. In different cultures it also means the "eye," symbolizing knowledge and insight. We aim to publish books that are accessible, constructive and that challenge accepted opinion, both that of academia and the "moral majority."

Our books are available in all good English language bookstores worldwide. If you don't see the book on the shelves ask the bookstore to order it for you, quoting the ISBN number and title. Alternatively you can order online (all major online retail sites carry our titles) or contact the distributor in the relevant country, listed on the copyright page.

See our website www.o-books.net for a full list of over 500 titles, growing by 100 a year.

And tune in to myspiritradio.com for our book review radio show, hosted by June-Elleni Laine, where you can listen to the authors discussing their books.

MySpiritRadio